THE CURIOSITY OF
SCHOOL

THE CURIOSITY OF
SCHOOL

EDUCATION *and the*

DARK SIDE *of* ENLIGHTENMENT

ZANDER SHERMAN

VIKING

VIKING
an imprint of Penguin Canada

Published by the Penguin Group
Penguin Group (Canada), 90 Eglinton Avenue East, Suite 700, Toronto, Ontario, Canada M4P 2Y3
(a division of Pearson Canada Inc.)

Penguin Group (USA) Inc., 375 Hudson Street, New York, New York 10014, U.S.A.
Penguin Books Ltd, 80 Strand, London WC2R 0RL, England
Penguin Ireland, 25 St Stephen's Green, Dublin 2, Ireland (a division of Penguin Books Ltd)
Penguin Group (Australia), 250 Camberwell Road, Camberwell, Victoria 3124, Australia
(a division of Pearson Australia Group Pty Ltd)
Penguin Books India Pvt Ltd, 11 Community Centre, Panchsheel Park, New Delhi – 110 017, India
Penguin Group (NZ), 67 Apollo Drive, Rosedale, Auckland 0632, New Zealand
(a division of Pearson New Zealand Ltd)
Penguin Books (South Africa) (Pty) Ltd, 24 Sturdee Avenue, Rosebank,
Johannesburg 2196, South Africa

Penguin Books Ltd, Registered Offices: 80 Strand, London WC2R 0RL, England

First published 2012

1 2 3 4 5 6 7 8 9 10 (RRD)

Manufactured in the U.S.A.

LIBRARY AND ARCHIVES CANADA CATALOGUING IN PUBLICATION

Sherman, Zander
The curiosity of school : education and the dark
side of enlightenment / Zander Sherman.

Includes bibliographical references and index.
ISBN 978-0-670-06643-8

1. Education—History. 2. Education—Social aspects.
I. Title.

LA11.S54 2012   370.9   C2012-903984-5

Visit the Penguin Canada website at **www.penguin.ca**

Special and corporate bulk purchase rates available; please see
www.penguin.ca/corporatesales or call 1-800-810-3104, ext. 2477.

ALWAYS LEARNING   PEARSON

For my mother, my alma mater

IT IS ACTUALLY A MIRACLE
THAT THE MODERN EDUCATION SYSTEM
HAS NOT YET TOTALLY STRANGLED
THE SACRED CURIOSITY
THAT DRIVES HUMAN INQUIRY.

—Albert Einstein

CONTENTS

INTRODUCTION

THE STORY OF SCHOOL begins in antiquity, when there was enough information in the world that someone was needed to copy it down. The job fell to the very first students, called scribes, who lived in what is now the Middle East and distinguished themselves through their ability to read and write.

The first teachers of general knowledge didn't appear for another couple of thousand years; they were the Greek sophists, who, for a few drachmas, delivered improvised lectures in the streets of Athens. Plato's Academy was what we might call the first school, and it remained in operation for nine-tenths of a millennium.

In 500 BCE, the philosopher Hippias taught that it was possible to argue for or against any cause, an idea so powerful that it remains the cornerstone of academia today. Hippias's Greek contemporaries evolved the idea of education—the process of teaching and learning—further and faster than probably anyone had before, and in ways that were unparalleled at the time.

School, in short, was looking pretty good.

But with the coronation of Constantine the Great and the beginning of Christendom, education took a marked turn for the worse. While schools existed, they were strictly for religious indoctrination. By 700 CE, the Church effectively controlled all that was known and disseminated knowledge (or what passed thereof) under the auspices of the local monastery.

Students who wished to attend universities had to meet the most trying of tests imaginable. Applicants had to "read, sing and construe well and also compose twenty-four verses on one subject in one day," in Latin. Assuming they passed and were admitted to the school, freshmen faced an even more gruelling initiation: incoming students were bound, gagged, and whipped until they bled, at which time they had urine splashed in their wounds and excrement smeared on their bodies.

Officials tried repeatedly to prohibit such hazing. At the University of Leipzig, one edict reminded students that it was an offense to "insult, torment, harass, drench with water or urine, besprinkle or defile with dust or any filth, mock by whistling, accost with a terrifying voice, or dare to molest in any way whatsoever" first-year students. But such pronouncements seemingly had no effect. One complicated ritual involved costuming a freshman to resemble a goat, singing, "May the devil shit all over you and piss on your stomach and feet!" and forcing the student to confess to crimes he hadn't committed, at which time he was finally offered salvation (provided he bought the older students dinner and wine).

Then, as now, university was prohibitively expensive, and students were pinched as it was. So often were parents begged for money that "A student's first song is a demand for money, and there will never be a letter which does not ask for cash" became a popular saying. One father criticized his son for preferring play over work, "and strumming a guitar while the others are at their studies ..." In a timeless display of the power of persuasion, the boy was told there would be no more money unless his marks improved.

Morning or night, students of all seniority wandered drunkenly through the streets looking for a fight. At a time when everyone carried a dagger, one observer recalled students "rush[ing] into conflicts from which armed knights would hold back," carrying off women, ravishing virgins, and slashing off each other's fingers and toes. When it actually came to attending class, students had to awaken before sunrise, attend chapel service, and study for twelve hours a day. At the University of Paris, the lecture hall was so dark that students couldn't see the quill in their hand, an almost incidental worry since paper was both expensive and scarce, and professors spoke too fast to copy anything down.

Provided you made it through first year alive, two or three additional years' worth of predawn lectures had to be memorized, with little or no notes to study from and presumably a great deal of distraction at any given time. The sum of a college education had to be delivered to a committee of examiners, at which time students were made to swear oaths in Latin, quote Plato in the original Greek, call to mind meaningful sections of the Bible, sing and dance, play the violin, argue persuasively, recite passages from Boethius and Donatus, swear more oaths, and finally bow to the judges. If even some of this was insufficient, the student failed and had to do it all again.

Since universities at the time possessed no fixed facilities, if ever there was an irresolvable grievance (and when wasn't there?), the entire school picked up and moved somewhere else. This is how Cambridge University was founded in 1209—students from Oxford simply packed their tents and books and walked sixty miles east. (The fact that they chose the middle of a marsh as their new home may attest to there being no geography as a course of study. That wouldn't come until the mid- to late nineteenth-century, which was then still over half a millennium away.)

School was guided out of the Dark Ages thanks to a number of unwitting luminaries. One was Martin Luther, who called schools "nests of gloomy ignorance" and then inadvertently improved them by helping abolish scripture from the curriculum. Another was Isaac

Newton, whose falling apple reordered the known universe—putting science ahead of religion—before it landed on teachers' desks the world over, proffered by obsequious students first known as "apple polishers." Yet a third accidental contributor to the evolution of school was John Rolfe, the tobacco-farming husband of Pocahontas.

Rolfe's crops depleted the soil, rendering large tracts of land good for only two things: schoolyards and cemeteries. The classic one-room schoolhouses depicted in popular culture were in fact built by Puritans—the radical sect of Protestants who drank beer at all hours of the day, burned witches at the stake, and practiced the abstinence of smiling. Puritans founded the oldest school on the continent, the Boston Latin School, in 1635, as well as three of the eight Ivy Leagues: Dartmouth, Yale, and Harvard, each designed to finish the religious education begun in grammar school. (Harvard's early motto, "Truth for Christ and the Church," was eventually shortened to just "Truth," at least partially in deference to such humorless beginnings.)

Puritans were looking for a way to inculcate their children with Puritan values, and school arrived at the right time. In 1646, Massachusetts legislated the Old Deluder Law, which asserted that it was the chief objective "of that old deluder, Satan, to keep men from the knowledge of the scriptures ..." To counter the ways of the evil trickster, the law required every town with fifty families to hire a schoolmaster, and every town with a hundred families to manage a grammar school at its own expense. The Old Deluder Law was the first time any attempt had been made to regulate education in the state of Massachusetts.

Puritans were famously draconian when it came to punishment, and considered bestiality, witchcraft, blasphemy, adultery, idolatry, sodomy, rape, and homicide all capital offenses. Puritans were especially concerned with anything to do with sex. A one-eyed man accused of bestiality was executed simply because a pig that was in his care had given birth to another pig who also had one eye. While burning at the stake and hanging were the severest forms of capital punishment, another favorite method of discipline involved clamping the head and hands of a culprit in wooden blocks. This was the fate of someone named Kemble who, in 1659, returned home to Massachusetts after three years at sea and, upon having his wife rush out from their homestead to meet him, kissed her on the mouth. He was put in the stocks for "lewd and unseemly behavior."

Because Puritans believed in original sin, children were viewed as essentially bad and at any time could be punished for the smallest offense, including lying, sucking on their fingers, being restless, and being idle. Children who whispered in class had a piece of wood lodged in their mouth and affixed to their head by the schoolmaster with a length of cord. Other students were whipped with buckskin, made to sit on a one-legged stool, forced to wear a dunce cap, rolled into a ball and kicked, and presumably punished in other ways that were never recorded. A child of sixteen years or older could be put to death simply for refusing to obey his parents. The letter *D* in *The England Primer* stood for "Death"; the illustration featured a skeleton chasing a schoolboy while brandishing a large spear.

Students who weren't being scared to death risked the less frightening but still just as real possibility of being bored to death. Some of the first instructional texts included the Bible, *The McGuffy Reader*, and other classics such as *Spiritual Milk for American Babes, Drawn Out of the Breasts of Both Testaments for Their Souls' Nourishment*. Readings from each were followed by the Lord's Prayer, the Apostles' Creed, and the Ten Commandments. Drill, memorization, and recitation were so tedious that some students were said to have learned to read by connecting memorized passages of the Bible with printed words. Mark Twain wrote memorably of a schoolchild under such duress who had apparently broken down and, in a fit of fevered delirium, described a circle as "a round straight line, with a hole in the middle."

Grammar schools were open six days a week and often began at six in the morning. Lectures started when the schoolmaster arrived at seven, could take three or four hours to deliver, and continued until four or five that night, depending on the season. Despite a break at midday, there was little relief from an otherwise exhausting schedule, which was repeated for almost ten months of the year: Mornings were occupied with Latin, Greek, and Hebrew; afternoons with reading classic works; Fridays were for review; Saturdays for writing; and Sundays for catechism. A total of seven years could be spent under such conditions, at which time students finally got to have some fun, go to Harvard, and become a minister.

Upon graduation, students often acquired STDs—sacred theology doctorates—which colleges and universities conferred to the exclusion of most other degrees. During much of the seventeenth and eighteenth centuries, higher education was simply outsourced to Europe. Those who stuck around either received an exorbitant education or none at all, depending on their status in society. The teenagers of wealthy families could be expected to recite Sallust in the original Latin; play the harpsichord and pianoforte; conjugate in Greek and Hebrew; read complex, multi-genre fiction; do math; write beautifully; and more. But the children of poor families, especially in the South, had almost no formal schooling, and knowledge—if it could be called that at all— came almost solely from the Bible.

By 1776, the year of the Declaration of Independence, the whole of the United States had a population the size of present-day Brooklyn. At the time, America was divided in many ways—over the issue of slavery, over the problems of government, over immigration and taxes and policy—and in an effort to make the nation more whole, it was decided that an actual *system* of education was needed. One of the earliest advocates of the idea was the politician Richard Rush, who claimed that an education system would "render the mass of the people more homogenous and thereby fit them more easily for uniform and peaceable government."

Another supporter from the period was Noah Webster, author of the first comprehensive American dictionary, who desired an education system that would "implant in the minds of American youth the principles of virtue and liberty," while instilling "an inviolable attachment to their own country." Webster's *Dictionary of the English Language* was the closest the author ever got to homogenizing mainstream society: its seventy thousand handwritten entries constituted the first American textbook, and led to Webster's name becoming synonymous with the word *dictionary* in both the United States and Canada.

But it wasn't until the 1850s that the compulsory, tax-funded, state-managed education system we know today came into effect. And, with the exception of this book's opening chapter, it's this exact system that I've devoted these pages to understanding.

Of the more revealing facts in this book are that America doesn't actually have an American education system; that the man who was involved in creating the Canadian public school system was also involved in creating its residential school system; that any college in the United States can buy information about you for twenty-eight cents; that the US government once equipped students with rifles and replaced teachers with war veterans; that teachers still have the legal authority to beat their students to the point of hospitalization; that in India, exam stress is so high that students have been known to hang themselves over a B–; and that at one time, Carnegie and Rockefeller spent more on American education than the federal government.

In the following pages, we learn that the history of school involves the history of eugenics; the rise of German nationalism; a secret plan by the president of Harvard to reorganize society; a court battle over the definition of Lucifer; the relationship between a school's ranking and the number of CEOs on its board of directors; a friendship between

Maria Montessori and Benito Mussolini; experimental programs in the United States Army; Christian fundamentalism; companies that profit from student debt; the role of corporations in higher education; a man whose books were found in Hitler's private library; a company with a dark secret; and much more.

When I had written part of this manuscript, I had a conversation with someone in the business of books and told them about my project on the story of school. I was informed, "But you don't have a degree in school. This book should be written by someone with a doctoral degree and years of formal schooling." I didn't have the heart to tell this person there is no such degree I could have. There is no school that school went to, no degree in the institution that invented degrees, no course in the history of courses. It's called *The Curiosity of School* because, of all the things we learn about in school, we never learn about school itself.

———————

For what it's worth, my own interest in this subject began when I was five and my mother gave me a piece of paper on which she had neatly and minutely written the alphabet. She said, "This is how words are made. Have fun."

I learned the alphabet, and then what to do with it, because my mother was also my teacher. On that day and for the next eight years, it was official: I was homeschooled. Everything I knew and didn't know came from my mother. If she was good with language and bad with history and geography, I was good with language and bad with history and geography. Rumi and Shakespeare could be recited verbatim, but the dates of World War II were a mystery, and even now neither of us is completely certain whether Cubism is a style of art or the political system of an island in the West Indies.

My brother Joshua and I grew up in Central Ontario, in the rural outskirts of a small town in Muskoka. We had no TV, microwave, or computer, let alone classes, lessons, or anything like a curriculum. A typical day consisted of my brother and me dressing up in homemade costumes and running through the woods behind our house. In the afternoon our mother might *bring out* the workbooks and even go so far as to *put them on the kitchen table*, but rarely did we settle down long enough to do the work or concern ourselves with anything other than which of our favorite superheroes we wanted to be that day.

As we got older and started talking about going to school, a tutor came to the house to teach us French. Those were the days we came away from the table with the feeling something big had just happened. We knew only sort of what school was and assumed the pulsing in our frontal lobes was part of it.

"Like Spidey sense," my brother told me.

When finally I ventured into mainstream life, it was at a small elementary school beside a deep ravine. It was hardly a rigid academic environment, but still it was a world away from my home-style education. Every morning my father dropped me off at the front of the building and watched as I held the door for the people behind me before walking in myself. Teachers thought it was quaint; students thought it was queer. It didn't help that I was a vegetarian, played classical guitar, and spent recess reading my grandfather's Marxist literature.

At the end of each year, our mother looked us over for signs of public-school contagion. Joshua was already finishing his fourth semester of high school and seemed to have developed an immunity. The key, I realized, was not to take school seriously, and for an unknown reason, I had recently been struck by the opinion—by the fact—that I needed to go to Harvard. My brother would come home and see me reworking an essay on *The Proletarian Revolution and the Renegade Kautsky* and slowly close his eyes in shame.

By the time I got to grade twelve, I had fast-tracked through so much schoolwork that for most of my senior year, I didn't have any classes. In my free time, I began to investigate school policies. In our public high school, students were prohibited from sitting down in the hallways. If we did, and there was a fire, the fear was that kids would panic, trip over each other, and get trapped inside the building. I supposed it made a certain sense, but at the same time, if ever there was a fire, who was going to stay sitting?

Another thing bothered me. There were more students in the school than there were seats in the cafeteria, where we went on our spares. No one had provided us with an alternative, so we chose the floor. This was of course against the rules, and anyone caught sitting on the floor was sent to the office.

Here was the superstructure of the Marxist struggle I'd been waiting for. I began writing essays, which I printed in the form of a pamphlet. The cover depicted a sinister administration puppeteering students forever unable to sit down. One fall morning, I stood on the steps of the school and handed out copies to students on their way to class. That afternoon, the secretary pulled me out of world issues. When I got to the office, I saw my pamphlet on the principal's desk (I'd called it, in a feverish moment of glory, *The Anarchist*).

"Come in," he said.

I sat down at the front of his desk. "This is nice," I said.

"What's nice?"

"Sitting."

I suggested that he open new rooms in the school where we could go and sit. I thought it was a reasonable compromise to what I really wanted, which, of course, was nothing short of revolution. The principal told me he'd think about it, and in the meantime I should stop distributing pamphlets on school property. The next morning I moved to the sidewalk across the street. If I couldn't give *The Anarchist* away on school property, I would give it away on public property while looking menacingly in the school's direction. On Friday the principal made an announcement. Beginning the following week, he would unlock rooms in the school where students could go and just *sit*.

A cheer rang through the hall.

It's in a similar spirit that I offer this work.

While my views have changed considerably since my days as owner, editor, and chief contributor of *The Anarchist*, my thrill in peeling back the layers, and getting to the origin of things, has not. It's this same spirit of inquiry that I've attempted to bring to the following pages. My hope is that you'll find it both accessible and informative—entertaining and yes, perhaps even a little educational.

Finally, discerning readers will notice this book has no thesis. It doesn't argue that school is bad, or that homeschooling is good, or any similar such thing. My intention is to simply present the story of school, and let you take away what you want. I've done this to avoid the problem of writing a book about school using scholastic methodology, namely, Hippias's notion of arguing for or against a specific proposition. Just because this is a book about school, it doesn't need to sound like it was taught there too. This isn't a lecture, but a conversation, a story. Telling you what to think would defeat the whole point.

So without further ado, please, sit back, relax, and above all: have fun.

1 | CURIOUS BEGINNINGS

The Prussian system of education is not rivaled by any in the world. This is the secret of her internal development.

—The New York Times, 1868

THE END OF HISTORY

History ended on the morning of October 14, 1806.

At least, that was the opinion of German philosopher Friedrich Hegel. Then a professor at the University of Jena, Hegel was describing the scene from his faculty window, where the streets of his otherwise peaceful town had erupted into chaos.

In the predawn hours, Napoleon Bonaparte had ordered a surprise attack on the Prussian army. Simultaneously, farther up the river at Auerstedt, in what is present-day Germany, French forces attacked another Prussian stronghold.

The conflict was over before nightfall. The French army was better organized and better trained, and suffered a mere fraction of Prussia's losses. On the other hand, virtually the entire Prussian army was either captured or killed. By the end of the month, Napoleon had claimed Berlin as his own, and the Prussian Empire—once a great and powerful force—had fallen.

But that was only the start.

Under the terms of the armistice, Prussia was humiliated even further. Half of its land—the nicer half—was divided up and gifted to the czar of Russia or turned into territories to be governed by Napoleon's favorite generals. Everything east of the Elbe River was now irrefutably French. After taking almost all of Prussia's money, Napoleon insisted on being paid 120,000 million francs to withdraw his own troops back to France. In a final humiliation, Prussia was allowed to have a standing army of forty-two thousand soldiers—less than a quarter of what it had before the Napoleonic Wars began.

Incredibly, this final stipulation would lead to the rise of today's education system.

———

Years earlier, Gerhard von Scharnhorst was born in a village northwest of the German city of Hanover.

His parents came from different social standings—his father was a peasant, and his mother a more respectable "free" peasant. Little more than this is definitively known, except that Scharnhorst's father was involved in a bitter, decade-long legal dispute over the inheritance of the family farm, which burned anyway in 1765.

It's been suggested, not altogether unreasonably, that to escape his unpleasant adolescence Scharnhorst joined the military. The commander was Count Wilhelm of Schaumburg-Lippe-Bückeburg, an unusually refined and educated man who was born in London and spent his life trying to introduce culture to his small and overwhelmingly uneducated principality. According to one historian, Wilhelm was the most important influence in Scharnhorst's life. As Scharnhorst himself would later write, "One will rarely find combined in one person that much kindness of the heart and greatness of the mind."

It was this combination of head and heart, education and culture, that impressed deeply upon the young soldier. During the next twenty-three years in the Hanoverian army, Scharnhorst developed a reputation as an expert teacher, strategist, and increasingly radical reformer. Though he had served in the frontlines of the War of the First Coalition, the experience had left him traumatized. "I can face danger without difficulty," he wrote his wife in a letter, "but I am enraged ... by the sight of innocent people moaning in their blood at my feet, by the flames of burning villages, which men have put to the torch for their own pleasure ..."

According to Michael Schoy, a lieutenant colonel with the Holzminden army, "This inner conflict between the exercise of power and the savagery of war confirmed to [Scharnhorst] the importance of his theory of *Bildung*," a German word meaning "education." To Scharnhorst, war was unnecessarily brutal, messy, and inefficient. If the army were only better educated, wars could be fought more efficiently (and fewer villages would have to be put to the torch).

In the spring of 1801, Scharnhorst moved to Berlin and joined the Prussian army. He was forty-six, and his idea of *Bildung* had had a chance to ripen. Soon after arriving in the country's capital, Scharnhorst approached the king with his plan. But according to Schoy, the king and his senior officers were unmoved by the lofty notions of the son of peasant farmers. Besides, the thought of France invading Prussia was so improbable that it wasn't worth their consideration.

Scharnhorst was dismissed.

Then, in 1807, a young philosopher returned to Berlin.

Johann Gottlieb Fichte had been staying in Königsberg while the Prussian capital was adjusting to its new French ruler. The fact that Fichte chose Königsberg as a safe haven was no coincidence. Königsberg was the home of the world's most famous philosopher: Immanuel Kant had published *The Critique of Pure Reason* in 1781, which Fichte had obtained, read, and admired deeply.

But the young disciple didn't stop there. By his own account, after reading *The Critique of Pure Reason*, Fichte hurled himself "head over heels" into Kant's philosophy. This was no small thing. As any philosophy student will tell you, Kant's writing is notoriously dense. Second only to his rigid prose was Kant's rigid personality, and Fichte spent ten years working up the courage to pay the older philosopher a visit. Finally, in the summer of 1791, Fichte traveled to Königsberg to visit Kant. Not surprisingly, it didn't go well.

But Fichte was as tenacious as he was smart. For the next four weeks, he threw himself into the writing of a two-hundred-page "introduction." Using Kant's own logical structure, in Kant's own narrative style, Fichte returned to Königsberg with his introduction—a manuscript entitled *Attempt at a Critique of All Revelation*. It was dedicated to Kant, or "the philosopher," as Fichte put it (as though there were only one).

By all accounts, this second meeting went considerably better. Kant was flattered by the attention and seemed genuinely interested in Fichte's work. He gave a copy of the manuscript to his own publisher and arranged for Fichte—who was incredibly bad with money—to have a job tutoring at the home of a wealthy count. *Attempt at a Critique of All Revelation* was published in 1792 and, much to everyone's surprise, became an overnight success.

Equally surprising was that the publisher had somehow neglected to identify the author—not correctly identify, but identify at all. Missing too was Fichte's preface, which explained to the reader how the book had come into being. Needless to the say, the public was bewildered. As the Fichte scholar Daniel Breazeale has noted, "Here was a new book, published in Königsberg by Kant's publisher, bearing an unmistakably Kantian title, and revealing an unquestionable mastery of Kantian terminology and modes of argumentation." The result was that Kant himself was credited with Fichte's work, and *Attempt at a Critique of All Revelation* was "widely hailed as yet another brilliant achievement by the author of the *Critique of Pure Reason* ..."

News of the book's brilliance had so entrenched itself on the reading public that, by the time Kant cleared things up, it didn't seem to matter that he wasn't the real author. Johann Fichte was the new hottest thing in philosophy. That would have been a considerable improvement of fortune for anyone, but for Fichte—a broke, unmarried theology student with no permanent address, no philosophical credentials, and no tangible prospects—it must have felt like winning the lottery. And things only got better from there.

Because of the book's controversial success, Fichte was invited to take an honorary teaching post at the University of Jena, which he did in the spring of 1794. For philosophers, there was nowhere in the world more thrilling to be. The University of Jena had and would produce such notable teachers and students as Friedrich Schiller, Friedrich Hegel, Wilhelm von Humboldt, Ludwig Tieck, and A. W. Schlegel. (And if that weren't enough, Goethe himself lived nearby.) By the time of his appointment, the philosopher's reputation had grown to the extent that Fichte's lecture rooms were packed with students "standing on tables, benches, and each other's heads."

For the young professor, it was good practice for what was to come.

As Napoleon's army marched toward the town of Jena, Gerhard von Scharnhorst seemed to have a premonition.

Scharnhorst was now a high-ranking officer in the Prussian army and charged with overseeing the battle's tactical aspects. This normally prestigious position was all but humiliating to Scharnhorst, whose army was too disorganized—too *uneducated*—to possibly win. As he wrote to his daughter, "What ought to be done I know only too well. What is going to be done, only the gods know."

What happened, of course, was that tens of thousands of Prussian soldiers were slaughtered. Scharnhorst himself barely escaped with his life. When Jena and Auerstedt fell, the Prussian Empire was close behind. Within a couple of weeks, Napoleon had claimed Berlin.

Then, immediately following the Treaty of Tilsit, Scharnhorst received some strange news.

Frederick Wilhelm III—king of Prussia—wanted to grant him the audience that had been denied years earlier. The lowly son of peasants was finally being listened to, and Scharnhorst was given both a promotion—to major general—and, more importantly, allowed to do whatever he wanted to the country's military system.

Thus began one of the most rapid and radical transformations of an army in modern history. Decades of planning finally had an outlet, and Scharnhorst wasted no time in bringing education to the military. Partly this resulted in his being given charge of the Berlin Institute for Young Officers. While this one achievement alone would have kept him busy—in the words of one commentator, Scharnhorst "selected the faculty, built the curriculum, monitored the instruction, and evaluated the students"—it was one of many reforms that would change forever the way the country's military system worked.

But Scharnhorst's overwhelming accomplishment after being given full command of the Military Reorganization Committee was in his instigation of the *Krümpersystem*.

The *Krümpersystem* was a brilliant way of getting around one of Napoleon's stipulations—the final and most humiliating from the

Treaty of Tilsit. When Napoleon had demanded that Prussia keep a standing army of forty-two thousand soldiers, he had neglected to say anything about training an army of reserves. That was what the *Krümpersystem* would do. Between 1808 and 1812, Prussia regained its military strength in total secrecy and did it by training soldiers as students.

————————

In the years since the authorship of his *Attempt at a Critique of All Revelation* had been publicized, Johann Fichte had grown increasingly radical.

As one colleague at Jena remarked, "He really intends for his philosophy to have an effect upon the world." In fact, Fichte's philosophy would do exactly that.

After returning to Berlin in 1807, Fichte began delivering a series of speeches in the amphitheater of the Academy of the Sciences. Hermann von Helmholtz described him as a "powerful" and "fearless" speaker who utterly captivated his audience. Addressing the emotionally dejected audience of former Prussians, Fichte professed to know why Prussia had lost to Napoleon—and moreover, how it could bounce back. "In a word, it is a total change of the existing system of education that I propose as the sole means of preserving the existence of the German nation."

The old system of education, established by the first king of Prussia, had led to an excess of "free will." Too many Prussians were thinking for themselves, and this was in turn leading to a disorderly and weakened country. "The very recognition of, and reliance upon, free will in the pupil is the first mistake of the old system." Squash individual identity, and you got a country full of people who were exactly the same. This was what Fichte proposed in the new system.

"By means of the new education we want to mould the Germans into a corporate body, which shall be stimulated and animated in all its individual members by the same interest." This new education was "the only means by which we can be rescued from our helpless condition."

Over the course of fourteen public lectures, one per week, Fichte's *Addresses to the German Nation* captured the spirit of national dissent. As Scharnhorst was educating the military, Fichte was calling for the militarization of education. If the government adopted a system of compulsory schooling, Fichte told his audience one night, "from the moment that a new generation of youths had passed through it, [we] would need no special army at all, but would have in them an army such as no age has yet seen." Fichte believed that compulsory education would be so powerful that only a single generation would need to experience it before its effects would replace the need for enforcement. "Moreover, compulsory military service, too, will thereby be ended, because those who are thus educated are all equally willing to bear arms for their fatherland."

These were, to say the least, radical ideas. As Bertrand Russell summarized Fichte from this period: "Education should aim at destroying free will, so that, after pupils have left school, they shall be incapable, throughout the rest of their lives, of thinking or acting otherwise than as their schoolmasters would have wished." Public, legally enforced education would substitute identity, free thought, and creativity with, as Fichte put it, "a fixed and unchangeable machine ..."

Fichte's lectures would eventually become his best-known work, surpassing even his *Attempt at a Critique of All Revelation*. As Gregory Moore notes in the introduction to a recent translation of Fichte's work, even the title—*Addresses to the German Nation*—was meant to be provocative since, at the time, there was no German nation to speak of.*

For once, no one was confusing Johann Fichte with Immanuel Kant.

––––––––––––––

By the time Scharnhorst was through, the *Krümpersystem* had trained tens of thousands of soldiers.

The process had been a resounding success. Quickly rotating soldiers through the ranks to form a secret reserve—in effect, a second army—was a stroke of genius, and by the spring of 1813, Prussia was ready to go into battle once more. For the first time in years, the country proved an effective combatant, thanks in large part to Scharnhorst's reforms. Unfortunately, Scharnhorst himself was wounded when a bullet entered his leg below the knee. A month later the wound turned infectious, and Scharnhorst died.

Leadership of the Prussian army fell to Scharnhorst's replacement, who was soon faced with the ultimate test: on June 18, 1815, Britain and Prussia joined forces against France at the Battle of Waterloo.

Napoleon's defeat—once an inconceivable outcome—was now a reality.

––––––––––––––

––––––––––––––

* Fichte's work was so provocative, in fact, that following the end of World War II, it was found in Hitler's private library, "the only serious work of philosophy" in a collection that once held sixteen thousand volumes.

The Prussian education system was officially overhauled in 1809, the same year Johann Fichte was given another honorary teaching position, this time at the University of Berlin.

Compulsory military service began in 1813—for the first time in Prussian history—and six years later, schooling also was made compulsory. Though Prussia had some form of mandatory education as early as 1763, this was the first occasion in which a division of the government—the Ministry of Public Instruction—was given charge of a publicly funded, legally enforced, nationwide school system. Likewise, while compulsory military service had been tried in other countries—notably, France—this was the first time that service in the army was legally binding.

The effect of both systems working together can hardly be overstated. Historians of the period called compulsory military service and compulsory public education the two "most characteristic" features of Prussian society; others seemed unable to tell them apart. The authors of the *United States Magazine and Democratic Review* wrote, in 1838, "All that we can say in favor of the Prussian school system is, that it is *military*, and as such productive of quickness and precision." Or as one officer told a journalist for *Blackwood's Edinburgh Magazine*, "What may be called our standing army is, in reality, nothing but a school, in which all citizens, without exception, between twenty and thirty-two years of age, are trained to be soldiers." As for the other half of the equation, one foreign commentator noted that in Prussia "the military spirit pervades the schools. The state rules its schools as strictly as it does its army." Or finally, as was summarized by *The New York Times*, "An educated nation in arms is stronger than a standing army, and common schools better even for war than Imperial Guards."

Indeed, after Prussia's victory over Napoleon in 1815, visitors began traveling to the country to figure out how it could go from being a tiny sliver of land, with half its people, half its money, and a fraction of its army, to one of the most powerful countries in Europe—and all in just under a decade. While Scharnhorst's *Krümpersystem* was initially considered to be the source of Prussia's astounding recovery, this theory was soon debunked by another. It wasn't the schooling of Prussia's army—the training of soldiers as students—that had unified the country and brought Napoleon to his knees; it was the militarization of Prussia's schools—the training of students as soldiers. To quote again from *The New York Times*, "The Prussian system of education is not rivaled by any in the world. This is the secret of her internal development." As the article continued, "Her great political purpose is the union of the German peoples into a single nation. And to a great extent this purpose has been accomplished."

Journalists from America walking the streets of Berlin were often struck by the city's eerie silence and unnatural orderliness. There were no beggars and no drunkards. There were no riots or public demonstrations. "And yet there was no appearance of pressure from the Government." The sentiment was echoed elsewhere. The American educator Horace Mann—about whom there is more next—was surprised that, although he had visited hundreds of Prussian schools, he "never saw one child in tears from having been punished, or from fear of being punished."

What the journalists seemed unaware of was that in Prussia, students who excelled in school could be exempted from two years of military service. Because of Scharnhorst's insistence that military training simulate actual battle as realistically as possible, even short periods of training were incredibly taxing. As the authors of a textbook on Prussian education noted, "The army service is generally conceded to be the most severe test and course of training that could well be devised. Any man who can stand two years' training in the German army need have no fears as to his physical stamina. The service is about as near actual warfare as could be imagined …"

But there was another reason to go to school.

The parents of truant children could be heavily fined or even thrown in jail. At the end of every week, truancy logs were handed over to the local police, who then showed up at the house of the child in question, and, if need be, hauled the parents—and sometimes even the children—off to prison. Even less severe punishment was still remarkably draconian. First-time fines could reach three marks. Under such circumstances, missing a day of school, or even stepping out of line, must have been all but unthinkable. As the textbook historians observed, "The number of children who escape school in Germany is very small; in fact, we might say that none do."

After Prussia's compulsory school system was decided to be the key to its astonishing comeback, word got out. "The school system in Prussia is said to be the best in the world," noted the American press. "France will undoubtedly hold forth this as one of the reforms which this terrible war has taught her as necessary, and the 'Prussian system' is already spoken of by reformers in Italy as among the improvements which must be adopted there." In Canada, it was declared, "the national system of Prussian schools has been the admiration, the envy, the model of other lands. Our own has to a great extent been formed from it ..."

By the end of the century, the Prussian model would be the basis for education in most countries of the world—thanks largely to one man.

THE GREATEST INVENTION EVER MADE BY MANN

American education reformer Horace Mann once called public schools "the greatest invention ever made by man," and many have since called him the father of that invention.

His famous *Annual Reports* reached an international audience, and attracted the attention of everyone from Charles Dickens to the president of Argentina. Just one of Mann's twelve reports is said to be "one of the key documents in the history of American education." As Paul E. Peterson, director of the Harvard Program on Education Policy and Governance, observes, "Public schools as we know them today owe their origin much more to Horace Mann than to the nation's founding fathers."

After creating the first board of education, which legislated the first compulsory school in North America, Mann retired into an accomplished old age. He claimed his invention—a precursor to the public school known as the "common" school—would become, in the words of Peterson, "the most successful of all the forces in the world." This was as bold a claim then as now, but Mann nevertheless insisted he was right; the effects of public education would be "as predictable as scientific experiment."

Following his death in 1859, public schools across the country were renamed in his honor, a postage stamp carried his image, and even today, at Antioch College, graduating students are reminded of Horace Mann's enduring motto: "Be ashamed to die until you have won some victory for humanity."

———————

Horace Mann was born in the spring of 1796, on a small farm in Franklin, Massachusetts. He was the fourth of a Protestant farmer's five children and later recalled being terrified of the local pastor's fiery sermons, which seem to have sparked in him a resentment toward Christian radicalism.

At the age of eleven, Mann's father died. Thirteen months later, Mann's seventeen-year-old brother, Stephen, skipped Sunday church in order to go swimming. He drowned. At the funeral, Reverend Emmons used the opportunity to suggest that Stephen was continuing to suffer "eternal torment" for breaking the Sabbath.

It was around this time that Mann experienced a spiritual awakening. "I remember the day, the hour, the place and the circumstances, as well as though the event had happened but yesterday," he later wrote, "when in an agony of despair, I broke the spell that bound me."

The spell was that of the reverend and his father's Calvinism—a religion that allowed Stephen to suffer eternally in hell. Suddenly free from this restriction, Mann began to exhibit the independence and determination that would serve him for the rest of his life. At the age of eighteen, he used his own money to hire a private tutor to teach him Latin, a prerequisite for attending nearby Brown College. After graduating with honors in 1819, Mann boarded with the school's president, Asa Messer, and made some money tutoring other students. He put himself through Litchfield Law School, where he was later remembered for routinely defeating his classmates in moot court. In 1823, Mann was admitted to the Norfolk County bar and moved to the quiet town of Dedham. Though Dedham had a population of just 2,500, there were already five full-time lawyers—more than there were doctors—and competition for clients was steep. But Mann was nothing if not hardworking, and within a few years he had won the community's respect. When he ran for the Massachusetts House of Representatives in 1827, he was elected by the town's overwhelmingly conservative citizens.

Following his assumption of office, Mann began searching for a public cause to champion, his own "victory for humanity." Under Massachusetts' law of the period, public drunkenness was a criminal offense and viewed as a moral crime of indulgence. There was a movement among the state's Puritans to treat "excessive drinking of intoxicating liquors" with the death penalty. Mann's idea was to strike a compromise by institutionalizing drunks along with petty crooks and the mentally insane. "If we recoil from taking human blood, we can take the blood of the vine before it maddens the human." Two years after his election, Mann opened one of the first asylums in the country, located in Worcester.

At around this time, Mann began thinking of marriage. In considering whom he would like to marry, he remembered Asa Messer's daughter, Charlotte, who had been ten years old at the time Mann had last seen her. Charlotte was now twenty, with a delicate nervous system like his own. As one historian has written, "For the ambitious farm-bred lawyer, winning the hand of a college president's daughter must have seemed the ultimate prize." In 1829, Mann sent Charlotte a letter confessing "to feelings whose utterance I can no longer repress." As Mann would later write of this period, "there was a light upon earth brighter than any light of the sun ..." The couple was married the following September, and in the spring, Charlotte was pregnant.

Mann had never been so happy. But unknown to him and everyone else, Charlotte was suffering from tuberculosis. In August 1832, before the baby was due, Charlotte died.

According to Megan Marshall in *The Peabody Sisters: Three Women Who Ignited American Romanticism*, "The trauma of those final weeks ... turned Mann's dark hair completely white—giving the thirty-five-year-old widower a spectral look." This single incident came to define Mann more than any other, and forever altered the course of both his professional and personal life. He resigned from the House of Representatives, moved to Boston, and fell into a deep depression. "That which gave light and beauty and reality to all is gone," he wrote. "I seem to stand in a world of shadow."

Three Summerset Court, Mann's new address in Boston, was a modest boardinghouse with a view of Charlestown. It also happened to be the residence of Mary and Elizabeth Peabody.

The Peabody sisters were the daughters of Nathaniel and Eliza Peabody. Sophia was the youngest, an artist who would later marry the writer Nathaniel Hawthorne. Mary, the middle child, would become a writer. Elizabeth, the eldest, became influential to the Transcendentalist movement and was tutored by Ralph Waldo Emerson, who later became the editor of her small publishing house. But in 1832, none of this had yet happened, and Sophia was living apart from her sisters.

Mann, with his unnaturally white hair and brooding eyes, "cut a tragic figure." Both Mary and Elizabeth fell in love. According to Marshall, "The smile he flashed in rare moments of levity captivated Elizabeth and Mary Peabody all the more for its suggestions of the depths of sorrow from which it had risen." Mann's knowledge and intelligence was appealing to Elizabeth but excluded Mary, who was more down to earth than her sister. In turn, Mann seemed to open up more to Mary, in a way that made Elizabeth jealous.

The situation proved to be too much for the Dedham lawyer, who left the boardinghouse and moved into his one-room office nearby. His reasons were also at least partly economic. Mann's brother had become a bankrupt alcoholic, meaning that it was up to Mann to support his mother and sisters, and he could no longer afford the rent at 3 Summerset Court. His life had already seemed to peak and now began to backslide. His political causes had not all been successful, and people had been resistant to the change he had called for, leading him to write to a friend, "Having found the present generation composed of materials almost unmalleable, I am about transferring my efforts to the next. Men are cast-iron; but children are wax." In other words, it was a desire to shape students, rather than giving them an education, that led Mann to his vocation.

In 1837, Mann resigned from the State Senate and was appointed secretary to the Massachusetts Board of Education, a position he would hold for the next twelve years. This was the work for which he is known and which changed the course of public schooling in the United States.

Despite having no formal training in education, Mann was chosen for the job over three other contenders and became the only paid member of the board. He was, it would appear, of great value. The reason for his appointment, according to one of his biographers, was that the movement to have a common school system, already underway, was "too important and difficult an undertaking to be placed in the hands of a mere educator." Instead, the board needed someone who could "overcome a small hostile minority opposed to public schools ..." Which is to say, they needed a good lawyer.

That same year, the board of education had been legislated at the request of the governor of Massachusetts, a man named Edward Everett, who then chose seven board members. There is no clear indication of why this exact moment was chosen to adopt a public system of education. Possibly it was because Massachusetts was said to have the best schools in the world, yet they were categorically underfunded, poorly managed, and run by teachers whose sole pedagogical technique was to "compel memorization through fear of physical punishment." Schoolrooms were so cold in winter that the ink froze inside students' pens, so hot in summer that suffocation was an actual risk, and so uncomfortable that half the state's schoolchildren were said to suffer curvature of the spine.

Under such conditions, many parents simply sent their children to private schools or shipped them back to England for education there.

But there was another reason to develop public education. Between 1820 and 1840, the population of Boston had more than doubled. Impoverished immigrants landed in the city's harbor "in masses of thousands upon thousands ..." Eighty percent of Boston's immigrants were Irish, and most of these Catholic, which contrasted sharply with New England's Protestant Puritans. Conflict was inevitable. Mann's own office had twice been set on fire. "In the face of the annual influx of immigration," it was decided, "further and more pertinent provisions by law are necessary to convert the great body of foreign-born, illiterate persons to intelligent, industrious citizens."

It was to this end that the state's board of education was assembled and to this end that it continues to assemble today. The board's job was not to create the idea of common schooling, but to convince the people of Massachusetts that such a system was necessary.

Horace Mann had been chosen for expressly this purpose.

As secretary of the newly formed and first-ever board of education, Mann had to gauge public reaction to the proposed common school system and refute criticism as it arose.

This he did by first collecting information about each of the state's school districts. The information Mann gathered went into an annual report, written by Mann and distributed by the board of education. Thousands of copies of each issue were printed, read widely, and even translated into foreign languages. The twelve annual reports of Horace Mann—one for each year of his incumbency as secretary—came to define both the author and the work he was charged with promoting.

Through the writing of these reports, Mann introduced "a playground, a bell and a well, a doormat, a woodshed, a classroom clock." He restricted the number of books that went into and out of Massachusetts' schools, "which he argued would cause cynicism about the very possibility of truth," as Charles L. Glenn, professor and chair of educational administration and policy at Boston University, has written. Instead, Mann "sought to ensure that only ideas he thought worthy would be presented in schools." Textbooks that conflicted with his own values were banned. He was especially adamant that anything overtly religious—material that may have reminded him of his brother's drowning—be abolished from the curriculum. The result was that, intentionally or not, Mann began to fashion a school system after himself.

He didn't always feel up to the job. His health was never perfect, but Mann also doubted whether he could sufficiently defeat critics of the common school. For one thing, the state's Puritans were vehemently opposed to centralization and had figured out—after reading three of Mann's reports—that this was one of the dominant features of the Prussian education system, which they now guessed was headed for importation into Massachusetts. In 1839, Mann took time in *The Common School Journal*—another of the board's publications—to refute these claims. "The allegation," Mann wrote,

> that the Board are attempting to fasten upon our
> schools the compulsory system of Prussia or France,
> is an extraordinary one … Having read these reports
> as they were published, from time to time, we will
> confidently say, we do not believe that the majority of
> our Committee, or any one else, can point out a single
> word which would show that the Board possess or
> desires any authoritative *control* over our school system.

The first part wasn't even remotely true. The Prussian education system had been in the collective consciousness of the board for some time. In 1817, the board's own director, Edward Everett, had become the first American to receive a foreign PhD, which he completed at the University of Göttingen, in Prussia. According to Messerli, "Having observed the efficient Prussian school system while a student at the University of Göttingen, Everett considered the establishment of a State Board of Education the first step in bringing some order and system into the common schools of Massachusetts."

Equally as significant, in 1835, a writer named Charles Brooks had happened to meet a doctor from Hamburg at a party in London. The doctor—whom the record refers to as "Dr. H. Julius"—had been commissioned by the king of Prussia to visit the United States "for the purpose of collecting information concerning our prisons, hospitals, schools, etc." The two men decided to spend the forty-one-day voyage back to Massachusetts as roommates, and by the time they disembarked in Boston, Brooks was convinced of the superiority of the Prussian system: "I was resolved to attempt the introduction of several parts of the system into the United States."

For the next four years, Brooks did little else. When he later met Mann at a conference, it was Brooks who suggested the idea of "normal schools," a precursor to teacher's training colleges. In at least Brooks's mind, normal schools were the very heart of the Prussian system: "I took my stand upon this Prussian maxim, '*As is the teacher, so is the school.*' I thought the whole philosophy was summed up in that single phrase; *and I think so still.* I accordingly wrote all my lectures with reference to the establishment of Normal Schools." Brooks went so far as to pay for advertisements in the papers that celebrated the Prussian normal school cause.

In 1838, he was successful. With twenty thousand dollars in funding, Mann petitioned the House Committee for the establishment of two normal schools in Massachusetts. The House came later to regret this decision, after normal schools caused outrage among the public; it produced a report that accused the schools of being "an unnecessary waste" since "If there were districts which desired more competent teachers than they now had, they should simply pay better salaries." In short, the House didn't believe that teaching would ever become a valid profession; in fact, thoughts to the contrary seemed to send the state's legislatures into a fury. The board of education was accused of attempting to place "a monopoly of power in a few hands," which the House deemed "contrary, in every respect, to the true spirit of our democratical institutions." The

House further accused the board itself of being "a dangerous power," and came within a whisker of shutting it down.

Mann didn't take it well.

In August of each year, on the anniversary of Charlotte's death, he would grow deeply depressed. Now he claimed in his journal to be "bereft" of even sorrow. "Nothing but the stern mandate of duty urges me forward …"

In his remaining reports, Mann developed an increasingly, almost ruthlessly, unemotional logic. In the *Fifth Annual Report*, of 1841, he wrote that the previous year had been spent collecting information from employers about "the relative merits of educated versus uneducated workers." Included in the report was a letter from one such employer, an industrialist who went by the name "H. Bartlett." Among other points, Bartlett argued that educated workers "were less likely to be drinkers and to damage machinery, and more likely to attend church and to provide a stable life for themselves and their families." Since educated workers were easier to control than uneducated workers, "Employers, therefore, could count on substantially fewer labor problems if they hired workers who had a common school education."

Bartlett concluded the passage by appealing to the employers' own self-interest:

> "Those who possess the greatest share of the stock of worldly goods" are deeply interested in this subject as one of mere insurance—that the most effectual way of making insurance on their property would be to contribute from it enough to sustain an efficient system of Common School education, thereby educating the whole mass of mind, and constituting it a police more effective than peace officers or prisons.

By linking education with capitalist values, Mann successfully convinced Massachusetts businessmen to support the common school movement; what had turned students into soldiers in Prussia would now turn them into hardworking, law-abiding citizens (a state not dissimilar to which we find them in today).

In another report, Mann employed other questionable tactics to deal with dissenting opinions. One was from "the rich man" who had no children and objected to "the extraction of a contribution from him, to educate the children of his neighbor ..." Another was from the rich man who *did* have children but "withdraws them from the Public School ... and then thinks it a grievance to be obliged to support a school which he condemns." Mann's solution was to remind the wealthy of their moral duty: "But for whose subsistence and benefit were these exhaustless treasuries of wealth created?" he wrote. "Surely not for any one man, nor for any one generation; but for the subsistence and benefit of the whole race, from the beginning to the end of time."

This was Mann at his finest—telling the wealthy Puritans that it was their moral imperative to support education for all. It was why he had been hired in the first place. Mann could invoke divinity when talking to people of faith; pragmatic capitalism when talking to businessmen; security when talking to the wealthy; and hope when talking to the poor, as he did in his *Twelfth Annual Report*. There, education was attributed with the power of "diffusing old wealth" by eradicating class distinctions. "Education creates or develops new treasures," Mann wrote, "treasures not before possessed or dreamed of by any one."

Mann could sound variously irate, detached, inspired, authoritarian, technical, religious, rational, and a dozen things more. He was so proficient at being enigmatic that even now it's hard to say what he really felt about what he was doing. But that wasn't the point. As Mary Peabody would write, he was simply "born to sway men."

Then Horace Mann did something odd. He proposed—to Mary.

Even at the time, the middle Peabody sister knew Mann "was still wedded to his memories of Charlotte ..." In an earlier fictional account by Mary of her romance with Mann, she wrote that she had "learned to repress all outward signs of emotion, for the one grand object of my existence was to contribute to his happiness ..."

For Mann, it was a marriage of convenience. Five weeks earlier, he had bought a ticket to Europe and didn't want to travel alone. On the day of the wedding, in the spring of 1844, it rained. That very afternoon the Manns departed on their honeymoon: a six-month tour of European schools, prisons, and mental asylums.

While abroad, the Manns visited England, Scotland, and Ireland, as well as Belgium, Holland, and France. Mary was pregnant immediately and over the next few years would give birth to three children—each of whom would be homeschooled. Though he was finished half the reports that he would author on the adoption of the Prussian system, when the Manns arrived in Berlin, it was the first time Mann had actually seen a Prussian school. Still, he felt Prussia stood "pre-eminent among the nations of Europe in regard to the quantity and quality of education." Prussian children "are born with the innate idea they go to school," whereas "this instinct is unknown to the American child."

It wouldn't be that way for long. By the end of his twelve-year contract with the Massachusetts Board of Education, his reports, articles, lectures, meetings, and travels had convinced the state of Massachusetts it needed a school system. Four years later, it had one.

In 1860, Mann's sister-in-law, Elizabeth Peabody, opened the first American kindergarten. Like the common school model, the kindergarten was a Prussian idea, imported to North America in such pristine condition that not even the word was changed.

In the century and a half since his death, biographers have variously referred to Mann as a "Protestant Republican," "Unitarian," "rationalist," "phrenologist," "nonsectarian Protestant," "profound Conservative," "visionary," "pragmatist," and more. Horace Mann may have been some combination of all of these things. At least occasionally, he appeared to be none.

Virtually all the images of Mann were created toward the end of his life. They show a prematurely aged man, his eyes hooded beneath a large forehead, an expression on his face that's neither a smile nor a grimace, but something in between.

As an eighteen-year-old, Mann sold straw he'd braided to raise enough money to learn Latin. Five years later, he was teaching Latin (as well as Greek). Five years after that, he was an established lawyer, and in another five years he was elected to the state legislature. Yet such was his incredible determination that all of this simply formed the basis of Mann's achievement.

To be sure, the extent of Mann's work is one of the few things that *isn't* debated in education. Even at the time, Mann seemed to know that the common school—his victory for humanity—was a profound achievement: "This institution is the greatest discovery ever made by man," he wrote in 1840, twelve years before the Massachusetts Board of Education had even legislated compulsory schooling. "We repeat it, *the common school is the greatest discovery ever made by man*."*

What made the common school model so great was its ability to produce whatever kind of student was required according to whoever was in power. In Mann's day that was the board of education, which

---

* Emphasis original. And while we're already here in a footnote, I'll add that I've kept the emphasis original in all of the quotations throughout this book, unless noted otherwise.

extolled the virtues of citizenship and democratization. But by the end of the century, as the Industrial Revolution became the new global zeitgeist, another interest group had elbowed its way onto the scene. At a meeting of the National Association of Manufacturers in 1905, it was decided "The German technical and trade schools are at once the fear and admiration of all countries. In the world's race for commercial supremacy we must copy and improve upon the German method of education ..."

A man named Georg Kerschensteiner was summoned for the task.

KERSCHENSTEINER'S SCHOOL

In 1900, a Munich superintendent submitted a paper to the Royal Academy of Sciences. In "Education for Citizenship," Georg Kerschensteiner proposed a radical new way of educating high-school-age students, who were next in line to enter the world of work.

By making select reforms to the existing *Berufsschule*—an early kind of vocational school—Kerschensteiner hypothesized that it was possible to create a society of not only efficient workers but also "useful citizens." In the words of Philipp Gonon, Kerschensteiner was arguing "that the realisation of an ethical, virtue-based community represented the ideal of the constitutional state and of national culture." Or, in Kerschensteiner's own words, "Educating for citizenship means educating the student to realize the ethical idea of the highest outward Good." Students, in devotion to their national governments, would be moral beacons for the rest of humanity.

At the time, Munich's principle industries were beer, lithography, leatherwork, glass staining, and artificial flowers. Heavy industries were clustered in Berlin and other northern cities. German electrical, chemical, and steel sectors were formidable by not only European standards but global ones. According to one source, the country's chemical plants generated nine-tenths of worldwide industrial dye production. In Germany, steel production was more significant than in Britain, France, and Russia combined. By 1913, Germany's share of global manufacturing was 14.8 percent, higher than Britain's 13.6 percent, and more than double France's 6.1 percent. The following year, Germany became the number one economic powerhouse on the continent—an almost inconceivable comeback for a country once decimated by Napoleon.

But Kerschensteiner, for one, didn't see the point in celebrating.

As a child, he had grown up in difficult circumstances: his parents were poor merchants, and along with his thirteen siblings, he lived in a one-room apartment. At the age of eight, Kerschensteiner had been arrested for "gang theft." This single incident appears to have permanently altered his outlook, and for the rest of his life, Kerschensteiner devoted himself to education, both other people's and his own. As a teenager, he dropped out of school to became a teacher's assistant in Bavaria, quitting the job two years later to finish his high school diploma. After working as a music instructor, Kerschensteiner wrote his doctorial thesis on "The Criteria for the Singularities of Rational Curves of the Fourth Order." He went back to being a teacher, then professor, before his election to the Munich council in 1895.

In a way, it was surprising that his seminal work, "Education for Citizenship," was received favorably at all. At a time when Germany had never been stronger economically—and was admired the world over—Kerschensteiner was claiming that vocational education, as it was then manifest, was leaving something out—namely moral integrity. Kerschensteiner felt "a useful citizen is one who contributes by his work, directly or indirectly, to the attainment by the State of its goal as a legal and cultural community." In his view, vocational schools should promote work not as an end, but as a means.

The problem with Munich's *Berufsschule*, Kerschensteiner argued, was that it made students "egocentric." Expressing such seemingly socialist ideas in a capitalist era made Kerschensteiner appear old-fashioned. As Diane Simons has summarized, "The nineteenth-century absolutist rule had trained the Germans to be useful, efficient State servants," an idea that had been fuelled by a misunderstanding of Nietzsche's superman theory, "which was avidly seized upon by the countless disgruntled intellectuals who were being churned out of university only to find that they were a common commodity on the employment market." This anger was ignited by a resurgence of interest in Johann Fichte's *Addresses to the German Nation*, which in turn was influential to the formation of the Pan-German League in 1894. Right-wing, extreme nationalists believed in letting the individual "rise to his full stature," and where their education was concerned, wanted as little interference from the government as possible.

In short, egocentrism was okay.

Despite his acknowledgement from the Royal Academy of Sciences, the fact that Kerschensteiner was envisioning a communist school model during an outpouring of pan-German individualism didn't make him especially popular. When the superintendent of schools presented his thesis to a group of German manufacturers, fifty-two out of fifty-eight voted against adopting his proposed reforms. Undeterred, Kerschensteiner learned the identities of the six who had voted yes and solicited their endorsements in private.

At the beginning of the twentieth century, the world was changing rapidly.

It used to be that a country's natural resources were shipped else-where for refinement, to places like Berlin. Now people—or more specifically, people who operated heavy machinery—were refining those same materials domestically, at which point they became consumable things and were sold to an international market.

This seemingly simple shift from a resource-based economy to one built on human capital had an utterly profound effect. Countries were suddenly competing with each other on a global stage. In the race for economic supremacy, school was seen as the means of achieving this end. Since everyone went to school, and school could be altered to engineer different outcomes, whoever changed the school system changed the world. This was the idea that occurred to two of its wealthiest citizens.

In the first twenty years of the twentieth century, Andrew Carnegie and John D. Rockefeller spent more money on education than the federal government. Newspaper headlines read like the call of an auctioneer: "Carnegie Gives $50,000 to College"; "Rockefeller Gives $50,000"; "Another Gift by Mr. Carnegie"; "Gets $100,000 from Rockefeller"; "Carnegie Gives $200,000"; "A New Rockefeller Gift"; "Carnegie Offers $400,000"; "Rockefeller Gives $600,000"; "Carnegie Gives $750,000"; "Rockefeller Adds $800,000"; "Carnegie Gift to Harvard"; "Rockefeller Gift to Princeton"; "Carnegie Gives $1,000,000"; "Rockefeller's Gift at Stake"; "Carnegie's $2,000,000 Offer"; "$1,000,000 for Harvard by J. D. Rockefeller"; "Carnegie Gives $3,500,000"; "Talk of Rockefeller Gift"; "A $6,000,000 Carnegie Gift"; "Paris Reports $6,000,000 Rockefeller Offer..."; "Carnegie's $10,000,000 Gift."

Then one figure brought the house down: "Thirty-Two Million Rockefeller Gift."

At the time, it was the largest single donation in history. Rockefeller gave the money to the General Education Board, which he had founded in 1902. Twenty years later, Rockefeller personally donated $129 million, and over the next four decades, he would give hundreds of millions more. The idea was that by supporting industrial training,

Rockefeller would turn the gears of capitalism—the same gears that had made him rich and would, with a few hundred million in support, make him even richer.

To this end, Rockefeller and other industrialists began meeting annually at a conference in West Virginia; the goal was to bring Southern educators together with Northern philanthropists. When, in 1901, the group announced a new effort to educate black Southerners, Rockefeller's General Education Board began directing philanthropy toward this new cause. Between 1902 and 1964, the board spent $324.6 million on black education.*

Although the money technically advanced the cause of Southern education, Elizabeth P. Harper has written that it "did so on a foundation of White supremacy, segregated schools, and Black industrial training." Rockefeller and the other industrialists' interest in education for African Americans "was driven by their need for Black labor for their railroads and cotton mills." By 1911, Rockefeller had a white supervisor in every black school in each of the former Confederate states. Meanwhile, Rockefeller's organization "repeatedly turned down grant requests from autonomous Black organizations ..."

It's worth taking a moment to consider the scene: normally, philanthropy and self-interest are incompatible causes, but here they were entirely codependent. The General Education Board saw black education not as a charitable cause but as an investment opportunity. In fact, an offshoot organization called the Southern Education Board scouted out precisely such arrangements. Both organizations traded board members and had representatives in related organizations and ventures: Robert C. Ogden, president and organizer of the North–South conferences, was also president of the General Education Board,

---

* Unless I've made a note of it otherwise, this figure, as with all others in this book, has not been adjusted for inflation.

Southern Education Board, and the boards of two historically black colleges—all in the same year. George Foster Peabody, who eventually became chair of the Federal Reserve Bank in New York, was an early fundraiser for Rockefeller's General Education Board and "has been called the investment banker of the Southern education movement."

Not to be outdone, Carnegie was soon funding his own organization.

At the first official meeting in 1906, it was decided to combine the various special interest groups vying for what had become known as "industrial education." The appropriately named National Society for the Promotion of Industrial Education (NSPIE) soon had four key causes: to raise public awareness of the role of industrial education; to discuss and study the phases of industrial education; to publish all relevant findings; and to establish schools of industrial training. By 1909, NSPIE had chapters in twenty-nine states and a membership of nine hundred.

The first president of the organization was a man named Henry S. Pritchett. Pritchett's father, C. W., was an astronomer and had a college named after him in Missouri. After graduating from Pritchett College, Henry Pritchett did astronomical work in New Zealand and eventually got his doctoral degree, in 1894, from the University of Munich. At the time, Georg Kerschensteiner hadn't yet written his famous essay, but the German educator must have made an impression soon thereafter. When he returned to the United States, Pritchett bought a house in Manhattan that was next door to Andrew Carnegie's sixty-four-room mansion. (Carnegie considered his palatial home "modest," "plain," and—the only adjective he got right—"roomy.") Pritchett soon became Carnegie's closest advisor. "You really don't realize how valuable you are to me," Carnegie reportedly told him. "You are one of the few people who tell me when I am wrong."

At the same time Pritchett was made president of NSPIE,

he was given the leadership of the Carnegie Foundation for the Advancement of Teaching (CFAT). These two organizations became the primary sources of Carnegie's educational philanthropy. CFAT alone was endowed with ten million dollars. The contributions of this single organization to American education could be the subject of its own book—suffice to say here that its influence is rivaled only by Rockefeller's General Board of Education. As for NSPIE, it began distributing funds into the Carnegie Institute of Technology in Pittsburgh. And, in 1910, it paid for the American speaking tour of Georg Kerschensteiner.

After Kerschensteiner had secured his investments in Munich, his model of industrial school was privately financed in Bavaria, Württemberg, Vienna, and Zurich.

In Kerschensteiner's hometown of Munich, where there had once been a single continuation school, there were now fifty-two. "It is the hope of the committee who invited him to come to America that some impetus may be given by his visit to the movement for industrial training in this country," recorded *The New York Times*.

The article painted a favorable portrait of Kerschensteiner, and showed images of students building chimneys and waiting tables. In Kerschensteiner's schools, students could become shoemakers, coppersmiths, oven builders, dentists, jewelers, secretaries, glove makers, woodcarvers, metal workers, locksmiths, furniture makers, carriage builders, printers, upholsterers, hairdressers, and tradespeople of nearly every variety.

To what purpose were these skills being put? "It may look at first sight as if my scheme was nothing more than a system of industrial education," Kerschensteiner told the reporter. It wasn't. Kerschensteiner's schools were designed for "the production of useful citizens." A useful citizenry would make money for the government, and a wealthy government would in turn look after its citizenry. Such reasoning made Kerschensteiner wildly popular for the two months he lectured throughout the Northeast and Midwest, from Boston to Cincinnati.

He was admired everywhere he went. George Herbert Mead implored the city of Chicago to adopt industrial continuation schools "of the same general character" as the ones in Munich. Kerschensteiner was featured on the cover of *Vocational Education*, where he was described as having "done more than any other" to promote industrial education. His school was called "world-famous," and as for Kerschensteiner himself, "No German educator had a greater American reputation ..." *The New York Times* said he had "revolutionized" school methods, and called his ideas "remarkable."

It is the irony of the age that the textbook heroes of American enterprise were importing a German model. Without Carnegie and Rockefeller's funding of German vocational schools, the United States might never have won the title of world's foremost industrial superpower. Yet despite his widespread popularity, Kerschensteiner himself had become increasingly neglected. The moral component of his industrial school model was repeatedly overlooked, and attention was instead directed toward the uncomfortably communistic undercurrent of Kerschensteiner's world view. In spite of his "repeated and detailed statements" to the contrary, critics still believed the industrial model would produce students whose sole purpose was to work for the state.

And this, as it turned out, was true.

In 1911, Holmes Beckwith was a student at Columbia University.

At the time, Beckwith was working on his doctoral dissertation for the Faculty of Political Science, for which he had chosen the subject of German industrial education. There is no indication of why this particular subject was chosen, apart from the fact that it was a new and increasingly popular topic in education. Beckwith, who later was said to have attended socialist meetings, was possibly drawn to Kerschensteiner's deeply authoritarian system. But unlike Edward Everett or Horace Mann, Beckwith had no prior connections or apparent reasons to be interested in Germany specifically. He had been born in Hawaii, the son of missionaries, and before becoming a student of political science at Columbia, he had studied economics at the University of California. His master's thesis was a portrait of domestic life in China. In short, and in the words of Beckwith's only friend on record, he was "extremely odd."

In Europe, the summer of 1911 was unusually hot, and Beckwith spent it on the train, visiting schools in Munich, Berlin, and Hamburg. His purpose was to "ascertain in what ways we in the United States may develop industrial education so that it may be of the greatest service to industry and to industrial workers, as well as to the whole people." After visiting Munich's industrial continuation schools, he wrote appraisingly of "the original and resourceful personality of Dr. Georg Kerschensteiner ..."

In *German Industrial Education and Its Lessons for the United States*, Beckwith made a number of remarkably unemotional observations. He noted he was primarily interested in "Industrial education for the masses, for the rank and file workers," an area in which he felt Germany "has [the] most to teach us." Derek S. Linton has described Beckwith as having a "single-minded dedication to the cult of efficiency," a phrase historians have used to refer to this period as one in which business and societal interests were routinely favored over actual education, setting something of a precedent for things to come. Of Kerschensteiner's philosophy of moral education, Beckwith's only comment was that he hoped it wouldn't interfere with "industrial results."

In terms of the promise of the dissertation's title, Beckwith was clear about which lessons the United States should adopt. "My inquiries into German industrial training have led me to wish that our own country had not allowed apprenticeship to go into such a decline, and to seek for its revival." Traditional apprenticeship programs in the United States, in which a master trained a dedicated novice, had declined with the rise of industry. Apprenticeship in the time of Beckwith's writing was being replaced with specialized labor, and it wasn't particularly in vogue of Beckwith to advocate the reverse. But the twenty-seven-year-old doctoral student was suggesting that the United States adopt not only compulsory industrial continuation schools but "workshops that could promote flexibility by introducing young workers to a wider variety of operations and procedures," as Linton writes in *German Influences on Education in the United States to 1917*.

Perhaps most significantly, to govern America's continuation schools, Beckwith wrote of the need for a separate vocational education board that was made up of both elected labor officials and business representatives. It was a contentious debate of the time, and polarized the question as one in which there was only one possible answer—either labor officials or business representatives should preside, but not both. The argument for having democratically elected labor officials was supported, not surprisingly, by the American Federation of Labor (AFL). The argument for business representatives, also unsurprisingly, was supported by the National Association of Manufacturers (NAM). By suggesting a union of both organizations, Beckwith felt he had struck a compromise that was, in his words, "both efficient and truly democratic."

Beckwith's report was published by the Bureau of Education in 1913. The following year, Congress created a "Commission on National Aid to Vocational Education," which comprised five NSPIE members, and four sympathetic members of Congress. By that time, NSPIE had solicited the support of both NAM and the AFL to create an almost unstoppable force for industrial education. As one historian has summarized, "the Commission's final report declared that vocational education was an urgent national interest that necessitated federal action." Kerschensteiner's school model would "promote industrial efficiency and national prosperity, decrease labor and social unrest, and promote a higher standard of living for workers." The Commission had two of its members—Senator Hoke Smith and Representative D. M. Hughes—introduce the proposed legislation.

The Smith-Hughes Act came into effect in 1917. It apportioned almost two million dollars for vocational training that year, and had increased the amount to over seven million dollars by 1925. Smith-Hughes was the first time the federal government initiated a "grant-in-aid" program, meaning that it was officially encouraging industrial education reforms. It also established the Federal Board for Vocational Education, an independent organization comprising labor and business interests, "along the lines recommended by Beckwith." More memorably, Smith-Hughes led to the introduction of shop and home economics into the everyday school experience.

Funded by Carnegie, NSPIE had successfully lobbied the government to implement reforms that were in keeping with its mandate. It was perhaps unfortunate for Kerschensteiner not only that his idea of promoting "the skill as well as the joy" of vocational training was left out, but that Kerschensteiner himself had been brought to the United States by an organization whose intention was to make neither happy nor educated students but rather students who were simply skilled enough to become part of a labor force. The Smith-Hughes Act prepared students for the working world from the time they entered high school. Carnegie had funded industrial training for whites, and Rockefeller had founded industrial training for blacks. As Rockefeller needed laborers for the railroad, Carnegie needed laborers for the factory.

The effect wasn't restricted to the United States. In Canada, the Royal Commission on Industrial Training and Technical Education recommended adopting similar measures, "for the promotion of the home and foreign trade of Canada with other nations." The Ontario Educational Association was told of the benefits of Kerschensteiner's school. "Let Canada accept the lesson that Germany has been teaching for years," the association was told. "Let her recognize the value of a higher technical training and make such a training possible for every worker in our land ..."

As for Holmes Beckwith, after delivering his report to the Bureau of Education, he strolled into the office of his employer, a dean at the University of Syracuse, and fired five rounds from an army-issue revolver. Then he turned the gun on himself.

2 | THE TEST, AND WHAT IT'S ON

If the unhappy day ever comes when teachers point their
students toward these newer examinations, and the present
weak and restricted procedures get a grip on education, then
we may look for the inevitable distortion of education in terms
of tests.

—Carl Brigham, creator of the SAT

BINET'S SCALE

John Harvard may have been many things, but lucky wasn't one of them.

During the bubonic plague of 1625, his father, three brothers, and sister died over the course of a single summer. That left his mother, brother, and Harvard himself. In 1626, Harvard's mother married a man named John Elletson, who died that same year, before she married the grocer Richard Yearwood, who also died. Harvard's mother died herself in 1635, the same year Harvard's first wife, Barbara Destyn, died. Thomas—Harvard's brother and last remaining relation on earth—died in 1637, and with seemingly no immediate alternative, John Harvard died the following autumn.

Before he did, he married a woman named Ann Sadler, who, after her husband's death, married the Reverend Thomas Allen. Allen had been the executor of Harvard's estate, which, considering the many deaths that had befallen the Harvard family and the wishes of relatives to bequeath their fortunes to John, the sole surviving heir, was not insubstantial. And so, after willing half of everything he had to his second wife, Harvard gave the rest to a college that was then under construction in the new town of Cambridge, Massachusetts. This amounted to 779 pounds, 17 shillings 2 pence. The school—which had been called "Newtowne College"—was rechristened in Harvard's honor.

But for the next three hundred years, Harvard College seemed cursed with the same luck as its founder.

The school's first director was a man named Nathaniel Eaton, who in fact was a close friend of John Harvard, and who, shortly after being sworn in, was fired for beating a student with a cudgel "a yard in length, and big enough to have killed a horse." Eaton was replaced in 1640 by Henry Dunster, who was also forced to resign after illegally opposing the practice of infant baptism. The seventh president of Harvard was Increase Mather, a Puritan pastor of Boston's North Church, whose son, Cotton, had enrolled in Harvard College at the age of twelve. Over the course of an exceedingly productive life, Cotton Mather wrote over four hundred books, one of which was a nonfiction account of the Salem witch trials that both he and his father were involved in, and which took the opposite view as his father's own work on the subject. The result was that Increase Mather burned his son's book in the Harvard Yard.

The 1680s were a remarkably unremarkable decade for the school in Cambridge. In 1682, not a single student graduated from Harvard College; two years later, John Rogers, president number five, happened to die during a solar eclipse, which the school indicates as the only noteworthy event of the year. Students created effigies of Harvard presidents fifteen and sixteen, and either hung or burned them in public. Abbott Lawrence Lowell, Harvard's twenty-second president, was a notorious combination of bigot, anti-Semite, and homophobe. As *The Harvard Crimson* has written, "Lowell attempted to ban black students from the Yard and place quotas on Jewish admissions." Lowell was likewise in favor of banning Harvard's gay students, as part of a covert operation known as the "Secret Court of 1920."

Unfortunately, the school's presidents weren't the only ones to experience the curse of John Harvard.

On a Monday afternoon in 1885, a Harvard sophomore was walking down the street in Boston when her dress suddenly and inexplicably caught fire, burning her to death. Some years later, Harvard chemistry students had the memorable experience of seeing their professor "suddenly throw his hands in the air," let out a piercing shriek, and fall dead to the floor. Chemistry was evidently a dangerous subject at the time: in 1886, a student burned by sulfuric acid sued the school for $50,000—a sum that must have constituted a fortune at the time.

In 1898, the son of Harvard's nineteenth president, Cornelius Conway Felton, managed to acquire a pistol while receiving treatment in a Boston hospital and shot himself to death. Another Harvard freshman shot himself in the head and survived. In 1901, a professor discovered flames emanating from a building on campus and called the fire department. The truck arrived promptly but ran over and killed a student in the process, by which time the blaze had fizzled out on its own. That same year a law school student named Morton Cressy shot an intruder who had woken him in the night, only to discover, after lighting a lamp, the intruder was actually his Harvard classmate. For the rest of his life, Cressy lived with the memory of his classmate's dying words, "You have shot your friend."

In retrospect, such accidents and errors in leadership were probably no more frequent at Harvard than at any other school. In fact, in total contrast with its reputation today, Harvard from its founding to the year 1933 was, in a word, mediocre. Offering one of the earliest criticisms of the school, Benjamin Franklin—just sixteen years old at the time—wrote sarcastically of Harvard being a "Temple of Learning," where, after spending a fortune on their education, students emerged "as great Blockheads as ever ..." The Anglican minister George Whitefield held a preceding and year-long debate with Harvard's ninth president, Edward Holyoke, who Whitefield believed had led the school into "impiety and sin." But the mediocrity of Harvard was perhaps best summarized by its sixteenth president, Edward Everett, a famously long-winded orator and rhetorician, who, in an unusual show of brevity, remarked, "When I asked to come to this university, I supposed I was to be at the head of the largest and most famous institution in America. I have been disappointed."

In an era when Exeter and Andover were considered the toughest schools in the country, the Ivy Leagues were places of relative hedonism. F. Scott Fitzgerald described Princeton University, his alma mater, as "the pleasantest country club in America." Another commentator called Stanford "a country club place, second rate and worse than you know." The Yale yearbook from 1904 bragged that it had produced "more gentlemen and fewer scholars than any other class in the memory of man." And in a quote attributed to Lincoln Kirstein, Harvard was described as "a kind of luxurious afternoon."

In response to the dwindling reputation of higher education, professors from Harvard, Swathmore College, and the University of Virginia wrote a joint letter to the American Philosophical Society, complaining of what they called "the tyranny of mediocrity ..." Two months later, in June 1929, Hans Zinsser, a professor at the Harvard Medical School, delivered a commencement speech in which he claimed, "The road to higher education has been paved so smoothly in our time, that many are impelled to enter it without considering the remote consequences to their lives." On an otherwise celebratory occasion, Zinsser dampened the mood considerably with his key point: "It is not easy to discriminate between those whose imaginations are quick with the lure of intellectual adventure ... and those whom we are apt to start on the road to disillusioned mediocrity, who will toil in growing discouragement to gather dull stores of dusty facts, as the convict accumulates his pile of dead stones."

But all that was about to change.

In 1905, a Frenchman named Alfred Binet, and his colleague Théodore Simon, made an important new discovery.

They called it the "Binet-Simon Scale of Measuring Intelligence." The scale associated a series of ordinary tasks with what the authors considered to be the underlying mental processes. A question that asked the reader to study a picture and determine which parts of a man's face were missing involved one part of the brain; a question that directed students to arrange a number of coins by value involved another; and so on.

Binet had arrived at this system after being commissioned by the French Ministry of Education to come up with a way to single out mentally disabled students for the purpose of putting them into remedial programs. Binet's solution was to administer his scale, which began with questions designed for young children and continued in order of difficulty. When the student couldn't solve any more problems, the level at which he stopped became his "mental age." Subtract this number from the student's biological age, and the Binet-Simon scale produced a mathematical score, thought to be an indicator of the student's general intelligence.

At the time of the Binet-Simon scale, Alfred Binet was the middle-aged director of a psychology laboratory at the University of

Paris's Collège de Sorbonne. Psychology wasn't what Binet had originally intended to do, nor was he technically qualified to do it. After
obtaining a law degree in 1878, Binet had abruptly changed fields and
enrolled in medical school, only to decide that wasn't for him either,
possibly the result of his father forcing him to touch dead bodies as
a boy. Whatever his reason for regularly changing vocations, Binet's
most formative years, as well as his least documented, were spent under
the tutelage of Jean-Martin Charcot.

Charcot, a swarthy, heavyset man, was a neurologist, pathologist,
and eccentric scientist. In 1882, he established a medical practice
in the Salpêtrière, a famous Parisian hospital located in the arron-
dissement des Gobelins. The hospital had once been a storehouse for
the city's gunpowder but in the late eighteenth century was turned
into an asylum for the mentally insane, as well as for a number of
Paris's seventy-five thousand prostitutes. At the time, it was popular
to believe that female sexuality was connected to a pathological
disorder known as "hysteria." At the Salpêtrière, Charcot proposed
that he had discovered a method to cure hysterical women, which
involved the application of pressure over certain "hysterogenic"
regions. According to Peter Kaplan in *Neurological Disease in Women*,
"Charcot used such techniques as well as suggestion to both treat and
provoke hysteria."

To assist him in his work, Charcot enlisted the help of two young
men. One was twenty-nine-year-old Sigmund Freud; the other
was twenty-seven-year-old Alfred Binet. Both students observed
Charcot's demonstrations with rapt attention. Nevertheless, two
opposing opinions were soon apparent: whereas Charcot and Binet
believed hysteria was a physical condition, Freud and another neurologist from the city of Nancy formed another view entirely. While
never denouncing the legitimacy of hysteria as a medical condition,
the so-called "Nancy school" contended that the alleged disorder was

a phenomenon of the mind (and not the womb, as the "Paris school" believed).

The Nancy school turned out to be right, with the result that Charcot was soon disgraced. For Freud, whose prior distinguishing contribution to academia had been the discovery of eel testicles—a small success he'd nonetheless managed to compromise by endorsing cocaine as a treatment for neurosis of the nasal passage—his siding with the Nancy school helped launch his career in psychoanalysis. While his differences with Charcot were substantial, Freud never entirely forgot his apprenticeship at the Salpêtrière. In his lengthy tribute to Charcot at the time of the hypnotist's death, in 1893, Freud claimed, "the young science of neurology has lost its greatest leader, neurologists of every country have lost their master teacher and France has lost one of her foremost men." Freud neglected to mention that he had named his son after Charcot: Jean-Martin Freud was born in 1889.

As for Binet, after six unpaid years in an asylum for hypnotized prostitutes, he didn't appear to know what to do with himself next. In 1884, he had married the daughter of an embryologist, and now had two young daughters. After leaving the Salpêtrière, he became interested in the study of magic and was involved in the first known recorded movie of a live magic trick, performed by the French entertainer Edouard-Joseph Raynaly. Binet also studied handwriting analysis, personality theory, the abstract reasoning capabilities of blindfolded chess players, and sexual attractiveness. He coined the word "fetishism," founded a regular journal of psychology, and took another unpaid job at the Collège de Sorbonne.

It was around this time that Binet grew interested in skulls. The famous anatomist Paul Broca had died in 1880, and Binet continued Broca's research on craniometry in his journal, *L'Année Psychologique*. In the span of three years, Binet published three articles on the "The relationship between the intelligence of subjects and the volume of their head ..." The articles constituted some of the earliest published work on the subject for which Binet would soon become internationally known. To assist the research, he began visiting schools and asking teachers to identify the smartest and densest students in the class. Binet acknowledged he hadn't questioned the foundation of what he was doing, and was simply following "the idea, impressed upon me by the studies of so many other scientists, that intellectual superiority is tied to superiority of cerebral volume."

It wasn't, and his study of craniometry was quietly dropped.

But Binet got a second chance when, in 1904, the Ministry of Education approached him about a way to single out mentally retarded students. By this time, Binet had had a chance to reflect on his earlier mistakes—and in addition, to read the work of Francis Galton. Galton was a scientist, adventurer, and half cousin of Charles Darwin. Fully literate by the age of two and a half, Galton could "say all the Latin Substantives and Adjectives and active verbs," as well as read in French, recite poetry in Latin, do mathematics, and "read any English book" by his fifth birthday. The following year, Galton was reading Homer, Shakespeare, William Cowper, and Walter Scott for pleasure; as his astonished sister noted, "by reading a page twice over, [he] repeats it by heart." At seven, Galton began a serious entomology collection, by the age of thirteen was drafting blueprints for rudimentary airplanes, and in his early twenties became a respected London scientist, by which time he had already rafted down the Nile, sailed from Egypt to Beirut, and ridden a camel caravan into Khartoum.

Partly prompted by a belief in his own intellectual superiority, Galton wrote a book called *Hereditary Genius*. In it, he propounded the seductively simple thesis that "a man's natural abilities are derived by inheritance ..." Rather than being acquired through learning and a nurturing environment, intelligence was a fixed, immutable property of nature, passed down from generation to generation. In Galton's mind, this explained why he and Charles Darwin were both brilliant: they were part of the same brilliant gene pool. The other, much darker side of *Hereditary Genius* was hereditary stupidity, and here, in the preface of his book, Galton admitted, "the idea of investigating the subject of hereditary genius occurred to me during the course of a purely ethnological inquiry, into the mental peculiarities of different races ..." Since intelligence was inherited through reproduction, it only made sense that stupid people shouldn't reproduce. Such thoughtless propagation led to groups of inferior races, which Galton ranked with his own marking system. African Americans were "a difference of two grades" lower than Anglo-Saxons, and "The Australian type is at least one grade below the African negro."

Published in 1869, *Hereditary Genius* was, according to multiple sources, a best-seller. More significantly, it announced its author as the father of two important new disciplines: eugenics and psychometrics. Eugenics, based on the idea that intelligence is a fixed and heritable property, was the supposed science of improving populations using two methods: one was the practice of controlled breeding (that is, ensuring that people of the same intellectual level reproduce together), while the other was sterilization. "Sterilization, surgically speaking, is an operative procedure in which the ducts leading from the organs of procreation are severed, or divided, thereby rendering the subject incapable of reproduction." Controlled breeding increased a population's intelligence while sterilization decreased its stupidity. Psychometrics, on the other hand, was the closely related study of developing, administering, and scoring psychological tests that allegedly determine intelligence, aptitude, and a host of other variables.

Aside from these two significant but primarily intellectual accomplishments, Galton's role in both of these fields was in the influence of more pragmatic students. After learning about a laboratory in which Galton had conducted his psychometric work, an American named

James McKeen Cattell contacted the author of *Hereditary Genius* to discuss their common interest. In 1886, Cattell was completing his PhD thesis, "Psychometric Investigations," and Galton quickly became a mentor figure. Cattell would later describe him as "the greatest man I have ever known." In 1887, Cattell established the first psychometric laboratory, located in Cambridge.

The degree to which Galton influenced Binet is difficult to know. In his history of the IQ, Stephen Murdoch writes that Binet "didn't believe that he was measuring a fixed quantity of intelligence." In Binet's own words, "Some recent philosophers appear to have given their moral support to the deplorable verdict that the intelligence of the individual is a fixed quantity, a quantity which cannot be augmented. We must protest and act against this brutal pessimism ..." It's been reasoned that Binet—whose reputation had been compromised along with Charcot's at the Salpêtrière—had learned to be cautious about declaring scientific breakthroughs, and was skeptical of the "pessimistic" view that intelligence could not be nurtured and couldn't change over the course of a person's life. Concerning his own opinion, Binet gave the analogy of a field that, in the hands of a good farmer, could grow from fallow to harvest. "It is in this particular sense, the only one that is significant, that we say that the intelligence of children may be increased ... namely the capacity to learn, to improve with instruction."

While it continues to be the source of contentious debate, the view that Binet opposed Galton has become increasingly mainstream. According to an introductory psychology textbook, Binet was hesitant about the use of intelligence testing on two counts. First, "He warned that IQ tests do not and should not be used to measure innate intelligence and that IQ tests should not be used to label individuals." While even now some mistakenly believe that Binet "invented the IQ test," this is technically wrong on a number of counts: he didn't invent a test, but rather a scale, and one in which intelligence was movable. Second, Binet's scale didn't measure IQ (the "intelligence quotient"), but gave a much more general indication of a person's intellectual ability at that particular moment.

But there soon began a long and systematic perversion of Binet's original intent. The English-language version of the Binet-Simon scale was translated by a eugenicist, revised by another eugenicist, and administered to millions of people by a third eugenicist. In short, it was used in the service of the troubling idea that humans are best treated as livestock—the prized specimens are to be bred to produce offspring with felicitous qualities, while the beasts who don't quite meet the standards of the breed are to be culled. The process by which steers could be made beefier and dogs more eager to retrieve could, it was believed, be employed to make the working class just as robust and pliable. In 1907, compulsory state sterilization laws were passed in Indiana, where it was declared "heredity plays a most important part in the transmission of crime, idiocy and imbecility." Two years later, Francis Galton was knighted. Fifteen other states had adopted similar legislation by 1917, and in 1933, following the American initiative, the Nazi Party began its official campaign of eugenic sterilization.

Intriguingly, it was in this same year that James Bryant Conant became the twenty-third president of Harvard.

Unlike Harvard presidents before him, Conant wasn't born into Boston's rich upper class (called "Brahmin"), but rather had grown up in working-class Dorchester, the son of a humble wood engraver. There was enough money to send Conant to Harvard, where he graduated at the age of twenty. He was not only the first Harvard graduate of the Conant family, but the first Conant-family graduate of any college.

In 1917, at the age of twenty-five, Conant became a major in the Chemical Warfare Service, a division of the army whose job was to create weapons for World War I. For the duration of the war, Conant lived in an industrial plant in Willoughby, Ohio, creating a weapon "more powerful than mustard gas," which at the time was the most lethal chemical weapon there was. No one knew the researchers were living in the factory, and their work was considered a national secret. When Conant's team resurfaced, they had created lewisite, an amber liquid that "carried the gentle fragrance of geranium blossoms but burst into flame when combined with water." The effect was an "intolerable agony" seventy-two times more lethal than mustard gas, a toxicity Conant specifically helped to achieve by harnessing the power of arsenic. The result was known to the public as the "Dew of Death," and, according to its class as a chemical weapon, has since been categorized as a "weapon of mass destruction." (Following the Iraq–Kuwait War, lewisite was found among the Saddam Hussein arsenal.)

During World War II, Conant was the de facto leader of the Manhattan Project. According to Joel A. Vilensky's history of lewisite, "There was a direct connection between lewisite, the atomic bomb, and the winning of the Second World War." Conant was awarded the highest honor of the American Chemical Society, the Priestley Medal, in 1944, as well as the Roosevelt Medal of Honor in 1948, and the Presidential Medal of Freedom in 1963. While his contributions to American society—"from Harvard to Hiroshima," as James G. Hershberg has put it in a book of the same name—can hardly be matched by another figure of the period, Conant was famously detached from his professional as well as personal life. When his 701-page autobiography, *My Several Lives*, was published in 1970, literary critic John Leonard commented, "Mr. Conant doesn't examine his life; he reports it as might an obituary writer." *My Several Lives* felt like it was written "in an airless room on some other planet ..."

One reviewer who joked that Conant had read one too many committee reports seemed to strike an unexpected nerve: Conant had in fact been asked to write his memoir by the Carnegie Corporation. Friends had arranged for two doctoral students to work through 527 boxes of personal correspondence. "I reacted with no enthusiasm," Conant later admitted. "I had a strong prejudice against people who wrote autobiographies." Conant's reticence was such that, when he announced his resignation from Harvard in 1953, his parting words to students of the school that had been his alma mater, home, and employer for decades was to "Never explain; your friends don't require it; your enemies won't believe you anyway."

But Conant began his presidency of Harvard on another note entirely. Within the first week of taking office, he set a plan in motion he'd been thinking about for some time. "We should be able to say that any man with remarkable talents may obtain his education at Harvard," he wrote in his first presidential report. The idea was based on what Conant called "the natural aristocracy," a phrase admittedly borrowed from Thomas Jefferson, who, in correspondence with John Adams in 1813, had written, "The natural aristocracy I consider as the most precious gift of nature for the instruction, the trusts, and the government of society ..." Jefferson, in other words, had wanted to reorganize society based on intellectual ability, not wealth.

While the plan had ultimately failed, Conant at once saw its applicability in higher education. Where the old Harvard had been an average school for many rich students, the new Harvard would select a small number of smart ones. As Nicholas Lemann has written, "Everyone would go to elementary and high school. Then would come a strict selection." This selection would prevent intellectually average students from attending Harvard while letting in the smartest ones. "The new elite's essential quality, the factor that would make its power deserved where the old elite's had been merely inherited, would be brains."

Conant's vision was radical. He wasn't proposing reforms just of Harvard, but—since Harvard students graduated into powerful positions in the working world—of society itself. Anyone who wanted to be powerful would first need a Harvard education. To this end, Conant instituted the "National Scholarship Program," a trust fund that awarded full scholarships, including room and board, to students who were intellectually—not necessarily economically—endowed (students, in other words, who probably reminded him of himself). Before Conant's arrival, Harvard had awarded no full scholarships, and any kind of handout whatsoever covered, at most, half the expenses a student could expect to incur. With the National Scholarship Program, Conant was remaking the entire admissions process of higher education. "If the fundamental purpose behind the national scholarship policy is to be finally achieved," Conant wrote in an annual report, "many other colleges and universities must obtain money for this same end and use their present scholarship funds along the same lines."

The only question, of course, was how to determine which students deserved the scholarships. Conant decided the primary criteria for admittance should be "potential for success in college," a contention that was controversial even within Harvard's own administration. But according to Jerome Karabel in *The Chosen: The Hidden History of Admission and Exclusion at Harvard, Yale, and Princeton*, Conant believed "This definition of merit sent the message that the quality Harvard valued most was academic excellence." Judging students' potential admission to college based on their academic success was how Harvard would distinguish itself, both from other colleges and its own past, and in 1934, two assistant deans were given the task of figuring out how exactly Harvard would go about doing this.

By his own estimation, Lewis Terman was a genius.

The twelfth of a farmer's fourteen children, Terman was born in 1887, in rural Indiana's Johnson County. In a later self-analysis, Terman aptly described himself as deeply peculiar. When a traveling phrenologist stopped by the farm, a pleasant evening was spent feeling the Terman family's skulls. When the phrenologist reached Lewis, he predicted "great things" for the boy with the oversized head. The experience seemed to awaken an introspective side of Terman, who began spending time in his room repeating the question "Am I living?—Am I living?—Am I living?" while rocking back and forth.

Terman left the family farm at age fifteen to become a public school teacher and principal before eventually entering Clark University, where he received a doctoral degree under G. Stanley Hall, the psychologist who famously compared children to "savages," and spent his summers rolling naked through the fields of Massachusetts. After graduating from Clark University in 1905, Terman moved to California (the drier climate suited his tuberculosis) and in 1910 was appointed to the Faculty of Education at Stanford University. One day, after hiking in the San Bernardino Mountains, a friend told him about the work of Alfred Binet. He "urged me to start some work at once with the Binet 1908 scale for measuring intelligence."

The scale had first been adapted by a man named H. H. Goddard. Like Terman, Goddard had been a teacher and principal, and also received his doctorate under G. Stanley Hall. In 1906 he became the director of research at an institution for the mentally handicapped, then called the Vineland Training School for Feeble-Minded Girls and Boys, and now called simply the Vineland Training School. Two years after assuming this position, Goddard made a tour of similar institutions in Europe. While there, he heard of Binet's scale and, realizing its application to eugenics, returned purposefully to the United States. Disregarding Binet's warning about the "brutal pessimism" of intelligence testing, Goddard supervised the English-language translation of the Binet-Simon scale.

The revised test was first administered to four hundred Vineland children, where Goddard discovered "the test scores corresponded quite closely with the informal diagnoses that had been arrived at by the professional staff," according to Barry J. Zimmerman and Dale H. Schunk. Next, Goddard gave the test to two thousand New Jersey public school students and compared these results with the students from his Vineland school. The results validated his supposition, and Goddard began work on his infamous book *The Kallikak Family: A Study in the Heredity of Feeble-Mindedness*, published in 1912. In *The Kallikak Family*, Goddard did what Galton had done in *Hereditary Genius*, except with the opposite end of the spectrum. He traced the family lineage of one of his mentally retarded students, whom he called Deborah Kallikak, in an effort to show the hereditability of intelligence.

In his book, Goddard followed Deborah's family back to Martin Kallikak, an American patriot of wholesome character and good breeding. But Martin had supposedly indulged in a one-night stand with a retarded barmaid and produced an illegitimate child. It was this child who tainted the gene pool, leading to generations of Kallikak criminals and defectives, including Deborah. Martin Kallikak had meanwhile remarried a Quaker girl and produced 495 morally virtuous descendants, nearly all of whom had normal intelligence levels and led happy, fulfilled lives. (*Kallikak* is an etymological mixture of the Greek roots for "good" and "bad," and illustrated the two hereditary lines.) Amazingly, Goddard's work was embraced by the academic community, and Goddard himself served on the Eugenics Section of the American Breeders' Association and the Committee for the

Heredity of the Feeble-Minded. Both organizations advocated brutal eugenics doctrines and helped advance the American sterilization laws of the 1920s.

But Goddard was even more famous for another reason. With the publication of *Feeble-Mindedness: Its Causes and Consequences* in 1914, he cemented the intelligence vocabulary we use to this day. It was Goddard who popularized the word *moron*, which referred to— at Goddard's design—the threshold of mental retardation. A moron was someone with the mental age of an eight- to twelve-year-old; one ratchet lower than moron was *imbecile*, and the absolute bedrock of stupidity was *idiot*. At the same time that Goddard was defining the lower spectrum of intelligence, Lewis Terman added another important piece: the intelligence quotient. By comparing a person's score on an intelligence test with the statistical average for his or her age, an "IQ" could be produced. Terman classified Goddard's definitions in the following way (all scores are out of 100): idiots were 25 points or below; imbeciles were in the 50 to 70 range; morons were in the 70 and 80 range; a "dull" person had an IQ of between 80 and 90; normal was between 90 and 110; above-normal was 110 to 120; very superior was 120 to 140; and finally, geniuses were 140 points and above.

Perhaps a result of his own phrenological giftedness, Terman was especially interested in people with high IQs. In 1921, he initiated one of psychology's most famous experiments: In what has been called the "longest-running repeated-measures" experiment ever conducted, Terman found 1,538 children in elementary and high schools whose average chronological age was eleven and average IQ was 151. For thirty-five years, Terman made detailed reports on each of his students' interests, family, health, personality, work, physical characteristics, and more. The students affectionately referred to themselves as "Termites," and some even wore termite pendants. Researchers took over Terman's "Study of the Gifted" following his death and continue their observations on ultra-high-IQ students to this day (whose lives, it turns out, are largely indistinguishable from our own).

But even back in the 1920s, IQ testing was not universally appreciated. Walter Lippmann, the Pulitzer Prize–winning reporter and critic, was the most noted opponent of Terman's revision of the Binet scale. "I hate the impudence of a claim that in fifty minutes you can judge and classify a human being's predestined fitness in life," he wrote in an article directed at Terman. "I hate the pretentiousness of that claim. I hate the abuse of scientific method which it involves. I hate the sense of superiority which it creates and the sense of inferiority which it imposes." Rather than defend his assertion, Terman tended to respond with sarcastic, personal attacks. "The validity of intelligence tests is hardly a question the psychologist would care to debate with Mr. Lippmann," he wrote in 1922.

For his part, H. H. Goddard's taxonomic choice of *moron* for the threshold category of mental retardation had repercussions that, given its continued colloquial usage today, are obviously still in effect. Interestingly, eugenicists had considered the word *fool* in its place, but Goddard had rejected it on the grounds that *moron* was a derivation of the Greek word meaning "slow." Meeting in 1910, the American Association for the Study of the Feeble-Minded voted in favor of officially adopting the word *moron* to describe borderline retardation. Following the meeting, however, a doctor named A. C. Rogers wrote a letter to Goddard in which he claimed that, in modern Greek usage, *moron* actually meant "mulberry." Rogers, who was the director of a competing school for the mentally retarded, proposed *aphron* instead. Goddard wrote a terse letter in response, reminding Rogers that the association had already voted, and "Personally, I must confess I do not see any good in discussing it. As far as I am concerned I would be perfectly willing to call them *stubs* or anything else."

At the beginning of the twentieth century, Robert Yerkes didn't quite know what to do with himself.

Having grown up on a farm in Pennsylvania, he had dreamed of becoming a salesman, preacher, or train engineer. In the end, he went to medical school, changed his mind and switched to philosophy, then biology, then psychology, only to discover his real passion was gorillas. Yerkes spent the majority of his professional life writing *Conjugal Contrasts among Chimpanzees* and other primatological classics. Progressive in his day, Yerkes came to believe that if relocated to human environments, primates would develop speech and other forms of human intelligence. To this end, and with the help of the Carnegie Corporation, Yerkes founded the Yale University Laboratories of Primate Biology (now the Yerkes National Primate Research Center in Atlanta*).

But by the age of forty, Yerkes was, as the late science writer Stephen Jay Gould noted, "frustrated." The profession on which he had settled—psychology—was still an inchoate discipline. If taught in university, psychology was often categorized as a "humanities" subject, alongside art, history, and literature. As one commentator summarized the consensus, "Psychology is a science only when it sticks to facts and scientific methods of investigation." This was precisely what Yerkes intended to do with it. Before the start of World War I, Terman and Yerkes jointly approached Rockefeller's General Education Board "for the support of a sort of school survey which would include the measurement of the intelligence of a good-sized group of pupils."

---

* Scientists at the research center eventually produced the computer language "Yerkish" to act as a medium between primates and humans. Chimpanzees and other apes press a Yerkish keyboard of symbols to communicate basic sentences to researchers, and vice versa.

Terman and Yerkes were friends—"kindred spirits," according to Terman—and both wanted to legitimize the psychology profession through the use of psychometrics. While the General Education Board expressed interest in helping with this endeavor, an even better opportunity arose with the onset of war. If Terman and Yerkes could talk the army into letting them administer IQ tests to new recruits, psychology would "transition from dubious art to respected science," in the words of Gould. Throughout the spring and summer of 1917, Terman and Yerkes met at Goddard's Vineland school to develop what came to be known as the Alpha and Beta exams. The Alpha was for recruits who could read and write, while Beta consisted of a pictorial exam; recruits who failed both were given an individual test, "usually some version of the Binet scales." In total, nearly two million army recruits were tested.

Still, the Committee on the Psychological Examination of Recruits—as the Terman and Yerkes outfit was called—wasn't an especially popular program. Three independent inquiries were made following the tests' implementation, reaching the conclusion that Yerkes shouldn't have been allowed to treat the army's recruits "as a hobby for the purpose of obtaining data for research ..." But this was exactly what had happened. Following the largest-scale testing operation ever conducted, Terman and Yerkes received a "steady stream of requests from commercial concerns, educational institutions, and individuals for the use of army methods of psychological examining or for the adaptation of such methods to special needs."

So Terman and Yerkes decided to start a business. In the spring of 1919, the General Education Board donated twenty-five thousand dollars to the National Research Council, "to be used for the preparation of methods of measuring the intelligence of children in the elementary schools." Terman, Yerkes, Thorndike (a pupil of Cattell's, who was the pupil of Galton's), and a man named Guy Whipple met to discuss the project. The exams were reconstructed from the Alpha and Beta material, and republished by the World Book Company as the National Intelligence Tests. The first print ran in the summer of 1920, and by June of the following year, Whipple estimated that two hundred thousand copies had been sold, though another estimate puts the figure at four hundred thousand.

In short, American schools were overrun with a variation of the same IQ tests used in the army. Both sets were multiple choice, and featured the same assortment of puzzles, substitutions, vocabulary and analogy problems, comparisons, sentence completion, math questions, and more. In the same way that the Alpha and Beta tests had classified new recruits based on their IQ, the National Intelligence Tests tracked students into average, advanced, and remedial classes, as we find them today. The similarity between army and school was so striking that one historian wrote, "The superintendent sits as commander of the armies, the principal acts as field commander, the teacher as officers, and below this command is a vast army of pupils. Orders flow from above, and pupils like soldiers receive privileges but are without rights."

Since part of the eugenics belief system was that people of inferior intelligence were more likely to be visible socially in the form of criminals, immigrants, drunks, prostitutes, and the like, Terman, Yerkes, Goddard, and Thorndike had no shortage of people from whom to extract data to support their claims. Goddard was infamously involved in the immigration process at Ellis Island and hired two women to single out supposedly retarded immigrants, a process they claimed to be able to do by sight. The result was that large numbers of certain ethnicities were sent back to Europe. One selection of 152 women determined that 87 percent of Russians, 83 percent of Jews, 80 percent of Hungarians, and 79 percent of Italians were idiots, imbeciles, and morons. Among other findings, Yerkes and company uncovered that "from 30 to 60 percent of prostitutes are deficient and are for the most part high-grade morons ..."

In *Psychological Examining in the United States Army*, Yerkes awarded an overall IQ score to the entire United States. According to his calculations, 37 percent of the white population and 89 percent of the black population were officially morons. Intriguingly, it was in a similar vein that Carl Brigham produced *A Study of American Intelligence*. Brigham had worked for the Committee on the Psychological Examination of Recruits, and helped administer Alpha and Beta tests during the war. Like Terman, Yerkes, and Cattell, Brigham used the intelligence data following the war to support his own eugenic philosophy. In his study—published by Princeton University Press—Brigham claimed that the population of the United States could be grouped into four ethnic categories: Nordic, Alpine, Mediterranean, and Negro.

As has been pointed out, Brigham appeared to have based his theory on the proximity of each group to the equator. "Nordics" were the farthest away—they were of Scandinavian and English ancestry—and "Negros" were the closest. Through immigration and interbreeding, the stupidity of the Alpine and Mediterranean races posed a serious threat to the United States, but Brigham reserved the most animosity toward Negroes. "We must face a possibility of racial admixture here that is infinitely worse than that faced by any European country today," he wrote, "for we are incorporating the Negro into our racial stock, while all of Europe is comparatively free from this taint." Brigham called the interbreeding of blacks and whites "the most sinister development in the history of this continent," and hinted at his preference for sterilization, claiming, "The really important steps are looking toward the prevention of the continued propagation of defective strains in the present population."

Brigham, a stocky New Englander, had moved to Canada in 1917, where he worked as a psychologist for the Military Hospital Commission. Brigham had recently graduated from Princeton, which was evidently a surprise to everyone who knew him. According to

Lemann, Brigham "had drunk his way through his first two years at Princeton." It was only after he became a psychologist that Brigham's life seemed to take on a new purpose. When Robert Yerkes traveled to Canada in order to collect data on military recruits, he took special note of Carl Brigham, and later asked him to become one of sixteen assistants to Terman and Yerkes's Committee on the Psychological Examination of Recruits. When Brigham authored *A Study of American Intelligence* in 1923, it was Yerkes who introduced the book.

In 1892, Harvard's twenty-first president, Charles Eliot, was chair of an organization called the Committee of Ten, a division of the National Education Association (NEA) that wanted to regulate the college entrance experience for high school students. Eventually, in the year 1900, twelve colleges and universities across the United States founded the College Entrance Examination Board, known today simply as the College Board.

The College Board's job was to create and administer an entrance exam whose results would be reported to participating colleges and universities. The institutions would then decide which students to admit. A rudimentary test existed from 1900 and 1915, consisting of nine content areas: English, German, French, Latin, Greek, math, physics, chemistry, and history. Students were asked to translate passages from Cicero and prove difficult physics problems by drawing them. Since multiple choice had not yet been invented, scoring all the paperwork could take months. In 1901, only 973 students took the College Board exam. By 1910 the number had grown to 3,731.

To standardize the admissions process further, the College Board approached Carl Brigham in 1922. After administering the Alpha and Beta tests to recruits during the war, Brigham had returned to Princeton, this time as a faculty member. His *Study of American Intelligence* had earned him a reputation, as had his association with veteran psychologists Terman and Yerkes. None of the members on the College Board knew anything about psychometrics and were presumably happy to give the job to someone who did. For Brigham, coming up with a standard admissions test can't have been an exceptionally difficult task. To complete his assignment, Brigham simply referred to Alpha and Beta exams, and calibrated a new test consisting of two components: verbal/linguistic and mathematics/science. The scores were tabulated on a scale continuum from 200 to 800, with a mean of 500 and a standard deviation of 100. He called it the Scholastic Aptitude Test, and on June 23, 1926, over eight thousand students wrote Brigham's SAT.

By the time James Conant assumed the role of Harvard president some seven years later, the SAT was the standard college entrance exam. When Conant appointed two assistant deans to find a way to admit the geniuses while excluding the morons, they didn't have far to look. In December 1933, Conant's committee members—Henry Chauncey and Wilbur Bender—met with Carl Brigham to discuss the SAT. By this time, Brigham had apparently had a remarkable change of heart and begun publicly renouncing *A Study of American Intelligence* as well as the entire discipline of psychometrics. "The more I work in this field," he wrote in 1929, "the more I am convinced that psychologists have sinned greatly in sliding easily from the name of the test to the function or trait measured." Three years later, Brigham recanted further in the justly entitled *A Study of Error*. Brigham called IQ testing, which he had helped to pioneer, "one of the most glorious fallacies in the history of science."

As we might expect, there has been some speculation about why Brigham suddenly saw things differently. In an article for *The Atlantic Monthly*, Nicholas Lemann offers the radically understated assertion that "Eugenics was passing out of fashion at the time." The closer the Nazi Party came to power, the more Brigham withdrew his earlier pronouncements. It didn't help that even Yerkes called German interest in psychometrics "the logical sequel to the psychological and personnel services in our own Army during 1917–1918." The relationship between the United States' program of intelligence testing and the Nazi program of eugenics was such that, according to the story, senior-ranking Nazi officials on trial at Nuremburg cited, in their own defense, that they'd gotten the idea from the United States.

Indeed, there exists another connection between Nazism and American academia. In 1909, Ernst Hanfstaengl, a close personal and political associate of Adolf Hitler, graduated from none other than Harvard University. A gifted pianist, Hanfstaengl allegedly composed both the Harvard fight song and the Nazi fight song. In 1934, Hanfstaengl returned to his alma mater to participate in a parade, where he was seen giving the Nazi salute to friends in the crowd, and afterward was invited to have tea with James Conant. The most senior-ranking Nazi to ever visit the United States, Hanfstaengl was even considered for an honorary degree—though in the face of student protests, Conant wisely declined, rejecting as well Hanfstaengl's proposal to establish a scholarship after himself (an equally wise decision, if only because of the difficulty of pronouncing "Hanfstaengl").

But it was before the visit of Hitler's right-hand man that Conant, in 1933, assigned one of his deans a task. Henry Chauncey, the primary subject of Nicholas Lemann's *The Big Test: The Secret History of the American Meritocracy*, was given the job of convincing the rest of America's colleges to adopt the SAT, which they did. (Carl Brigham, in keeping with his newfound sense of right and wrong, was against the idea of using his test as an entrance exam and stood in opposition to Chauncey until his death in 1943—at which time Chauncey could proceed without Brigham's approval.)

While Henry Chauncey once admitted the SAT was "essentially an intelligence test," the College Board has understandably wanted to distance itself from the idea that the test taken by millions of students every year is a product of the eugenics movement. In 1946, when the College Board replaced the SAT's logic problems with reading comprehension, they insisted that the IQ component had been replaced by something called "reasoning ability," which they claim is different from intelligence. R. J. Brodnick, former director of institutional research and planning at Shippensburg University, found a "substantial relationship" between SAT scores and the general intelligence factor (known as "g") when he coauthored a paper on the subject. In a more recent study published in the journal *Psychological Science*, Meredith C. Frey and Douglas K. Detterman found "a striking relation between SAT scores and measures of general cognitive ability."

In fact, SAT-to-IQ calculations are so easy to make that many websites offer an algorithm for tabulating the conversion.

But discussions of the disturbing origins of the SAT are often lost amid other complains. The accuracy of the SAT as a predictor of a student's success—one of the College Board's most consistent assertions—continues to be a hotly debated issue. A 1980 study deduced that the SAT was "a third-rate predictor of college performance." The same year, a 555-page study conducted by Ralph Nader concluded the entrance exams "do not, in fact, predict much of anything." *The Case Against the SAT*, which appeared in 1988 and was written by James Crouse and Dale Trusheim, argued that high school grades are a better indicator of success than the SAT, a claim that has been repeated often since.

But for every argument against the SAT—and there are many—a seemingly equal volume of supporting material exists. A study in 1989 found that the correlation of the SAT with first-year grade point average (FYGPA) was strong initially and only decreased over time. A 2001 report synthesized three thousand validity studies, with data from over a million students, "and found that the SAT is a valid predictor of FYGPA, with multiple correlations corrected for range restriction and attenuation ranging from 0.44 to 0.62," in the psychometric jargon of the College Board.

Still, just what the SAT is and does is one of the most enigmatic and controversial riddles of higher education. At times famously biased toward wealthy white males—prior exams have asked students about polo ponies, cummerbunds, and pâté de foie gras—the makers of the SAT have so far only attempted to rework and recalibrate, rather than remake. Since its debut in 1926, the SAT has undergone no fewer than twenty major revisions, and—owing to the highly contentious nature of the SAT's history and philosophical contentions—has had its name changed on multiple occasions. "SAT" has variously stood for Scholastic Aptitude Test, Scholastic Achievement Test, and Scholastic Assessment Test, and now doesn't stand for anything. The absence of a literal meaning of "SAT" reflects the inability of the College Board and wider psychometric community to produce a cogent explanation as to what the test actually measures.

Oddly, this hasn't prevented its use as the standard admissions test for well over half a century. Considering its beginnings in one of the darkest periods of American history, it's hard to think of a more divisive, more offensive, more objectionable idea than the SAT. It seems likely that many students who write the exam today are unaware of its origin as a tool of racial, intellectual, social, moral, and merito-cratic segregation, its initial purpose as a device to support the eugenics cause, and its evolution as Brigham's interpretation of Yerkes's admin-istration of Terman's revision of Goddard's translation of Binet's scale. Nor is it likely that many students are aware that standardized tests, which began with the SAT, presuppose the same Galtonian principle of a fixed, immutable intelligence that can be assessed through psycho-metrics—a point of view Binet referred to as "brutal pessimism."

Following the establishment of the SAT, Conant left Harvard to work on the Manhattan Project; Yerkes returned to his gorillas; and Terman died of tuberculosis. As for Carl Brigham, he became head of the College Board. In 1947, the Harvard dean who had brought Brigham's SAT to Conant—Henry Chauncey—became the president of an organization called Educational Testing Service, or ETS for short.

SERIOUS BUSINESS

Testing is serious business.

In China, exams can take many days to write, during which time entire districts are closed down, traffic rerouted, and noise levels restricted citywide. Students running late may receive a police escort to the exam center, where tests are guarded by armed officers, monitored under closed-circuit surveillance, and classified "top secret" by the Chinese government.

Each year, thousands of cheaters are caught and arrested. These students are not scribbling notes onto napkins but are involved in something more closely resembling the montage scene of a spy movie. Networks of highly organized students have been caught with miniature high-definition cameras, scanning their exam in real time to a prearranged team of experts who debate the questions in a remote location before relaying the consensus back through a wireless earpiece.

Far from being student-run operations, Chinese cheating networks involve parents, teachers, and even (it's been rumored) high-ranking government officials. In 2009, a plot two years in the making was thwarted when a network of parents and teachers was caught by police doing a radio sweep of the exam building. Jail terms for the offenders ranged from six months to three years—an improvement over earlier eras, when anyone caught cheating was simply shot.

The students of the Beijing scandal were writing the college entrance exam. By number alone, it is the biggest test in the world. The *gao kao* is written by over ten million high school students annually, takes two days to complete, and is "key to social mobility in China," according to *The Guardian*. Exam results mean the difference between getting into a good school—and having access to a good job—and not. Because space is limited, students are competing against each other, and only three in five make the cut. A Chinese proverb describes the process as "thousands of soldiers and tens of thousands of horses [stampeding] across a single log bridge."

Preparation for the *gao kao* begins at age five and represents a truly staggering level of devotion considering that, after twelve years of all-day cram sessions and countless hours of study, students might catch a cold on either of the two days of their exam; or not make it in time and be locked out (as happened, in 2007, to a student who was four minutes late); or sit down only to discover they suddenly can't recall a thing. Not to mention, of course, the possibility of simply being outdone by another student, either one who studied longer, harder, and better, or one who spent the last twenty-four months assembling a team of academics (possibly including the teacher himself) and is at this moment sending them images of his exam sheet from a camera imbedded in the button on his collar.

With so much intensity, it is not surprising that these types of tests are described as "high-stakes." In her blog, a teacher from the province of Gansu summarized the situation by writing that "students consider scores as something as important as life itself." In fact, exam scores seem to be in another category altogether. On the day results from the *gao kao* are announced, rashes of suicide break out across China. It is the country's fifth most common cause of death and first among people of a student age. There are no official numbers provided by the Chinese government, but considering the exceptionally high stakes—*gao kao* means "high test," after all—we can assume the number is likewise not low.

India keeps a more thorough record of its high-stakes victims. The national newspaper, *The Times of India*, reported 5,857 suicides "due to exam stress" in 2006, or sixteen per day. The following year it was seventeen; the year after, eighteen. Expectations are so high that students have been known to jump from the Gandhi Bridge rather than face their parents with a B–. Some don't even wait for the results to come in. A "bright mechanical engineering student" leapt to his death thirty minutes before his exam took place. In the spring of 2009, another student hanged himself shortly after breakfast. "His friends said they were completely clueless about any possible reason," *The Times* noted, "for he secured 70 per cent marks in high school, was a brilliant student, and was an IIT-JEE aspirant."

The JEE is the entrance exam to the Indian Institute of Technology and, by some estimations, the hardest test on earth. Students are required to write two papers on four subjects in six hours. A sample question reads: "A proton and an alpha particle, after being accelerated through the same potential difference, enter a uniform magnetic field the direction of which is perpendicular to their velocities. Find the ratio of radii of the circular paths of the two particles." Students preparing for such questions are reminded to "keep depressing thoughts away" by breathing deeply, performing gentle stretches, and engaging in "light chit-chat" with friends.

"First of all," the official website cautions, "realize that you are not the only one facing anxiety. Each IIT-JEE aspirant is facing the same dilemma." Of the half-million students who apply to the Indian Institute of Technology, only 8,295 get in—to be reminded of this fact just before writing the entrance exam can't be much of a comforting thought. Competition is so stiff, and expectations so unreasonable, that eighteen-year-old Joginder Singh, who received a coveted acceptance letter after passing the world's most difficult exam, committed suicide anyway: he'd wanted to get into the Delhi campus, and not the one in Kharagpur.

Testing is serious business.

Based out of Lawrence, New Jersey, Educational Testing Service earns over $1 billion annually. It is the world's biggest testing company, with 9,000 locations in 180 countries (including India and China). It designs, develops, administers, and scores 24 million tests each year, about three million of which are the college entrance exam. The SAT is the company's original and best-known product, though there are numerous other abbreviations as well: the SLEP, SLAA, SLS, SSA, TFI, TOEFL, TOEIC, TOPT, TASC, to name some from just two stations in the alphabet.

ETS, as the company itself is abbreviated, distinguishes between and has separate categories for tests of achievement, adaption, and aptitude; standardized, norm-, and criterion-referenced tests; licensure and certification tests; and tests scored by either a human or machine. ETS makes tests for students ranging from junior kindergarten to grade 12, to those entering a technical college, to those entering Ivy League grad schools. There are tests for non-anglophones learning English as a business language, English as an academic language, and English as an idiomatic language; separate and numerous tests for non-francophones learning to read, write, listen to, and speak French; and a test for people who want to teach sign language in the state of Texas. ETS administers tests that simply prepare you to take more tests and tests you have to take should you want to administer tests yourself. Through data collected from many of its small tests, the company creates one very big test, the National Assessment of Educational

Progress, whose results are published in the form of "The Nation's Report Card."

These are clearly people who like tests, and not just the ones you get in school. In practical terms, you cannot become a firefighter, police officer, marine, naval officer, soldier, librarian, travel agent, realtor, mechanic, golf instructor, barber, or beautician without taking an ETS test. A reporter for the UK *Telegraph* sounded surprised when he discovered the company "even supplies the English and civic values tests that immigrants have to take before they become US citizens." No one seems to have told him that ETS at one time administered tests to the CIA, NSC, Department of Defense, and Institute for Nuclear Power Operations.

In the global education community, ETS is at the center of a long and heated debate, making it the target of attacks from multiple fronts. Books with titles such as *The Reign of ETS: The Corporation That Makes Up Minds* and Nicholas Lemann's *The Big Test: The Secret History of the American Meritocracy* speak to the scandal that is ETS. The company reached a plateau of villainy in 2004, when it was portrayed as the bad guy in the (equally bad) film *The Perfect Score*. It doesn't exactly help the company's public relations that its American headquarters, in Lawrence, is situated on 376 acres "of woods and rolling hills." The grounds were at one time a country club belonging to Princeton University—the campus is just eight minutes away by car—and still feature pleasant lakes, geese, and "cavorting deer," according to the journalist David Owen.

One reason why ETS is so often maligned has to do with the company's status as a nonprofit organization. ETS profits 11 percent on the one billion dollars it grosses internationally—or 155 percent the industry average. "As a nonprofit [organization]," noted *The New York Times*, "ETS does not have to pay corporate income taxes, which saves it tens of millions of dollars, freeing up cash to hire workers and develop ever more sophisticated tests." But this is only half the equation. Nationally, ETS is a nonprofit organization, but internationally it has many for-profit subsidiaries, which sell for-profit test-prep material and for-profit official guides to its own exclusive line of test products. The question arises: is it a private company or a nonprofit organization? For a testing service that makes students choose A, B, or C, ETS, it would seem, is all of the above.

The close working relationship between the College Board and ETS has also raised more than a few eyebrows. The College Board cofounded ETS in 1948. (In a testament to the times—the Cold War had begun just three years earlier—the company's mission statement assured the government it would "continue to function" in the wake of an atomic holocaust.) The two other founding bodies were the American Council on Education and the Carnegie Foundation for the Advancement of Teaching—contributions that gave ETS national attention. The College Board donated startup money and gave ETS members of its own staff, and today it is the testing company's biggest client, representing $250 billion of its annual revenue. This sum, of course, comes from students, in the form of registration fees, administration fees, test fees, late fees, postage fees, optional fees, rescore fees, retest fees, and various other fees and expenses. Between the two organizations—the College Board and ETS—supply and demand are pretty well covered. ETS supplies, while the College Board ensures demand by making ETS products prerequisites for entering and exiting the levels of school, from state final to SAT to Graduate Record Exam. In his classic four-hundred-page study, *The Reign of ETS*, journalist Allan Nairn characterizes the situation as "student consumers in captivity."

But testing is only one of ETS's areas of expertise.

On the ETS Global website, the company asserts that it is an expert in a total of five areas, including test design and development;

test administration and scoring; statistics and psychometrics; instructional products and services; and educational research and development. Point three—statistics and psychometrics—is the work for which the company is probably least known, but is nevertheless a source of importance and value.

Almost from the day it began, ETS used the results from students' tests to amass a treasure trove of data. Some of the data was used to make new tests—or create statistical averages from which new tests are calibrated—and some of it was used to conduct very peculiar research. The trouble was that for a long time no one knew anything about it: the public wasn't allowed near the Lawrence headquarters, let alone inside. One of the first journalists to gain admittance, in 1974, was Steven Brill, whose first impression was of a room full of wailing babies. "In the same building where the test for the CIA agents is written," Brill wrote, in an article for *New York* magazine, "infants are observed behind one-way mirrors as part of a foundation-funded project to examine the initial processes of human learning." (With keenness of observation, the project concluded "a baby will smile more at a normal face than at a cyclops.")

Though comprising just one-fifth of the company's expertise, research—however strange—constituted enough space even then to fill a book 184 pages long. Other oddities included studies such as "Attachment Behavior in Thirteen-Month-Old Opposite Sex Twins," "Relationship of Height to Criteria of Anti-Social Behavior," and, with considerable mystery, "Sex Chromosome Anomalies in a Male Prison Population."

Of greater importance to us, ETS was two years into the trial of a program called Student Search Service. The SSS used ETS's repository of data "to supply participating colleges with names of high school seniors with special qualities that the college is looking for." At the time, the cost was seven cents per name. Representatives from a college or university simply went to ETS, searched the databank, and selected which students it wanted. Searchable criteria included race, gender, income, level of education, zip code, financial background, religion, and so on. The school would then buy thousands of names in order to appeal directly to specific demographics—and still does. Though the price has risen, ETS clients—some 1,700 colleges and universities—continue to use the program (as do mostly unwitting students and third parties of the testing company's choosing). In an article entitled "How All Those Colleges Got Your Name," *The New York Times* recorded an unspecified university that bought the information of 300,000 students for $84,000. The following year, in 2006, the University of Pennsylvania bought 1,000 low-income names and profiles for $280 to mail each student "a letter, brochure, and DVD about the University"—information that no doubt emphasized the school's generous bursaries and scholarships.

In his article for *New York* magazine, Steven Brill asked ETS if it would erase his own financial information, which the company had gathered from a scholarship application he filled out in college, plus his high school transcripts, and any other statistical data it had collected. He felt, not without reason, the information technically belonged to him and should therefore be his to delete. ETS felt otherwise. He was informed "[The data] belongs to ETS as well as the applicant." Brill pressed further and was put through to the executive vice-president, who told him the statistics were too valuable to be deleted. Valuable how? Brill asked. "The information," he was told, "is essential to research."

In present times, the College Board and ETS collect data on just about everyone, from just about everywhere. Students make especially easy targets since so much of what they do is on the web. Email addresses, Facebook profiles, blogs, tweets, online surveys and forms are all mined for data, but this isn't to say offline methods are overlooked. Americans for Educational Testing Reform have upbraided ETS for packing a forty-five-minute "research program" into the GRE, the three-hour entrance exam for students applying to US grad schools. ETS refers to the program as the "Unidentified Unscored Section" because it looks just like an exam question and doesn't count toward your final grade. In order to avoid filling out the program, however, you would have to first be able to distinguish the survey from the rest of the exam, which of course you can't, and we don't imagine many students are willing to risk a zero by skipping over a real question, thinking it was part of the program.

The Student Search Service is even sneakier.

Officially begun in 1972, it is the biggest, "most effective recruiting and admissions search tool" in the education business. The SSS is technically voluntary, but to remove yourself you have to uncheck the appropriate box, and the College Board, which currently runs the program, would prefer you didn't know that. Arriving at the official website, we can select separate pages depending on whether we're a student, parent, or university representative. If we choose the site for students, we are given the impression that the SSS isn't something we could say no to: "Say Yes to Student Search Service" the banner reads. And why wouldn't we? Students are virtually promised their choice of college as the SSS plays matchmaker to schools "that are looking for students like you." Or more to the point, schools looking for data like yours. As an admissions director at the College Board reminded *The New York Times*, "This is not just colleges looking to put buns in the seats, but for very selective colleges to target specific students."

On a different section of the website, the College Board appeals to the other half of the match. "Student Search Service is a powerful, economical student search tool," college and university representatives are told—one that "allows you to reach qualified, college-bound prospects of all backgrounds. With SSS, you can shape your incoming class by conducting customized searches at any time and effectively reach students by mail or email with targeted communications." On the page for students, the College Board neglects to mention the fact it's been selling student email addresses since the year 2000. But back on the page for post-secondary representatives, the point is almost celebrated: "Each year more than 6.3 million students—4.5 million with email addresses—and 1,700+ colleges and universities participate in SSS."

To be more specific, 80 million customized invitations are sold each year, for $17 million. The cost to schools is $185 flat, plus 28 cents per student.

Shortly after Steven Brill's article appeared in *New York* magazine, Educational Testing Service was forced to do an uncomfortable, and unfamiliar, thing.

Beginning in 1979, ETS was ordered to give exams back to students after they'd been marked. Up until that time you wrote your test, got your score, and took the company's word for it. Considering the trove of data ETS still withheld, it was a pittance. This single added degree of accountability, however, led students to uncover something strange about ETS's premium product, the SAT.

To start, it was preferential toward wealthy white men—the kind of prospective student, say, that Princeton University, with their Carnegie Lake rowing team, wanted to attract. An SAT question from the 1990s famously singled out this exact group. During the now-defunct analogies section, students were asked to select the equivalent of a runner to a marathon, and presented with the choices (A) envoy: embassy; (B) martyr: massacre; (C) oarsman: regatta (D) referee: tournament; and (E) horse: stable. More than half of white students chose the preferred C—an oarsman is to a regatta as a runner is to a marathon— but 78 percent of black students chose something different, and went to different schools. (They were, it seems, unfamiliar with a sport normally reserved for British gentry.)

The SAT and ETS have been plagued ever since.

In 1991 a professor at the Lynch School of Education named Walter Haney warned ETS it was in violation of professional standards. He was "politely told to buzz off." In the same year, ETS refused to release to colleges the entrance exam score of a student suspected of cheating. The second time he took the SAT, Brian Dalton nearly doubled his score—in the point system of the day, he'd gone from 620 to 1030. Dalton was sick during the first attempt and before his second attempt took an expensive, six-week course. But ETS claimed that Dalton's test jump was statistically so improbable someone else must have written it for him. Since he needed to go to college and needed his SAT score to get there, Dalton took the testing company to court. In a trial that lasted what would have been the duration of his college years, he lost.

In 2001, students taking an online version of the entrance exam for business school came to the end of the three-and-a-half-hour test, clicked submit, and were given the message "a fatal error has occurred." It was not only a fatal error, but an expensive one: the association of schools that had contracted ETS found a new supplier, and each year 250,000 applicants buy a different company's test.

In 2005, 27,000 new teachers writing the Praxis exam received 27,000 incorrect scores. Over 4,000 were told they had failed, including Rob Mitchell from Dayton, Ohio. Mitchell lost his job teaching social studies at Stebbins High when the district found out he flunked the exam. The only thing was, of course, he hadn't—he just didn't know that yet. In the meantime, his wife had taken a job at General Motors, they'd had a child, sold their house, and moved 350 miles to a town in the middle of Tennessee. An $11-million suit was filed, and this time, the judge ruled against ETS.

Earlier in the same year, an MIT professor had attended a conference of educators. The topic was the SAT's new essay-writing section, and here Les Perelman discovered something odd. By studying the samples given out at the seminar, he found nine out of ten times he could predict the mark the student was about to receive based solely on the length of the essay. He went back to his hotel room and phoned *The New York Times*. When the reporter arrived, Perelman made him stand across the room and hold up the exam. Perelman squinted. "That's a four," he said—and it was.

Even more incredibly, when Perelman further scrutinized the SATs, he noticed that factual errors went unchecked. A Civil War essay that received a perfect grade had two mistakes in the same sentence—describing how America was plunged into conflict by "the firing of two shots at Fort Sumter in late 1862." As noted by the reporter, it was actually early in 1861 and something more like four thousand shots fired over thirty-three grueling hours. Not that we're counting. In fact, ETS *doesn't* count factual errors, longer essays *still* receive higher scores, and Perelman, who continues to work at MIT, advises students about to take the test to write as much as possible "and include lots of facts, even if they're made up."

The SAT is administered not only in the United States and Canada, but in the United Kingdom (where it's pronounced *sat*), as well as Asia, Africa, and the Middle East. In the winter and spring of every year it is possible, though perhaps undesirable, to write the SAT in Baghdad, Cairo, and even the West Bank. These are places where the stakes are high as it is, but with denser populations, fewer elite schools, and so much pressure, it isn't surprising that ETS exams—with the power to funnel students into good and bad schools, good and bad jobs, and good and bad futures—are taken, and written, quite seriously. "By and large," Steven Brill wrote, "those who do well on the tests will get where they want to go. Those who don't, won't."

In earlier eras, there existed a debate about whether tests measured the actual ability of a student. The debate ended in 1987, when the

Center for Fair and Open Testing "was able to demonstrate conclu-sively that test preparation did in fact lead to higher scores, thereby challenging the original premise on which the SAT was built." After ETS began administering test-prep courses to its own exams, and after it was shown that students who prepared for these exams received higher scores because of their preparation, ETS should have toppled. The "A" in SAT might well have stood for *affluence*, not *aptitude*, since students who could afford test-prep did better than students who couldn't.

It's hard to imagine a more dangerous tool than a test designed to weed out the stupid from the smart. If the SAT were relegated to some corner of antiquity, it—along with various eugenics societies and lewisite—would be part of our history of shame. But ETS continues to reign. Even after it's been demonstrated that the SAT doesn't measure intelligence or aptitude—even after the company changed its name to S-A-T, in quiet submission of the letters' meaninglessness—the entrance exam is still the Western world's most administered test. As David Owen and others have noted, ETS is "probably the largest unregulated monopoly in America." Together with the College Board, the company steers the course of the country's students—the schools they get into, the jobs they qualify for, and the kinds of lives they can have. *The New York Times*, which ran a sixteen-week investigation into ETS, concluded the testing company has the power to "determine the future of millions of Americans and foreigners."

Foreigners like Joginder Singh, the student who passed the impos-sible IIT-JEE, was admitted into India's top school, and committed suicide because he didn't get into the right campus. Or Tusi Roy, a Bengalese student who couldn't find her name on an exam-results website, assumed that meant she failed, and hanged herself. BBC News reported, "Tusi's mother arrived at the school to find her daugh-ter's name in the list of successful candidates who had in fact passed the exam." And Americans like Elizabeth Shin, a student in residence at MIT, who had a nervous breakdown in 2000 and set herself on fire. It was the tenth MIT suicide in ten years. In 2010, Cornell had six suicides in six months, leading to a reinstitution of the moniker "Suicide School." (In the preceding decade, a total of twenty-seven student suicides took place on the bridges surrounding Cornell's campus.)

In 2011, Staffordshire student Nathan Lightfoot, "who became stressed about his A-level exams," died of a drug overdose. The following year, exam stress drove Jitendra Sai, a student at the Amrita Institute of Technology and Science, to hang himself from the ceiling fan. Days later, the same fate befell sixteen-year-old Anita Nadar, "who was stressed about her upcoming exams." In Kenya, two fourteen-year-old girls committed suicide just days apart, after learning their score on Kenya's exit exam for middle school. And in China, on the first day of the *gao kao*, three separate suicides were reported within hours of each other: One student jumped from the top of a building because he was fifteen minutes late to the exam centre. Revealingly, the police said they were reluctant to provide further details about the suicide until after the *gao kao* was over, lest the other students be unable to finish the exam.

CURRICULUM VITAE

If you were single, well-off, and dashing—and lived in Britain during the 1800s—you might well have owned a curricle.

A kind of evolutionary cross between a carriage and a bicycle, curricles featured a light wooden frame on top of two five-foot wheels and were held together by a network of poles and rope. Their winning combination of speed and danger ensured the curricle's popularity with Britain's gentry class. Sir John and Lady Lade were on their way to Hendon when their curricle came apart and spooked the horses. As recorded in volume 34 of *The Sporting Magazine*, the two leapt from their seats while the horses "continued running furiously to Sir John's house with the curricle, a distance of near four miles, and entering the yard, got into a pond, from which they were got out with difficulty."

In 1828, *The Sydney Gazette* reported a more grizzly story, in which Joseph Pigott was accused of killing someone named Mary Berry, "by driving a curricle and pair of horses over her body." Another story from *The Sporting Magazine* involved a man accused of "running with a gig upon the plaintiff's curricle, whereby he, the plaintiff, was thrown to the ground, had his collar bone broken, etc. etc." Several issues later it was impressively noted that a captain of the Worcestershire regiment, stationed at Portsea, walked 60 miles in 12 hours, after which, for 120 guineas, he climbed into his curricle and did half of it again.

But curricles also appealed to the romantic types. The now all-but-forgotten Georgette Heyer, in her book *Venetia*, kills off two characters in separate curricle incidents. Likewise, the heroine of an especially disposable romance novel—a cultured Frenchwoman named Marguerite—implores her courtier to "dash over to the Cascade, and fetch some water, and champagne, and brandy." (The vehicle of dashing is of course a curricle.) Perhaps more memorable is Jane Austen's *Northanger Abbey*, in which Catherine and Henry escape for a country drive in Henry's dad's curricle, making Catherine "as happy a being as ever existed."

As a word, *curricle* is a derivative of *currere*, "to run," and the basis of a number of words in a number of languages including *courier*, *current*, and *curriculum*. For many centuries, curriculum meant "a course," but not a course of scholastic study. Rather this course was one on which a curricle could be raced, what we now would call a racetrack. It's amusing to think that *curriculum*—a word that strikes immobilizing boredom into the hearts of schoolchildren the world over—really means something as exciting as "racing chariot." This was a giddy irony that lasted for the duration of the curricle's popularity, which, given its history of mowing people down on the streets of Hendon and Sydney, wasn't very long.

The first time the word *curriculum* appears in English with the meaning we ascribe it today was when John Russell, First Earl of Russell and later Britain's prime minister, traveled to Germany in 1824. There he dutifully noted, "When the student finishes his curriculum, [he] leaves the university." Some thirty years later, in June 1855, *curriculum* made its way across the Atlantic in the form of a complaint directed toward the day's youth and printed by the popular press. "Our young men press into life too early," the person wrote, under cover of anonymity. "They learn a little Latin (which they forget), and can demonstrate the propositions in Euclid or Legendre (which they also forget), but I think no direction is given to their minds. They do not learn what the world is doing, and what it is made of." The writer expressed concern that the college curriculum wasn't helping: "The system of a College curriculum [does] not remedy this evil."

By 1875, curriculum was not just on the editorial page but featured in significant articles for the general public. A protest "against the exclusion of the German language from the public schools" drew three thousand concerned citizens to the Cooper Institute in Dallas. As reported by *The New York Times*, "3,000 persons last evening assembled in the large hall ... and during the whole of the evening listened with great attention and apparently great satisfaction to the long and, in most cases, interesting speeches." The first was by a man named Clark Bell, who "endeavored to find one good, sensible reason why the study of the German language should be erased from the curriculum of the public schools." Unable to do so, the case was closed, and everyone went home.

Then, in 1876, James and Martha Bobbitt had a son named Franklin.

The Bobbitts were originally from England and Wales, and relocated to Virginia during the 1600s before migrating south. James grew up on a farm in rural Indiana, the seventh of thirteen children. A family genealogist records the appearance of the typical Bobbitt male to be "over six feet tall, blue eyes, brown hair, and of a strong medium build," but a photograph of James Bobbitt taken at middle-life depicts a heavyset patrician, with a handlebar mustache and small, discerning eyes. A farmer, clergyman, schoolteacher, superintendent, politician, and auditor, James was said to be "efficient and progressive" at all he endeavored, words that just as easily could have described his son.

John Franklin Bobbitt—or Franklin, as he was called—was the eldest of James's eleven children. He was born in the very small town of English, Indiana, and other than this, little of his adolescent life is known. The trail picks up again in the fall of 1900, when Franklin, suddenly now twenty-four, became a teacher at a high school in Randolph County. There he stayed for two years while completing his undergraduate degree. Then—it would seem to us abruptly—he left Indiana and moved to the Philippines to accept a teaching position there. As he later recalled to *The Phi Delta Kappa*, "I went to the Philippine Islands, where I was jarred out of the ruts and gained an entirely new vision of the purposes and nature of education." Bobbitt realized he had been teaching "a stereotyped and lifeless chronology" back in Indiana, "but arriving on the Philippine scene, it was at once obvious that a textbook of American history would not serve our purposes." After discovering he had brought nothing else to teach, Bobbitt used a more modern curriculum—a hint of things to come.

After five years abroad, Bobbitt returned home, bringing with him Sarah Annis, a woman whom he'd married in Manila. Sarah gave birth to a girl they named Margaret, and the family moved to Massachusetts so Bobbitt could finish his graduate studies, which he did at Clark University in 1909. Bobbitt's PhD thesis was "a statistical study of the physical growth of several hundred Filipino children." Supervising his work was the psychologist Charles Judd; impressed, he offered Bobbitt a professorship at the University of Chicago, where Judd himself had just made chair. The Bobbitt family moved again and by the end of the year were living in Chicago's Kenwood neighborhood.

It was through Judd that Bobbitt met G. Stanley Hall, the influential psychologist who enjoyed naked romps through the fields of Massachusetts and had supervised the doctoral theses of Lewis Terman and H. H. Goddard. As a eugenicist, president of Clark University, and sometime editor of the *Pedagogical Seminary*, Hall agreed to publish one of Bobbitt's papers. In "Practical Eugenics," Bobbitt asserted that society was doing itself a disservice by "keep[ing] alive multitudes of weaklings that formerly were weeded out by hard conditions." Morons weren't just a waste of schooling but a danger to the well-being of society: "To-day we save weak lungs, weak muscles, weak eyes and ears, weak minds and weak wills, weakness in general, and weakness in every particular, and permit it to reproduce itself in heredity, further corrupting the next generation."

Though the paper received little in the way of scholarly attention, it served to reveal the deep workings of Bobbitt's character: here was someone who believed that people were born with intrinsic and immutable qualities, some of which were inherently better than others. The people with keener minds, quicker instincts, and whiter skin— people like himself—ought to be at the top of the social pyramid, whereas the others beneath him should perform the work that befit their intelligence. Each person had his or her own special place, and each place was based on a series of heritable properties: cradle to grave, you lived the life you were born into and couldn't escape or change your fate in the grand social order.

After the publication of his paper in 1909, Bobbitt turned his attention back to the curriculum, bringing with him the ideas of "Practical Eugenics." In his native state of Indiana, public schools were operating "at about 50 per cent of efficiency," and after conducting a study, Bobbitt reported his findings in an article published by the University of Chicago. "There were two ways of meeting the situation," he wrote in 1912. "One was to build inferior buildings, omit playgrounds, school gardens, laboratories, workrooms, and assembly halls, to employ cheap teachers, to increase the size of classes, to cut down the yearly term to eight months, or to accommodate two shifts of children in the same building each day by doing half-time work." Or they could do it his way.

Namely, Bobbitt recommended incorporating the ideas of Frederick Taylor. A pro-level tennis-playing Quaker with the training of a lawyer, Taylor is best remembered as an industrial consultant. His job was to advise factory owners how to make their workers more productive, a process he outlined in *The Principles of Scientific Management*. Bobbitt read Taylor's book and later wrote excitedly of it in his own: "This system is looked upon by many factory managers as the most perfect that has yet been devised." If the schools in the city of Gary adopted Taylor's system, they could double their productivity. "Under the so-called 'Taylor-System' of scientific management," Bobbitt wrote,

> all the thinking is done by specialized officials in the
> "planning-room." Decisions are there made as to what
> is to be done every hour during the day by every man
> in the shop. Instructions are typewritten, and sent out

to the workmen. The latter are not expected to do any
thinking or judging or deciding; this is all done for
them; they are only to obey orders.

Though it had been applied to fields outside the factory, Bobbitt's
endorsement of Taylor's model marked the first time such a system
was used inside the classroom. The result was the industrialization of
education: each person fulfilled a specific role in a hierarchy of order
and efficiency. This included faculty as well as students and would lead
to an education system in which the emphasis was placed on "outputs,"
a word in pedagogical parlance that refers to a student's benefit to
society. Education had to go somewhere—it had to lead to a profession or, if nothing else, be put to use in the form of skilled manual
labor—and was no longer viewed as a benefit unto itself.

Bobbitt helped to pioneer the prototype of this model, known as the
"Work-Study-Play School," or "Platoon School." While one platoon
of students did rigorous academic work, another did calisthenics and
went swimming. By alternating the curriculum, productivity appeared
to rise from 50 to 100 percent, since at any given moment there was
twice as much going on.

His success with Gary schools brought Bobbitt into wider renown.
Platoon schools were adopted in New York, and he was asked to super-
vise a national study of education, whose aim was to "have for the first
time a scientific curriculum." What had happened in Indiana would
now be applied at the federal level. Once again, the idea was to treat
schools like factories: in order to make society run with machine-like
efficiency, schools would produce students with varying specializa-
tions and degrees of refinement, "as in the factory." A teacher himself,
Bobbitt compared his profession to the factory equivalent of foreman,
where students were the end product:

> The first teacher in line receives the original raw
> material in the kindergarten and performs the first
> process. It is then taken by the I-B primary teacher for
> a half-year. She passes it onto the I-A primary teacher,
> who gives it her half-year of effort. And so the product
> in more and more finished form is passed down the
> long line of specialists. In the later years of departmental
> teaching, the tasks are more minutely specialized and
> the material passes through many hands.

This was Bobbitt writing in his 1918 *The Curriculum*, which averaged sales of between one thousand and three thousand copies a year, figures that in its day made the book a bestseller. *The Curriculum*'s popularity prompted an author speaking tour, which in turn made Bobbitt something of a national sensation.

In his follow-up *How to Make a Curriculum*, Bobbitt expanded on his educational philosophy. Society needed certain kinds of labor in certain quantities, and the way to achieve this was by taking control of school and then reverse-engineering the outcome. School, operating like a factory, would produce the commodities demanded by society. More specifically, the things schools taught were of critical importance, since any extraneous material—anything that constituted an actual education—was deemed "inefficient."

To this end, Bobbitt created a list of fundamental subjects students needed to know "according to their social and vocational destiny." Here Bobbitt's eugenic ideals came into full view. Through implementation of the modern curriculum, Bobbitt was standardizing the educational experience by giving students uniform curricular content. The factory model produced the "outcomes" demanded by society, each student inheriting their predetermined vocational identity—their "destiny" in society—upon graduation.

For Franklin Bobbitt, science was the highest good, and in his time and place, this was the faulty science of eugenics. Everything could be broken down, quantified, and measured. Every person was fated for work, and every job fated to be either of maximum or minimum benefit to society. Even pleasure, Bobbitt believed, could be mathematized. In a chapter called "The Function of Play in Human Life," he divided the workweek into exactly forty hours of leisure—2,400 minutes—in which it was possible to reminisce quietly about the day, plan social activities, or spend time in "the consideration of one's current problems."

On December 1, 1915, Franklin's father died on the Bobbitt farm. According to *The English News*, James had eaten "a hearty dinner," gone out to do some work around the house, and "sank down suddenly in the yard." *The English News* recorded the return of "his son, Doctor Franklin Bobbitt, [who] drove through from Chicago in his car." The car was noted with particular interest since it was only the second time anyone in English had seen one—the first being when Franklin had returned the summer before.

After burying his father on a hill overlooking the farm, Franklin drove back to his house on Kenwood Avenue, not a block away from the University of Chicago. A homebody, the only other time Bobbitt left the neighborhood was to take a four-month leave in 1922, and again in 1923, in order to advise the superintendent of schools in Los Angeles. As part of his work, Bobbitt began a program that used Terman and Yerkes's scholastic tests "to place children in specific classes from the beginning rather than rerouting them at a later stage." The industrialization of the classroom—Bobbitt's hallmark on education reform—was beginning to be manifest in standard measures of achievement, or standardized tests (to be discussed later on).

Bobbit's relationship with his family was never cozy, and if his writing is any indicator of Bobbitt the poet, it wasn't difficult to see why. In a chapter called "The Mother Tongue," he begins with the sentence "The mother-tongue is man's primary instrument of social intercourse and intercommunication." In a photograph from about this time, Franklin is holding a doll at arm's length for his wailing daughter. While technically smiling, Bobbitt's expression is probably more accurately described as a grimace: his teeth are clenched, his neck muscles tight with exertion. Another shows his wife in a similar setting, with a toddling Margaret dressed in a lace gown. In contrast to her husband's tableau, Sarah is genuinely smiling, and Margaret is too.

But as time went on, Bobbitt had an ever-increasing amount of leisure time in which to consider his problems.

In 1937 Sarah sued for divorce, accusing Franklin of "extreme cruelty" and asking for a court order "to restrain her husband from molesting her." *The Chicago Tribune* followed the story with the undetached sensationalism of the day. "Prof. Franklin Bobbitt Sued by Wife; Accused of Beatings." "Home Is Hers, She Says."

Sarah told the *Tribune* their marriage had taken a nosedive in 1914, when she'd become ill with an unspecified condition. That was when Franklin had started hitting her, calling her names, and "making her face black and blue." A few days after the story came out, Franklin publicly rebutted the accusation, filing a legal denial. A month later he drove home from work, pulled into the garage with the windows up, and left the engine running. The maid, a woman named Moselle Keyes, had seen Bobbitt drive in but not enter the house. She waited fifteen minutes and then went in after him. "Prof. Bobbitt Periled by Gas; Saved by Maid," was the next day's headline. "U. of C. Educator Is Taken from Garage." "Maid Helps Him from Car."

Bobbitt was rushed to the hospital, where he was tended to by a nurse named Mabel. As the Bobbitt family genealogist, John William Bobbitt, observed: "Human relationships are so complicated that we all know that association with one person can make one ill, whereas association with another person can make one well. [Mabel] was honest and open in her dealings with all persons. She had the healing qualities and touch of a skillful nurse and soon she had cured the physical and mental illnesses of John Franklin Bobbitt." Thirteen years his junior, Mabel married Bobbitt in 1941, and the couple eloped to a farm in the country. There they lived quietly until the spring of 1956, when Bobbitt died of a heart attack.

In the life of Franklin Bobbitt—his curriculum vitae—the line between personal and professional grew increasingly faint—an act of permeation that must have been particularly excruciating for a man of puritanical principles.

As an educator, Bobbitt's real success wasn't in suggesting which courses be taught in the present, but in structuring an environment for their teaching in the future. By implementing Taylor's factory model in mainstream public education, Bobbitt industrialized the classroom, instilling the atmosphere of an assembly line it continues to exude.

His influence was about the "how," not the "what." In his own increasingly antiquated view, the curriculum should be unabashedly ambitious. For literature, it was recommended children be given books on war, poverty, commerce, industry, adventure, "the struggle with nature and with disease," science and technology, and "the other major ingredients of human existence." For foreign language, it was the standard Latin and Greek, but also French, Russian, Italian, German, and Spanish, in addition to proper translations of Dante,

Homer, Virgil, Tolstoy, Ibsen, Freitag, Maeterlinck, Bjornsen, Balzac, Cervantes, Khayyam, Plato, and the Old Testament, plus the usual Shakespeare and Dickens.

But soon these subjects were viewed as extraneous. Knowledge of Shakespeare was of little benefit in the everyday workplace—perhaps it was even a hindrance. As Bobbitt's life fell apart, so too did his work. Though it hadn't been that long ago that languages such as German had been viewed as an essential curricular requirement by the general public, soon even the teaching of Latin and Greek—the curricular backbone of formalized education for thousands of years— was under fire. And leading the assault was a man named Abraham Flexner.

THE RISE OF LOW LITERACY

In practical terms, from the level of the individual all the way to the level of government and country, education is most commonly measured by the degree, and definition, of literacy.

The trouble is that no one can agree on what literacy *is*.

Of course, the definition used for centuries has been the ability to read and write. "Unfortunately, if the scholarship of the past fifty years is anything to go by, the matter is not that simple," says Peter Roberts, a professor at the University of Canterbury's School of Educational Studies and Human Development. Roberts and much of the academic community now believe that defining literacy by reading and writing alone is an oversimplification, and more importantly, that it ignores the latest developments of society.

In an effort to bring literacy up to speed with the times, scholars have broken the word into a dizzying number of iterations, classes, and subclasses. To begin with, there's high and low literacy. High literacy, as we might expect, represents a sophisticated blend of linguistic, rhetorical, and arts-based skills—the sort of abilities we associate with fluency in Latin and Greek (and for a good reason, as we shall soon discover). Low literacy—the prevailing literacy of today—is more technical and skills-oriented. Within the category of low literacy are three important subcategories, defined by their quantitative, qualitative, and pluralist approaches.

For most of the twentieth century, quantitative literacy—the prevailing approach worldwide—was defined simply by the number of years one spent in school, called "reading ages." In 1975, the United States had a literate reading age of seven. Two and a half decades earlier, the reading age in Britain was nine. Of course, the problem with the quantitative approach to literacy is its preposterous faith in the school system. "Clearly," Roberts has written, "the number of years one has attended school in no way provides a definitive picture of one's abilities in reading, writing or anything else."

The failings of quantitative literacy gave rise to the qualitative approach. Here literacy isn't measured by the number of years spent in school—it isn't measured at all. As the anthropologist Louis Dupree described it, "Qualitative literacy means the ability to use literate sources in order to consider political, economic, social, and psychological alternative solutions ..." In other words, qualitative literacy is the ability to think creatively. This was certainly a more lively definition, but the only problem was there was no way of telling who was literate and who wasn't: qualitative literacy can't be measured (that was why it was invented in the first place). Having arrived back at the beginning, scholars devised a third solution.

Pluralist literacy sees virtually everything as a potentially useful skill. A frequent and knowledgeable traveler is *culturally literate*, an environmentally conscientious consumer is *ecologically literate*. Other categories include survival literacy, health literacy, religious literacy, multimedia literacy—multimedia literacy itself has many offshoots, and encompasses computer literacy, which again has more offshoots—and so on.* The point is not to define what literacy is generally but only in specific scenarios. The ability to use Adobe Photoshop can be referred to as *Photoshop literacy*, since it makes no statements about the essential nature of literacy outside of Photoshop.

Such thinking is at once impossibly narrow and impossibly broad: broad in that it sees everything as a potential source of literacy, and narrow in that it ties literacy to specific uses, "and hence the specific contexts in which it is learned and applied," according to Ulrike Hanemann, head of the Literacy Cluster at the United Nations Educational, Scientific, and Cultural Organization (UNESCO).

But scholars, not to mention administrators, teachers, and pretty well everyone else, would no doubt find it helpful to have a single, universal definition of literacy—no matter how exactly it's defined. Unfortunately, none exists.† Though its goal is to achieve universal literacy, UNESCO is in the uncomfortable position of being unable to define what that means. "A universal definition of literacy does not seem possible," writes Niels Lind, a professor at the University of Waterloo, and Fellow of the Royal Society of Canada. What's more, "There can never be a single, fixed, timeless definition of literacy," since the prevailing wisdom about what literacy should define, in a rapidly evolving world, is likewise in a state of constant change.

According to Suzanne de Castell, Allan Luke, and David Maclennan in a joint paper for the *Canadian Journal of Education*, the lack of a fixed definition is the very problem: "Current responses to the so-called

---

* In a revealing statement of the times, *survival literacy* refers not to the skill of roughing it in the wilderness but to surviving in the midst of present-day society.

† However—at the risk of being parenthetically obsessive—it is interesting to note that traditionally, the word *illiterate* preceded the word *literate*. So at one time, it would appear, literacy was so common it didn't warrant a description, and illiteracy so unusual, so rare, that it did.

literacy crisis in Canada originate, we believe, in a failure to define or frame the problem appropriately." They might have indicted not just Canada, but the whole planet. Despite an effective campaign to reduce global illiteracy since the 1970s, about 20 percent of the world's population continues to be unable to read or write. The overwhelming majority of the world's illiterate people live in just eight countries—Bangladesh, China, Egypt, Ethiopia, India, Indonesia, Nigeria, and Pakistan, as *The World Factbook* lists them, a touch thoughtlessly, in alphabetical order.

The United States and Canada, by way of contrast, have a pleasingly high literacy rate of 99 percent—but then so does Uzbekistan, Albania, and Guam. If we define literacy by the ability to read and write at the age of fifteen, most countries' populations are literate to the ninetieth or even ninety-ninth percentile. Even so, the 1 percent who are illiterate cost Canada and the US ten and twenty billion dollars a year respectively.

As shocking as these figures are, they of course represent an even greater shock when we consider the following: the people who *are* literate are meeting a drastically reduced standard. Literacy has not only devolved from high to low, but descended farther from low to what can only be described as very low. Despite the best efforts of UNESCO and other organizations to stop the spread of illiteracy, no one—not even the most optimistic educator or theorist—is addressing the bigger problem: namely, how to have a planet full of highly literate people.

———

In the spring of 1916, Abraham Flexner published a report that revolutionized education.

"A Modern School" was the most important education paper not only of its own time, but possibly of any. Never before had the contents of the report been suggested, nor in such a striking manner. With "A Modern School," the progressive era was effectively launched, guided by Rockefeller's General Education Board, whose members were instructed to spend "whatever it takes" to make Flexner's idea come true. (And as we may recall, the General Education Board had thirty-two million dollars at its disposal.)

Abraham Flexner had arrived to education quite by accident. The sixth of nine children, Flexner left his rural home in Lewisville, Kentucky, to enroll at Johns Hopkins University. He graduated in 1886 at age nineteen and thereafter opened his own private school, which he named after himself. Graduates of the Flexner School were often sent to Harvard, where its twenty-sixth president, Charles Eliot, noted their academic excellence and wrote Flexner to congratulate him. It was to be an important connection.

In 1905, Flexner completed his graduate studies at Harvard's psychology department, under the direction of primatologist Robert Yerkes. He was also tutored by his brother, Simon Flexner, a scientist at the Rockefeller Institute for Medical Research. Two years later, traveling with his wife, Flexner relocated to Berlin, where he wrote a pedantic and vociferous work entitled *The American College*. It would have attracted no notice at all had it not been for Henry Pritchett, neighbor and confidant of Andrew Carnegie.

Where no one else had liked, or even noticed, Flexner's book, Pritchett at once saw its value. In a passing comment, the author had assailed the medical departments of American colleges and urged the overhauling of research laboratories. Flexner had no direct experience with medicine at all—in fact, when Pritchett commended him on his work, Flexner thought he had been confused with his brother Simon. After being reassured he was indeed the right fellow, Flexner was sent back to North America, where he secretly toured 155 medical schools. The resulting report, published by the Carnegie Foundation in 1910, caused a scandal: the schools Flexner had critiqued had to consolidate their departments or risk being shut down. "Seven schools in Louisville became one; fifteen in Chicago consolidated into three," noted Franklin Parker in his portrait of Flexner for the *History of Education Quarterly*.

The Flexner report brought its author to the attention of another financier. Just as his contract with Andrew Carnegie ended, J. D. Rockefeller hired Flexner for his own purposes. Like many at the time, Rockefeller was perturbed by the escalation of crime and prostitution in his home state of New York and had traced the problem back to the Old World. Flexner was thus sent to Europe. With customary diligence, he took it upon himself to make an exhaustive, two-year study of the continent's brothels. Upon his return home, Flexner's advice was adopted by New York and a number of other states, and the level of prostitution was eventually curbed. Rockefeller was so pleased that Flexner was given a job as assistant secretary on the Rockefeller General Education Board. As he wrote to his wife, "Thus all doubt as to our future is removed."

One of his first jobs, in 1916, was to visit a school in Gary, Indiana. This was the platoon school of Franklin Bobbitt's admiration. The school's superintendent—one William A. Wirt—claimed the superiority of his work-study-play method and wanted the endorsement of the General Education Board. Flexner was supposed to give a favorable report, but when it was published and Wirt was given a copy, he was shocked to discover Flexner had been punishingly critical (likely because of the platoon school's ambitious, classically centered curriculum, which Flexner viewed as being outdated and irrelevant). As with medical laboratories and European brothels, the platoon-school paper had a damning effect, and Wirt's institution was immediately closed down. But "If the Gary survey was a tearing down," Parker wrote, "the Lincoln School was a building up."

Lincoln was the "Modern School" of Flexner's report, and the most experimental—and influential—in American history. It was built in 1917 and formally affixed to Columbia University's Teachers College. The Lincoln School of Teachers College, as it became known, was a radical experiment in education. To start, as was noted by the General Education Board, "The school will frankly discard that theory of education known as 'formal discipline.'"

In education, "formal discipline" refers to the ability to learn something unintended. As the renowned educator John Dewey wrote in *Democracy and Education*: "According to the orthodox theory of formal discipline, a pupil in studying his spelling lesson acquires, besides the ability to spell those particular words, an increase of power of observation, attention, and recollection which may be employed whenever these powers are needed."*

At the Lincoln School, Flexner had to go to considerable lengths to remove formal discipline from the curriculum: The teaching of grammar was struck. Literature and history were reconstructed. Algebra and geometry as separate disciplines were struck as well. The biggest and most shocking change, however, was that Latin and Greek—curricular staples since the beginning of Western education—were now gone too. Flexner's reasoning was that students were no longer particularly good at Latin and Greek, and as he wrote, "It is, therefore, useless to inquire whether a knowledge of Latin and mathematics is valuable, because pupils do not get it."

Flexner had come to this opinion by studying college entrance exams. Students used to have to write short passages in the classical

---

* The theory was so called because it assumed the ability to learn was latent in everyone, and all that was needed of a teacher was to train—to discipline—the mind through formal education.

languages, and after comparing the grades of these sections over a period of time, Flexner had discovered what would have been—had it been true—one of the first modern examples of literacy in decline. However, according to Andrew Fleming West, then a dean at Princeton University, Flexner intentionally and elaborately misinterpreted the exam results, excluding the data that showed students continuing to perform well in Greek and Latin. Intrigued, another of Princeton's faculty, an assistant professor of economics and statistics, made a study of Flexner's findings, and discovered "the statistics have been misused in a very extraordinary way." (A year later, in 1918, at a meeting of the National Education Association in Pittsburgh, West openly accused Flexner of waging a war against classical learning and pleaded for Americans to "stand on one side or the other" of the debate. Either you were for a classical education, or you were for the "Modern School"— one led to literacy while the other led to its opposite.)

Perhaps not surprisingly, Flexner's idea was hotly contested. *The New York Times* began covering the story with the headline "Rockfeller Board to Revise Education." It didn't take long before the debate had progressed to the paper's editorial section, where someone at the *Times* called the plan "radical and dangerous." Readers' letters soon began pouring in, with one writer saying the idea was "evil," and another that it was the death of scholarship. Critics—and there were plenty—were outraged by both what was being cut out of the curriculum and what was being stitched in.

What the Lincoln School would teach instead of Latin and Greek were courses designed to fit students to work. The public was assured that every effort would be taken "to give the pupils sufficient contact with their natural, industrial, social, economic, vocational, and domestic environments so as to derive the basis for their schoolwork from real situations, and thus make school work constantly real to them." Flexner was persistent, even strangely proud of how the modern school would emphasize social integration while de-emphasizing the core educative elements of literacy. "The man educated in the modern sense will be trained to know, to care about and to understand the world he lives in," Flexner again wrote. "He will forgo the somewhat doubtful mental discipline received from formal studies; he will be contentedly ignorant of things for learning which no better reason than tradition can assign."

By associating formal discipline with traditionalism, and progressivism with the "Modern School," Flexner successfully convinced the public that the former was outdated—*medieval* was the word in use—and so no longer worth keeping. *The Classical Weekly*, a New York publication, took issue with the association of datedness and efficacy. An issue from 1918 doesn't mention Flexner by name, but evidently alludes to him and the entire cause in a section called "A Plea for the Classics; and Remarks on Formal Discipline." The author, a professor at Swarthmore College, took offense at the idea that classical education was outdated, arguing, "Classical education is not, as is so often thoughtlessly said, an inheritance from medievaelism. It was the principal engine of revolt against medievaelism."

What is noteworthy about this comment, of course, is that the writer—who would go only by the initials C.K.—clearly attributes formal discipline to a state of self-empowerment. And according to UNESCO, empowerment is the feeling of being literate. (Among the organization's many campaigns is the Literacy Initiative for Empowerment.) There was something distinctly Prussian in Flexner's desire to crush formal discipline; it was inefficient to have a school model based on individual needs that empowered—through discipline—one student at a time. Sever modern languages from their Latin and Greek origins and what you got was a servile population too estranged from its own past—its own history and identity—to think for itself. As the Lincoln School, and the others that soon followed suit, removed formal discipline, high literacy began to fall. As modern schools introduced the Lincoln curriculum of Spanish, French, German, "science, industry, and the domestic arts," low literacy began to rise.

In 1928, Flexner retired from education. He was asked to speak on the prestigious Rhodes Memorial Lecture and Taylorian Lecture at Oxford, where he also resided. In between lectures there was a tour of Europe, plenty of reading, and the publication of another book.

Then, in 1930, a brother and sister approached Flexner to ask his advice about what to do with five million dollars; the two evidently didn't know what to do with it themselves. With the confidence of someone who had been employed by both Carnegie and Rockefeller, Flexner told them to give the money to him.

With it he built the Institute for Advanced Study, a center for experimental academic work in Princeton, New Jersey. Unlike the universities Flexner was famous for criticizing, the institute was designed to be a place where "highly selected scholars would work in their own way to inquire freely into truth." Famously, the first such scholar was Albert Einstein, whom Flexner personally convinced to emigrate from Berlin. (Einstein was happily employed at the institute until his death in 1955, and Flexner himself was its first director.)

The impact of the Lincoln School was great. Public education began to phase out the teaching of Latin and Greek, with all but a few private schools refusing—a state we find both systems in today. What's more, post-secondary education stopped requiring students to know either language upon admittance, though some exceptions existed. New York's Hamilton College, for instance, continued to require incoming students to know both languages and considered the aversion to such requirements "rank Philistinism" (a word, incidentally, that is both Latin and Greek).

But predominately, the ancient languages were ushered out and the modern ones ushered in. Though modern languages such as English, French, German, and Spanish are Indo-European, and share roots with Latin and Greek, the modern school of Flexner's design saw them as separate, outdated, and unworthy of study. Though his research was falsified, many of us still consider the ancient languages as just those things. There is no way of knowing whether we might still be a highly literate society today if we had kept Latin and Greek. What is for certain is that literacy has virtually plummeted from high to low since the founding of the Lincoln School in New York.

It's worth keeping in mind that this was an era when even the averagely literate spoke three or four languages, wrote lengthy letters by hand, and read impressive works of both fiction and nonfiction. As is sometimes mentioned, one of the period's bestsellers was *The Last of the Mohicans*, which expects the reader to follow along—for three hundred pages—with prior knowledge of the Seven Years' War, geography of Western Europe, and historic, political and religious life, as well as the ability to read French.

It is a sobering thought that two of the most educationally restricted and oppressed groups of the twentieth century—women and immigrants—were more highly literate than their comparatively unrestricted and unoppressed counterparts today. Near the beginning of the century, touching on this very issue in *The New York Times*, was a woman who expressed dismay about her own limited education. In her study of Greek, the article claimed, she "never got beyond the irregular verbs," had only made it up to "the first three books of 'Euclid,' and in algebra had gone as far as quadratic equations, but not into them." Immigrants, in a similar state of restriction, were given a literacy test upon reaching Ellis Island. They were instructed to read twenty to twenty-five lines of the United States Constitution and explain them back to the officer on duty, a feat many graduate students—or indeed politicians—might struggle with today. But amazingly—for such was the state of literacy at the time—many of them could do it quite ably.

As for the Lincoln School itself, after numerous mergers and rechristenings, it closed down in 1991. In its place today, on West 110th Street, stands the Lincoln Correctional Facility—a grim, eight-story prison.

3 | CITIZENS AND SOLDIERS

*There was very little of indecorous behavior, such as winking
or laughing in a clandestine manner; but the sobriety appeared
to me to come more from fear than from repentance.*

—Horace Mann, upon visiting a Prussian prison for students

INDIAN TROUBLES

A lodger in the town of Fredericksburg once awakened in the night
to discover a group of Indians absconding with his horses. He hastily
gave chase, "without his gun, pistol, or knife—pantless, coatless,
shoeless, and hatless, and with the rear portion of his shirt playing in
[a] graceful horizontal position." After a mile-long pursuit, the horses
were reclaimed, and the lodger returned to his lodge.

Encounters between whites and Indians were an everyday occur-
rence in nineteenth-century North American life. *The New York
Times* kept track of the conflict in a regular column entitled "Indian
Troubles." An example from 1874 told of a routine circus act gone
afoul when a band of Warm Spring Indians happened to attend a
performance in which an actor was deprived of his wig, looking to
the Indians as though he'd lost his scalp. "They rose to their feet, drew

their scalping-knives, and with terrific war-whoops were about to rush into the ring," recalled a terrified reporter. "It was only with the utmost difficulty they could be quieted down."

But Indian troubles were not always so agreeably resolved. In 1851, two Indians from Yuba City stole watermelons "near Rose's or Brophy's ranch." They were caught, beaten, and thrown in the river. By the time the story made news, it wasn't clear if anyone had survived: "Whether the Indians got out of the river or were drowned, we do not know, but they have not been heard of since." Another incident, from 1885, involved a group of Apaches who stormed a fortified barracks in Tombstone, Arizona, "with the object of rescuing their squaws, who [were] prisoners there." Sixty miles north in Wilcox, on the same day, the sheriff of Graham County was discovered to be alive after it was commonly believed he had been murdered by Indians, a fact that seemed to be corroborated by the cadaver of a man named Kilton, who either in death or life had resembled the sheriff. Yet again on the same day, a lengthy chase between Blackfoot Indians and someone named Plenty Cones came to an exhausting end when Cones and his men overtook the Indians at Crazy Mountain and reclaimed the horses that had been stolen from them.

Suffice to say, Indian troubles were costing the government a lot of headache, and a lot of money. This was true in Canada as well, where the question was raised during the country's fifth parliamentary session, when an elderly Sir John A. Macdonald spoke of "Indian troubles in the northern part" of British Columbia. Unprepared for such disturbances, the provincial government had borrowed a gunboat from the United States—a favor Macdonald felt wasn't proper for a country that was then all of sixteen years old. "I would ask the attention of the Government to this question," he said. "Disturbances internal or external would seriously interfere with our trade and commerce, and anything which might injure any part of the country would injure the whole."

While there was no mention of the expense to Canada's government, Indian troubles in the United States were costing a hundred thousand dollars a day—and that was in the money of the 1800s. At a meeting in Congress, one speaker estimated "if the Indian depredations are continued for two months longer, they will have cost the Government not less than one hundred millions of dollars." Even if only half true, this was indeed a staggering sum, and the government was desperate for a way to avoid having to continue paying it. In 1867, a special committee concluded that "the Government had better bring all the tribes together on liberal reservations, where they can be cared for at a mere fraction of the present expense."

After the tribes had all been brought together, the question was what to do with them next. "The favorite Western idea of extermination" was considered at some length, but rejected primarily because of logistics, to say nothing of cost. So the committee came up with a new idea: "The scheme proposed embraces one of education for the rising generation of Indians." Instead of extermination, the government would put Indian children through eight years of compulsory schooling. "By such means," it was hypothesized, "the savage red man of the plains will soon be a thing of the past, and in his place we shall have a hardy, intelligent, industrious race of his dark-hued sons."

What followed would be nothing short of cultural genocide.

———————

In 1803, Egerton Ryerson was born in the pleasant town of Norfolk, Ontario.

His father fought for the Loyalists in the American Revolution, and afterward fled to New Brunswick where he married a woman named Mehetabel Stickney. The colonel and Mehetabel traveled west to Ontario, where they established themselves on a large property awarded through a land grant. Five children were soon available for chores.

Egerton, the youngest, heartily embraced the work, arising every morning at three to study until six, before putting in a fourteen-hour day on the family's 2,500-acre farm. As he later recalled in his auto-biography, "I ploughed every acre of ground for the season, cradled every stalk of wheat, rye, and oats, and mowed every spear of grass, pitched the whole, first on a wagon, and then from the wagon on the hay-mow or stack."

The young Ryerson showed the same enthusiasm in the classroom. Eager to win over his teachers, he became one, filling in whenever the lead instructor was ill. Ryerson himself was a sickly child, perhaps as a result of his long days of work coupled with a self-imposed regiment of fasting and little sleep. On his eighteenth birthday, Ryerson felt sure he was on his deathbed and struck a deal with God: "I then and there vowed that if I should be restored to life and health, I would not follow my own counsels, but would yield to the openings and calls which might be made in the Church by its chief ministers." He had only to think the words before "the cloud was removed" and "the light of the glory of God shone into my mind." His health miraculously restored, Ryerson set about living up to his end of the bargain.

In 1824, Ryerson moved to Hamilton, where he joined a group of Wesleyan Methodists. On Easter Sunday, Ryerson chose a medita-tion from Psalm 126—"They that sow in tears shall reap in joy"—and delivered his first sermon. For the next year he traveled throughout the Niagara region preaching by horseback. Between regular bouts of unspecified illness, and an exhausting two-day search for the horse he had somehow managed to misplace, Ryerson was invited to a meeting in which a clergyman from Ancaster spoke to Mississauga and Mohawk Aboriginals. The clergyman had successfully converted sixty Indians to Christianity, a fact that seemed to impress Ryerson. As he later recounted in his journal, with what seems a touch of surprise, "These Indians thanked the white people for sending them the Gospel."

Following the meeting, Ryerson began to expand his riding circuit. He ventured into the United States, where, with an objection any visiting foreigner can appreciate, he complained of the rudeness of its people. Preaching to whites made Ryerson uncomfortable, and he turned to Ontario's indigenous population for a more receptive audience. The Ancaster rider Peter Jones was building a mission at Credit River and offered Ryerson the job of missionary. Ryerson wasn't sure if it was the right decision, but "if the Lord will open the way," he promised to follow, believing he could convert the "children of the forest." Again in his journal, Ryerson noted, "My soul longs to bring them the Word of Truth."

At the Credit Mission, Ryerson waited until after Sunday worship to assemble the Mississaugas. Sitting on the head of an upright barrel, he lined the Indians up and took a collection, "to build a house for the double purpose of the worship of God and the teaching of their children." The elders paid with shillings they'd earned from selling moccasins and blankets, but the younger generations had to pay in freshly caught salmon. Ever thinking of the Bible, Ryerson compared the event to King David calling upon the Israelites to build the Temple. After the collection was over, Ryerson formally began his work, converting Indians through the fall and into the winter. On December 16, he noted how he had been "trying to procure for the Indians the exclusive right of their salmon fishery," which conveniently secured his own continued stipend. Ryerson was successful, and the Indians thanked him at a special ceremony:

> The old Chief arose, and approached the table where
> I was sitting, and in his own tongue addressed me in
> the following manner: 'Brother, as we are brothers, we

will give you a name. My departed brother was named Cheehock; thou shalt be called Cheehock.' I returned him thanks in his own tongue, and so became initiated among them.

Successfully converted himself, Ryerson was asked to attend an annual meeting between Indians and the government. Addressing the assembled tribes through an interpreter, Ryerson tactfully "contrasted the superiority of the religion we brought to them over that of those who used images." There were murmurs of agitation, but Ryerson— or Cheehock—continued: "I explained to the assembled Indians the cause of their poverty, misery, and wretchedness, as resulting from their having offended the Great Being who created them, but who still loved them so much as to send His Son to save them, and to give them new hearts, that they might forsake their bad ways, be sober and industrious; not quarrel, but love one another, etc."

The room erupted, and death threats were shouted in Ryerson's direction.

Then, in 1829, Ryerson was made editor of *The Christian Guardian*. In its day, the *Guardian* reached three thousand readers per issue and established Ryerson as a Canadian icon.

Adding to his reputation was Ryerson's willingness to embrace controversial political topics and fill the pages of the *Guardian* debating them. One such topic was the government's possession of three million acres in Southern Ontario, which it was reserving for religious officials. Ryerson negotiated their sale in 1831, and as a result Wesleyan Methodists received a generous nine hundred pounds a year. This won Ryerson the patronage of a number of prominent Wesleyan Methodists, such as one Adam Crooks, and two successive governors general, including, to begin with, Sir Charles Bagot.

In 1842, the year he took governorship, Bagot's job was to "inquire into the Affairs of the Indians in Canada and the application of the annual grant of money made by the Imperial Parliament for the benefit of that Race." The Bagot Commission, as it became known, was presented to Parliament in 1845. In it, the government was urged, in the consideration of Indian troubles, "to form a judgment upon any scheme proposed for their future management." The scheme Bagot had in mind was twofold: "First, to collect the Indians in considerable numbers, and to settle them in villages, with a due portion of land for their cultivation and support," and "Second, to make such provision for their religious improvement, education, and instruction in husbandry as circumstances may from time to time require ..."

Unfortunately for Bagot, he died before completing his paper, which was then finished by colleagues and presented by his successor as governor-general. Under Sir Charles Metcalfe, Ryerson was promoted to chief superintendent of schools, a position that enabled him to write his own report based on a number of trips to Europe. His first was in 1844 and included the requisite stop in Prussia, where Ryerson visited schools, prisons, and institutions for the mentally insane. "All the Prussian children are treated by the government as though they belonged to Prussia and would in the future become Prussian citizens," he wrote, upon his return. "The Prussian government takes it for granted that it has the right, yea, more, that it is a public duty to establish schools in which every child may receive such a culture as will fit him to be a good Prussian citizen."

Horace Mann had made the same observation on his own voyage to Prussia during the previous decade. It was the ability of the school system to produce "good citizens" that had attracted Georg Kerschensteiner and the financiers who used his vocational model to create the world's foremost industrial superpower. With students sorted by the adapted version of Binet's scale and a curriculum purged of formal discipline, institutionalized education could be anything anyone wanted it to be, and Ryerson seemed to sense the potential.

In *The Journal of Education for Ontario*, under the heading "Superior Education," Ryerson argued for adopting the Prussian model to Canada's public education in schools from primary through post-secondary. Referring to the opinion of an expert, he wrote "if we adopted the Prussian system, it should be adopted in its entirety." But Ryerson wasn't just thinking of public schools: "I returned to Hamilton more deeply impressed than before with a sense of the capability of the Indian for civilization," he wrote, again in *The Journal of Education*, "and yet more clearly cognizant of the slow and almost imperceptible degrees by which alone an Indian population can ever be actually absorbed by our own race."

Such views were met with ferocious contention. It didn't help that Ryerson himself was the subject of considerable criticism. While in Europe, it seems that Ryerson had used taxpayer money to buy 236 paintings of a brooding, old-master vintage. (Though there is no record of the amount he appropriated, *The New York Times* reported the interest alone to be 1,500 pounds). This apparently rampant corruption on the part of a public figure was predictably scandalous, and if it weren't for Ryerson's considerable stature and influence, it seems likely that this single incident would have marked the end of his career as superintendent of schools.

But for Ryerson, it was only the beginning.

Under the editorship of George Brown, *The Globe*, now *The Globe and Mail*, launched a particularly aggressive assault. The subject was Ryerson's importation of the Prussian school system, which Brown felt was "about as well suited to Canada as it is to Kamschatka." The gravest of Brown's accusations was in claiming that, when Ryerson introduced a Prussian school system to Canada, he necessarily introduced Prussian despotism. As Ryerson recollected in his autobiography,

"It was represented that I had plotted a Prussian school despotism for free Canada, and that I was forcing upon the country a system in which the last spark of Canadian liberty would be extinguished, and Canadian youth would be educated as slaves." In the preface to *Dr. Ryerson's Letters in Reply to the Attacks of Mr. Brown*, Ryerson—with characteristic enthusiasm—responded by calling the accusations "the most insidious conspiracy and formidable attacks which have ever been witnessed." Addressed to the entire nation of Canada, he began, "Our system of Public School is not the decree of a despot enforced upon you ..."

But this was a difficult argument for Ryerson to uphold.

At the time, the controversial Gradual Civilization Act—"An Act for the Gradual Enfranchisement of Indians"—was already in effect. It included the suspiciously despotic statement that Indians "shall no longer be deemed Indians within the meaning of the laws," and that each individual shall declare "the name and surname by which he wishes to be enfranchised and thereafter known." Even for the time, this was a bold step and, as scholars have occasionally noted, absent in the biographies of Canada's best-known educator. Another of the law's provisions granted land to the Canadian Indian based on "the degree of civilization to which he has attained, and the character for integrity and sobriety which he bears."

The Act for the Gradual Enfranchisement of Indians was so titled because it determined "enfranchisement" based on the government's opinion of the Indian's moral character, and as *The New York Times* noted, "Precisely what constitutes moral character is an open question." In white society at the time, Connecticut, for instance, was believed to have a higher moral standard than Montana, "although it is barely possible that, while three-card monte, horse-racing, and profane swearing are not so openly countenanced in the Land of Steady Habits as in Montana, the Territory does have the advantage over the State in the matter of poisoning and wife-murder." As was quickly added, however, the standards for Indians were different: "If the bill now before the Senate shall become a law, the Indian applicant must prove that for two years he has not killed anybody, has taken no scalps, [and] has not beaten his wife." (Still relevant for today, the *Times'* own wish for the Indian was that, "Before he swears to his morality and intelligence, let him prove that he subscribes to a daily newspaper, has a church-sitting, and wears trousers.")

So it was with some courage—if not a kind of willful self-deception—that Ryerson could claim not to have enforced a despotic state in either the public or Indian school system. The rise of government-run compulsory schooling meant that whatever the government wanted its citizens to think, it could effectively push a button: "It is the omnipotent power of the State over all the educational operations of the country that has brought the Prussian System to its present maturity," Brown wrote. "The blind advocates of Prussianism have awakened a desire in some simpletons to sacrifice their liberties for the sake of a foreign despotic school system," he wrote, "a system in which none would be troubled with the sometimes very annoying interference of the people."

A century and a half after the debate between Ryerson and Brown, the prime minister of Canada did something remarkable: he apologized.

Standing before the Speaker of the House of Commons in 2008, Stephen Harper offered a belated and not particularly expansive 3,600-word apology. This wasn't for Canada's public school system, of course, but for its residential school system.

"The Government of Canada built an educational system in which very young children were often forcibly removed from their homes and often taken far from their communities," read the official transcript. "Many were inadequately fed, clothed and housed. All were deprived of the care and nurturing of their parents, grandparents and communities."

Of the many things Harper made no mention of was the fact that residential-school students in the last stages of tuberculosis were finally given their wish and sent back to their families, and that this was to both lower the schools' mortality rates and spread the disease into Aboriginal communities. Nor did he mention that after their deaths, the whereabouts of children's bodies was withheld from their parents in order to prevent some semblance of healing from taking place. Nor did he mention the darkest secret of them all: that the man who created Canada's public school system also helped create its residential one.

In fact, the view that Ryerson was involved in *both* systems is hugely contentious. As we might expect, Ryerson University's professors of history at most will admit only to Ryerson's partial responsibility. Alternatives are often hastily proposed: Sir Charles Bagot, for instance, or Nicholas Flood Davin—or before either of them, one Major-General Darling. What can be said definitively is that Darling, Bagot, Ryerson, and Davin, respectively, wrote the ideological blueprint—the commissions and reports—that led to the horrific Indian Act of 1879.

But it was Ryerson's report to Indian Affairs, back in 1846, that coined the term *industrial school*. Something between a missionary and boarding school, industrial schools were designed to be equal parts "learning and religion." Ryerson called them "industrial" because, as he said, "they are schools of more than manual labour; they are schools of learning and religion; and industry is the great element of efficiency in each of these." By combining industrial pedagogy with religious inculcation, Ryerson believed that industrial schools could transform the wild, godless Indians into hardworking Christian citizens—and other people thought so too.

Located in Carlisle, Pennsylvania, and founded in 1879, the Carlisle Industrial School was the first of its kind and set the tone for non-reservation-based education. Run with Ryerson's combination of "learning and religion," the school was presided over by Colonel R. H. Pratt. After morning mass, "The boys learn the trades, and the girls are taught laundry work and sewing," as a teacher at the time recorded. "Regular instruction is given in carpentering, blacksmithing, painting, tailoring, baking, shoemaking, farming, gardening, and all kinds of house work," on top of recitations from the Bible.

Pratt, a deeply unpleasant man, is famous for creating the slogan "Kill the Indian, save the man," which first appeared in "The Advantages of Mingling Indians with Whites," in which he pens, "All the Indian there is in the race should be dead. Kill the Indian in him, and save the man." It says something of the times that Pratt was considered a warm, father-like figure to the Indians and kept in touch with a number of the twelve thousand students he superintended. In 1903, he wrote to President Roosevelt, demanding to be retired with a promotion by 1905; Roosevelt's reply was to retire him immediately, without promotion, as well as remove him from Carlisle. The school itself shut down shortly thereafter, but not before its features were borrowed and adapted elsewhere. Pratt's "outing system" was especially popular. An outed Indian student was put in the foster care of a wealthy white family, completing the process of conversion. "Pupils are placed in families to learn English and the customs of civilized life," a Carlisle memo reported, though accounts of abuse and other misconduct are too numerous to mention.

Part of the motivating force behind the outing program was the fear that children, after being released from an Indian school, would regress into their former ways, "joining the dog dances and other dances with an enthusiasm that makes them worse Indians than they were before." F. W. Blackmar, at one time a professor at the University of

Kansas and president of the American Sociological Society, recorded supposedly failed outings in an article for the American Academy of Political and Social Science. A Cheyenne boy who attended Arapaho, Carlisle, and Haskell industrial schools ended up back on the reserve, where he "resumed the habits and customs of his tribe and draws his rations with the other worthless wards of the nation." A Pawnee girl from Haskell returned to her reservation, where she abandoned her school uniform and was last spotted in a wigwam, kneading bread on a blanket and cooking over a bed of coal. "It is needless to say that dust and ashes were the principal seasoning," Blackmar sniffed. An Osaga girl who—according to Blackmar—loved Haskell so much she wanted to return, was apparently refused by her parents, who then sold her in exchange for some horses. Soon thereafter the girl died, "and thus passed to a world where, we trust, her education will be of some use to her, as it was doubtless of little benefit here."

The residential school system that Ryerson helped establish lasted 130 years, killed thousands of Aboriginal students, and left scars that cut "like merciless knives at our souls," in the words of Phil Fontaine, former national chief of the Assembly of First Nations.

In total, some 150,000 children were taken from their homes and forced to attend 132 schools across Canada, where they were physically, sexually, and emotionally abused. In the United States, white control over Indian education peaked in 1973, at which time an estimated 60,000 Indian students were being schooled with the same horrific results. Incredibly, a select number of Indian boarding schools still exist, including Haskell, which became a tribal university in 1993.

It speaks to the nature of government that its relationship with First Nations has never developed past a dollar amount: in the 1980s, it was reported that each year Indian troubles were costing the American government $19,000 per Aboriginal student, "a cost that Congress figured was exorbitant." When the Canadian government finally agreed to compensate its own Aboriginal community, the cost threatened to bankrupt four Christian churches. The 16,000 Indians who were still living received nearly $2 billion in recompense. Probably the money helps, but it can't undo the damage that can only be described as indescribable.

As for Ryerson, following his retirement as editor of the *Christian Guardian*, chief superintendent of schools in Upper Canada, and president of Victoria College (now part of the University of Toronto), he settled into a respected old age. When at last he died, in 1882, his funeral was attended by thousands of clergymen, statesmen, and leading public figures—though no Aboriginals were present.

OLD-SCHOOL DISCIPLINE

The world may be changing rapidly, but our school system is not. Take, for instance, scholastic corporal punishment, better known as spanking, strapping paddling, popping, caning, whipping, beating, smacking, swatting, rodding, hitting, shoving, dragging, hurting, and otherwise punishing the body.

At a grammar school in 1647, students could receive such treatment for talking during class. Today, in a surprising number of the world's territories, students can be hit for exactly the same reason.

In 2003, William Rini, a forty-seven-year-old middle school teacher in New York City, was arrested for taking students into his van and spanking them with a hairbrush. Also in 2003, a ten-year-old from East Texas, who was interviewed by Human Rights Watch as "Tim L.," forgot his asthma medication at home and was beaten by his teacher to the point of bleeding. The following year, eighteen-year-old Jessica Serafin, a student at San Antonio's School of Excellence in Education, violated a school rule by walking off campus to buy her breakfast. When she returned, she was held down by two assistants as principal Brett Wilkinson spanked her until bloody. During the same year, a student in Chennai, India, made the unthinkable transgression of skipping school on his birthday. When Ram Abhinav returned the next day, he was punished in front of the whole class and shortly thereafter committed suicide.

In 2008, a Canadian principal and teacher were charged with assaulting seven students at a private school in Malahide Township. Two years later, Bernadette Camacho, a teacher at Hillcrest High School in Queens, was forced to attend anger-management therapy for excessive corporal punishment. (Camacho was later fired for verbally abusing her students, among much else.) In India during the same year, Rouvan Rawla hanged himself after being caned at a private school in Kolkata. In 2011, Tyler Anastopoulos, of Wichita Falls, skipped detention and was sent to the assistant principal's office. "The blows were so severe that they caused deep bruises and the boy wound up in the hospital ..." In 2012 in Pakistan, Zahid Malik—principal at a public school in Mansehra—fractured the arm of an eighth-grade student, sending him to the hospital, after the student accidentally broke a flower pot.

The international status of scholastic corporal punishment is a telling example of how little our school system has evolved: It wasn't until the twenty-first century that Canada disallowed Section 43 of the Criminal Code in the defense of teachers who used "reasonable force" against a student. Two Canadian provinces, Alberta and Manitoba, have yet to confirm this Supreme Court ruling, and corporal punishment in the private sector has not been explicitly prohibited in any provinces or territories. During the previous century, hitting students was so commonplace that instances of specific abuse went largely unnoted, though the memories of an older generation suffice.

During the 2005–2006 school year, at the time of the last census, the United States reported 223,190 instances of scholastic corporal punishment, making it the developed world's leader in state-sponsored violence against children. During the following academic year, African American students, who made up 17.1 percent of the total schooling population, constituted 35.6 percent of all those paddled. According to Human Rights Watch, "Although girls of all races were paddled less than boys, African-American girls were nonetheless physically punished at more than twice the rate of their white counterparts ..." In a particularly grotesque display of injustice, students with mental or physical disabilities were also found to receive punishment disproportionate to their overall demographic. In Texas, special-education students comprise 10.7 percent of the total schooling population, but during the 2006–2007 school year, received 18.4 percent of the beatings.

America's draconian treatment of school-aged children puts it in the same category as Malaysia, Singapore, and Iraq. As a late associate justice of the United States Supreme Court pointed out, prisoners have more rights than students. But this isn't to say the issue is nonexistent elsewhere. According to a study from 2007, two out of every three schoolchildren in India are physically punished by their teachers, despite restrictive legislation and guidelines. A more recent study by the Society for the Protection of the Rights of the Child found that thirty-five thousand Pakistani high school students drop out of school yearly due to corporal punishment. With hundreds of thousands of examples of beatings in North America alone, the use of physical punishment in private and public schools is a painful reminder of our Prussian past.

In his *First Annual Report*, published in 1838, Horace Mann remarked on his travels to Prussia.

"In almost every German school into which I entered, I inquired whether corporal punishment were allowed or used, and I was uniformly answered in the affirmative." But Mann was struck by a peculiarity: While teachers were allowed to flog their students, rarely was such punishment required. That was because, at the time of Mann's visit, there existed an institution called a school-prison, where misbehaving children spent twelve-hour days picking wool and subsisting on bowls of bean porridge. "At the expiration of the sentence," Mann explained, "the children return to the school whence they came."

Under such circumstances, there was no need for corporal punishment in regular public schools. In Scotland, which was visited on the same European tour, there was no such thing as a school-prison. Without the fear of imprisonment, any particular student was less inclined to be obedient, and wrong answers or other infractions were met with "a retributive blow on his head by the teacher's fist ..." Mann's summative observation was wry in its understatement: in Scottish schools, "the criminal code seemed to include mistakes in recitation as well as delinquencies in conduct."

Years later, Egerton Ryerson embarked on his tour of Europe's prisons and schools. In his *Report of 1846*, the Canadian superintendent of education quoted Mann at length and repeated many of the same arguments—the chief being, of course, that the Prussian system should be adopted in Canada as it had in the United States. It wasn't enough to simply have educative legislation: in order to oversee and reinforce acts of Parliament, an administrative system should be established as well. Such a system would naturally accompany compulsory school attendance, which Ryerson argued was in the interest of all Canadians to endorse. Here, in addition to receiving the criticisms of George Brown, he was accosted by the politician Malcolm Cameron, who objected to what Ryerson sarcastically referred to as "the enslaving elements of my Prussian school system."

Both Mann and Ryerson, representing the United States and Canada respectively, wanted teachers to take issues such as corporal punishment into their own hands (literally). Legislation and administration could propose and reinforce the rules, but when it came right down to it, local school officials should be the ones in charge. This was how principals initially came to use the paddle, rod, switch, strap, cane, or other disciplinary instrument—or sometimes just the back of their hand. While punishment existed in schools prior to Mann and Ryerson, it was sanctioned not by the government, but by the Church.

In the seventeenth and eighteenth centuries, recalcitrant students could expect to be dragged by the ear out of the classroom, where, on bright, cloudless days, the teacher would burn them with a magnifying glass. Psychological traumas included the threat of eternal damnation. Students who stole might be made to endure a public whipping, only to then be ridiculed further by having a *T* stitched into their clothing. Two thieving students in 1645 were beaten by their Harvard schoolmaster. In 1672, a blasphemous student was both whipped and suspended, with the additional order that, henceforth, his meals be taken both naked and alone.

By the end of the following century, schoolhouses were being built with whipping posts included. One schoolmaster kept a meticulous record of each of his beatings: in a career that spanned an unfortunately long 51 years, he was said to have administered 911,517 blows with a stick, 136,715 blows with his hand, 24,010 with a rod, and another 20,989 with a ruler. Other punishment included making students kneel on peas or forcing them to stand with their arms outstretched, a heavy book placed on top. When all else failed, students were tied up in the schoolhouse closet.

When Horace Mann became secretary of the board of education, he visited a school in which 328 beatings were suffered over a five-day period. In the same year, 1837, the State upheld the authority of teachers to abuse their students, provided the children had no lasting injuries. This would seemingly set the tone for all future scholastic corporal punishment. Following the passage of common school legislation in Canada and the United States in the middle of the nineteenth century, the only difference was that violence toward children was government sanctioned. Teachers, *in loco parentis*, could effectively do whatever they wanted.

At the end of a school day in 1886, one Kentucky principal released all but three of his students. The girls—ages eight, nine, and ten—began to cry, thinking that a whipping would follow. Instead, over the course of the afternoon, each was sexually molested. When the girls eventually escaped, the townspeople assembled into a mob and lashed the man within an inch of his life. In 1895, at an Indian school near Arkansas City, a fifteen-year-old who had become "a chronic violator of all rules" was sentenced to fifty lashes, administered by his classmates. At a time when such brutal measures were routine, another student was sentenced to the same number of lashes, plus a twenty-day imprisonment that included menial chores—work that was doubtlessly made more difficult by the clasping of an iron ball to his ankle.

The following century saw only a slight decrease in the severity of punishment. In 1907, a principal at a school in Pittsburgh took to whipping identical twins because he couldn't tell which had committed an offense. Closely related to teacher–student beatings are, of course, student–student beatings, also known as hazing or, in slight variation, bullying. In 1913, a group of senior Cornell students sent a freshman to the hospital after pushing his head through a window. A decade later, a teacher in Bourbon County, Kentucky, married one of his students and then—when she drew a caricature of him on the blackboard—whipped her in front of the class. In a testament to the supreme patriarchy of the times, the woman was said to find the punishment "just."

By the 1930s, whipping was so common that when one

Pennsylvanian teacher refused to corporally punish, a committee of parents petitioned to have him removed. And by the middle of the century, paddling, caning, whipping—and in particular, spanking—had become entrenched in the prevailing ethos, associated with the adopted Biblical adage "spare the rod, spoil the child." In other words, physically abusing children was viewed as the best way to turn them into morally virtuous citizens. Speaking to a class at Columbia University in 1945, Bernard Montgomery, the first Viscount Montgomery of Alamein and a field marshal in the British army, claimed that "a good beating with a cane can have a remarkable sense of awakening on the mind and conscience of a boy."

But it could, of course, have the opposite effect. While the horrors of public school punishment are at least partially recorded, the greatest abuses occurred, and continue to occur, in the private sector.

In the early 1990s, a Canadian journalist named James FitzGerald began recording an unofficial oral history of Upper Canada College, arguably the country's most elite private school. What followed were some three hundred conversations with UCC alumni—students who had graduated over an eighty-year period in the twentieth century. The resulting book, entitled *Old Boys: The Powerful Legacy of Upper Canada College*, was so explosive that it led to the arrest of three teachers and a class-action lawsuit against the school that was settled in 2002. (FitzGerald had attended the school himself, as had his suicidal father, who once returned from a vacation to Mexico, walked wordlessly past his family, and climbed the stairs to his bedroom on the second floor. Before closing the door, he left a note that read simply, "Daddy ded.")

In *Old Boys*, FitzGerald got his subjects to reveal some alarming things. "UCC was a murderous establishment, absolutely brutal," recalled John Macdonald, a civil servant who left the school in 1930. "Very quietly going on all the time was a homosexual undercurrent, which mostly came from the headmaster." "Duke Somerville, the prep headmaster, was a peculiar fellow," recalled another former student. "After the canings, he would put the kid on his lap, fondle his bum and kiss him in a way that was rather peculiar." Patrick Johnson, UCC's principal from 1965 to 1975, recalled that "One of the history masters used to take boys on trips out west. God knows what happened on those trips ... In one isolated case, a boy was raped by this master."

But sexual abuse was just part of the equation. Conrad Black, the media baron convicted of fraud in 2007, got his start at UCC. "After a series of vicious canings, I became completely and perniciously insubordinate and undermined the school in various ways, culminating in stealing the final examinations and selling them to the boys in the school." Robert Martin, a professor of law at the University of Western Ontario, told FitzGerald that "The relish with which some of the masters caned little boys was quite extraordinary. There were some very unpleasant men who clearly derived sadistic pleasure out of bullying and beating little boys." John Schaffter, a UCC prep master, headmaster at St. John's Ravenscourt School in Winnipeg, and headmaster at St. Michael's University School in Victoria, recalled accidentally breaking a student's hand during a corporal beating. The boy told an inquiring nurse that he'd broken it catching a ball. "He saved my career," Schaffter observed. "That was a turning point ... I stopped beating boys from that point on."

What is most disturbing about a book like FitzGerald's, of course, is how many could be written, but never have been.

In the fall of 1970, James Ingraham was a student at a junior high school in Dade County, Florida.

He and some other students were loitering on the school stage when a teacher asked them to leave. They did, though evidently not fast enough: the students were taken to the principal's office for corporal punishment. While the other students allowed themselves to be spanked, Ingraham refused. The principal—a man named Willie Wright Jr.—called two assistants to force the fourteen-year-old down. They held his face and legs across the table while Wright produced a paddle. Ingraham was struck twenty times—so severely that he had to be taken to the hospital, where the doctor discovered the boy had developed hematoma.

Seven years later, the case had made its way to the United States Supreme Court, where it was presented by the plaintiffs as a violation of the Eighth Amendment to the US Constitution. Did scholastic corporal punishment constitute "cruel and unusual punishment"? If it did, it would be an infringement of the Constitution, and the Court would be forced to prohibit paddling across the country. But in a shocking upset, five Supreme Court justices ruled "the spanking of schoolchildren, no matter how severe, by teachers or other school officials does not violate the Constitution's Eighth Amendment ban against cruel and unusual punishment." Or to put it another way, Willie Wright Jr. had the constitutional authority to send James Ingraham to the hospital.

In the spring of 1987, Mary Sue Bruno, principal of a public kindergarten in Jacksonville, spanked two students, Crystal Cunningham and Ashley Johnson—aged five and six—for "snickering in the hall." Later the same day, the girls were spanked again by their classroom teacher, Rosa Cook. By the time they got home, Cunningham and Johnson were in serious pain. Their parents pulled them out of school for six days, took them to see the doctor, and reported the incident to social workers, who said it was a clear case of child abuse. But when the children's parents brought the issue to federal court, the presiding judge once again upheld the right of the state to hit children, stating *Ingraham v Wright* as precedent.

In fact, *Ingraham v Wright* has prevented an explicit ban on scholastic corporal punishment ever since. While the Eighth Amendment does prohibit the use of cruel and unusual punishment, beating children to the point of hospitalization does not seem to fall into this category. Justice Byron White criticized this view by pointing out that "if a prisoner is beaten mercilessly for a breach of discipline, he is entitled to the protection of the Eighth Amendment, while a schoolchild who commits the same breach of discipline and is similarly beaten is simply not covered." With perfect logic, White continued:

> By holding that the Eighth Amendment protects only criminals, the majority adopts the view that one is entitled to the protections afforded by the Eighth Amendment only if he is punished for acts that are sufficiently opprobrious for society to make them "criminal." That is a curious holding in view of the fact that the more culpable the offender the more likely it is that the punishment will not be disproportionate to the offense, and consequently, the less likely it is that the punishment will be cruel and unusual. Conversely, a public school student who is spanked for a mere breach of discipline may sometimes have a strong argument that the punishment does not fit the offense, depending upon the severity of the beating, and therefore that it is cruel and unusual.

In other words, it is deemed more cruel and more unusual to beat a hardened criminal than to hospitalize a kindergartner.

In 2011, Canadian and American researchers released an important new study.

"Effects of a Punitive Environment on Children's Executive Functions: A Natural Experiment" compared two West African private schools: one used corporal punishment, while the other used a gentler, nonphysical approach. The results indicated that students who were corporally punished performed "significantly worse" when it came to abstract thinking, planning, and delaying gratification. As Victoria Talwar, a coauthor of the paper and associate professor at McGill University concluded, "This study demonstrates that corporal punishment does not teach children how to behave or improve their learning." Considering the duration of government-approved violence in schools, this was indeed a revolutionary breakthrough.

In light of similar findings, the rest of the world's countries are prohibiting scholastic, as well as domestic corporal punishment—if they haven't already.

In 1979, Sweden set the trend by banning corporal punishment both in schools and private homes, and by 1983, Finland had done the same. By the turn of the millennium, most of Europe had banned scholastic corporal punishment and strictly monitored its domestic equivalent. In the United Kingdom, scholastic corporal punishment was prohibited in public schools in 1986 and in private schools in 1998. By 2007, Uruguay, Venezuela, Taiwan, Namibia, and other countries in the developing world had followed suit, and over the next three years, Costa Rica, Moldova, Kenya, Tunisia, and Poland could be added to the list.

Yet the United States and, to a lesser extent, Canada have remained conspicuous anomalies. Nineteen states, primary in the South, still condone corporal punishment, and only two—New Jersey and Iowa— have expressly forbidden it in both public and private schools. While Canadian provinces have made a more concerted effort, private school students continue to be at the mercy of their teachers (and considering the track record of UCC alone, this is indeed an alarming thing). While studies exist, it doesn't take a team of researchers to point out that beating children into being "good citizens" is an egregious act founded on an erroneous supposition. Trying to teach someone something while abusing him or her are clearly incompatible activities. Taken in isolation, the sheer existence of scholastic corporal punishment is evidence that our school system came from another century—and that it was adopted to manufacture a wide variety of outcomes, from the production of a useful citizenry to the production of an obedient army, as we shall see next.

THE WAR MACHINE

On April 2, 1917, Woodrow Wilson stood before Congress and declared war against Germany. In the words of one spectator, "As the President recommended the declaration of war, applause, which seemed universal, rolled through the whole assembly from floor to gallery."

The spectator was no doubt among those cheering. His name was Newton Baker, and he was secretary of war, head of the War Department, and in the eyes of General Hugh Johnson, one of "the greatest Lords of War that ever trod the earth."

Two months earlier, Baker had established a branch of the War Department called the Committee on Education and Special Training. Comprising a colonel, a deputy marshal, a lieutenant colonel, and a major, its job was, in Baker's words, to "mobilize the country's schools and colleges behind the army." In nineteen months they turned thirty-two thousand Americans into four million, "the largest war machine that the United States had yet known."

———————

Newton Diehl Baker was born in 1871, in the town of Martinsburg, West Virginia. If we are to believe the celebratory biography by C. H. Cramer, which really we shouldn't, Baker's mother "was an unreconstructed rebel who once boarded in the same house with John Wilkes Booth, ran the blockade, smuggled quinine and other necessaries to Confederate prisoners in Fort McHenry, and until her death in 1922, never saw a good-looking Negro girl without a desire to buy her." Baker's father appears to have been more conventional. A volunteer soldier in the Confederate army, he fought in Gettysburg and was captured, traded amiably for another prisoner, and sent home.

Their son, Newton Jr., was small and slight, with spindly legs and an uncomfortably large head. Cramer describes him as "Puck with a book," an odd comparison since the one time Baker tried out for a play, Shakespearean or other, he was turned away on sight. "There are no cupids in this show," the manager is said to have told him, though in fact probably didn't. Cramer seems to want us to think of his subject as a cherub; early on and with an entirely straight face, he refers to Baker as an "angel child." As an undergraduate student at Johns Hopkins, Baker happened to share a boardinghouse with Woodrow Wilson. Baker seems to have made an impression on the future president, though evidently it was a hazy one. Years later, when Wilson was scrambling to assemble his cabinet, he first considered Agricultural Secretary David F. Houston and Interior Secretary Franklin K. Lane for the role of secretary of war. But both men were deemed more valuable in their present positions, and so Wilson picked his old bunkmate instead.

Though he sent millions of young soldiers into war, Baker himself never fought. The closest he came was during the Spanish-American War, which he evaded on grounds of moral objection. "I am a pacifist," he sniffed, neglecting to mention that the army didn't admit soldiers with poor eyesight. Instead of storming San Juan with Roosevelt and the Rough Riders, Baker practiced law in Martinsburg, spending idle moments reading in foreign languages and thinking about a novel he'd always wanted to write. Its only two characters spent the duration of the story sitting beneath a tree while "saying wonderful things to each other" (an idea that seemed appealing to Baker's biographer, for one). Woodrow Wilson's telegraph interrupted all this, and Baker was summoned to Washington, leaving his legal career—and romance novel—behind.

Wilson's opponents protested his appointment of the forty-seventh secretary of war. It didn't help that Newton Baker had never so much as held a rifle and was publicly, if dubiously, opposed to war. In the milder rhetoric of the day, Baker was criticized as a "pacifist at heart," a "lamb-like gentleman," and "a lover of flowers." The American ambassador to Britain compiled these and other smoldering attacks in an article that compared Baker to a peaceful monk, "serene in his certitude," "unvexed by gross passions," and "ruminating on the Golden Rule."

Newton Baker set out as if to prove them all wrong.

As head of the Committee on Education, his work was twofold: (1) provide the army with men, some who had special training and others who did not; (2) keep the factories busy. Baker's genius was in connecting the one to the other, linking the older and previously established Federal Board for Vocational Education with the War Department's Committee on Education and Special Training. The first group was made up of the industrial lobbyists who oversaw the adoption of Kerschensteiner's school. The second group consisted of Baker and the colonels and deputy marshals mentioned earlier. By joining the two together, students from industrial schools such as the Carnegie Institute of Technology would transfer directly into specially designated war schools. Instead of smelting iron for the automotive industry, they would go to a different school and smelt iron for bomb casings.

With World War I raging in Europe, war schools couldn't be built fast enough. Baker acted as foreman during the construction of the first thirty-two. The Kentucky war school that stationed F. Scott Fitzgerald was built in an hour and a half, "from timber that had been standing in Mississippi forests one week before." (The training facility gets a mention in *The Great Gatsby*.) War schools were built so fast there wasn't time to print textbooks for them. Instead, the army used its own encyclopedia of military professions, taught by retired army generals and industrialists from the Federal Board for Vocational Education.

For principals, Baker hired department heads from schools across the country. One was Frank Sheppard, of an agricultural school in Oregon. Sheppard must have been surprised to wake up one morning to a telegram from the secretary of war—one in which he was offered a job. "Pay not to exceed that of Major," the transcript read. "Plan involves mobilization of educational facilities of the nation to meet army demand for technicians which now exceeds one hundred thousand and is increasing." Sheppard left for Washington, where Baker informed him he was now district director of war schools in Oregon, Idaho, Montana, and Wyoming. No doubt adding to the shock, Sheppard was given total charge, with no boss or superior. "We frankly state to you that unless there is a good and sufficient reason the War Departments [sic] Committee on Education and Special Training will never reverse one of your decisions."

Sheppard seems to have been the type to do well under pressure. By the time the war was over, his districts alone had produced thirteen thousand soldiers (with the exception of Wyoming, which, for an unknown reason, didn't produce any). Given all the power he wanted, Sheppard and the other district directors chose to manage war schools with the emphasis on *war*. An inspecting committee made a tour of three dozen facilities "from Maine to California" soon after Sheppard had settled into office. The resulting report admitted "the extension of military discipline to the class room was an experiment watched with keen interest by the authorities." Overall, the inspectors were "thoroughly convinced of its success," noting in particular how alert and attentive students were. This is not very surprising when we consider the inspecting committee was made up not of teachers or even government officials, but military officers, including one Lieutenant-Colonel Payne.

By the time they were up and running, each of the 32 war schools was its own small city, with 1,400 trucks, 1,200 outbuildings, and an abundance of bunk beds. To fill them, Baker created the first organized draft. Students needed to be registered before they could become soldiers, so Baker developed a system that still gets used today: the Selective Service System was designed to "secure the co-operation of the educational institutions of the country and to represent the War Department in its relation with such institutions." The SSS collected your name, age, level of education, and prior work experience. Then it issued a registration card which you took with you to war school. There, the commanding officer paired you with a special training program. Before the system was in place, 32,000 American men volunteered for the war. On the day of registration, the SSS inputted, sorted, and put on a waiting list—a very long waiting list—9,586,508.

In September 1917, the first 6,000 were chosen, trained, and shipped to France. Three months later the number of war schools grew from 32 to 157, "delivering about 25,000 trained men each month to the army." The following year, 10,000 new American soldiers arrived in France each day.

War schools featured a total of 565 military programs. Program A was for infantry and heavy artillery; Program B was for air service; Program C, quartermaster service; Program D, engineering corps; Program E, motor transport; and so on. Whatever the army needed, it got: the student was schooled with that particular program to become that particular kind of soldier. There were programs for non-soldiers too. In every combatant division of 36,000 men, there were 691 chauffeurs, 360 telephone repairmen, 167 mechanics, 156 radio operators, 128 machinists, 122 truck masters, 78 auto mechanics, and 67 blacksmiths, not to mention a smattering of mathematicians, electricians, firemen, policemen, detectives, physicians, psychologists, meteorologists, photographers, artists, rubber workers, steelworkers, metal workers, gunsmiths, sailmakers, boatmen, and writers. The standard training term consisted of twelve fifty-three-hour weeks. Then you graduated war school and got to go to the real thing.

Since the training of war school students made their involvement with the war more peripheral than direct, the army needed another *kind* of soldier altogether, one who was able-bodied and otherwise not terribly bright. Here again schools were the place to go. Baker wrote letters to colleges and universities at Christmastime, commending athletic students for "the continuance of all kinds of sports ... not only the sports which they have been following usually, but also boxing, rifle shooting, and wrestling." Athletic students were physically fit, used to competitive and combative role-play, and thought to be more brawn than brain, a point Baker reinforced when he silently passed over Harvard, Princeton, and Yale, whose students were too intellectually valuable to be wasted on the front lines.

The new year brought new challenges. Colleges across the country were empty and broke, since there were no students left to attend or pay for lectures. War schools, on the other hand, were completely stuffed, not to mention expensive. Though students were fed, housed, and schooled for as little as $1.20 a day, the bill added up considerably. In 19 months, the government spent $25 billion on war schools (rather more than it had spent on education since it began). There was another thing. Germany had advanced 40 miles into the Western Front. In a report filed by the War Department's Committee on Education and Special Training, this news was noted with customary detachment: "Class I of the first draft was exhausted," and by this they didn't mean merely tired.

So Baker came up with a new idea. The Second Plan, as it was called, drew students out of high school by enticing them with a private's salary, in effect bribing them. In an amendment to legislation of the previous year, Woodrow Wilson lowered the age of enlistment from twenty-one to eighteen. "High school graduates of 18 years and over will be eligible," Baker told the deans of the schools in question. To reduce the cost of training, Baker—with admirable inventiveness, it must be said—turned public schools into makeshift war schools.

Heading up the Second Plan was the Students' Army Training Corps, a group of senior military officers who went around converting schools into training centers with barracks, mess halls, laundry rooms, firing ranges, bakeries, marching fields—even urban schools were overhauled. It is a strange sight to see photographs of students at Cornell lying in a row on a field, squinting down rifle barrels at some unseen target, or a teary exchange between a young soldier and his lover as his unit departs from the University of Kentucky. Baker so thoroughly blurred the line between student and soldier that newspapers printed the words jointly, with a hyphen between. At the behest of the Students' Army Training Corps, thousands of .30-caliber rifles arrived in over five hundred American schools. Teachers were replaced by war veterans who "equipped and encouraged" students "in body and mind for service." Boys of seventeen who weren't old enough to draft were still trained, as were boys who were intellectually slow and boys with only a grammar school level of education.

All of this was still extremely expensive. The Second Plan cost the War Department fifty-four million dollars and gave the army an extra five combatant divisions—or two hundred thousand student-soldiers.

———————

On November 11, 1918, the war was over.

Baker's role as secretary of it was over too, as was the Wilson administration. The president made a postwar tour of Europe, where, according to the suspect opinion of C. H. Cramer, he "was idolized by adoring crowds which regarded him as the King of Humanity," and Baker was considered for a peace prize. In fact, it was Wilson who was awarded the Nobel Peace Prize and Baker who went to Europe.

But first Baker went home to Martinsburg, where he took up his old law practice and wrote a book. A far cry from his romantic best-seller, *Why We Went to War* was a retrospective analysis of World War I, including much of his own thought on the subject. In its two hundred or so pages, the word *school* appears on just five of them and in each instance is meant in the sense of a philosophical movement—a school of thought. At first this appears to be a considerable oversight. After all, Baker was the man who invented war school. However, in Baker's defense, *school*—referring to an actual building, where people go to learn—may have appeared more often if he'd called his book *How We Went to War*.

School was the *how* of the Great War. It was how the army turned young men into student-soldiers. It was how they got so many able-bodied men to populate the front lines. It was how, in twelve weeks, a college grad could become a sailmaker or infantryman. It was how eight-and-a-half-pound rifles with two-foot-long barrels ended up in the hands of boys who must have struggled just to hold them up. School was also *where* nearly ten million Americans were registered for war. It was where the army went to find most of its soldiers and where it converted them—in number and type—into whatever it needed. Even the War Department seemed pleasingly astonished. "The system was surprisingly successful," Baker's committee concluded.

But why wouldn't it be? School was designed to be a war machine: In Prussia, it was school that enabled the secret training of soldiers. In America, it was school that was seized to create an educated labor pool, thanks to the financial contributions of Carnegie and Rockefeller. In Canada, it was school that was used to convert Native Canadians into just regular ones. In Asia, India, and the rest of the world, school is the gatekeeper of power, privilege, and prestige. The people who control it, control the world. The fact that Baker was a trustee of the Carnegie Foundation and that C. R. Mann, a representative of the same foundation, was part of the War Department's Committee on Education and Special Training attests to the fact that the school model was versatile, while the system itself was so singularly appealing it could attract Puritans and warlords alike.

Baker's work—especially in the registration, organization, and conscription of students—was profoundly effective not only in World War I but in the following war as well. "In World War II," Cramer wrote—truthfully, for once—"the educational program of the Special Services Division was to be built on the foundation that Baker had laid."

4 | THE CORPORATE EQUATION

*French fries: Lemon & Herb, Sweet Chili Pepper, Smokin
BBQ, Tex Mex, Outbacka, Chili & Cheese, Poutine, Sweet
Potato, Hamburger Poutine, Curly Fries, Regular Fries.*

—menu at Potato World, Florenceville, New Brunswick

MOUNT A+

Mount Allison University is a small school with a big name. Per
capita, it's Canada's top-ranked undergraduate university and has
produced more Rhodes Scholars than any university in the British
Commonwealth.

A survey by *The Globe and Mail* awarded the school an A+ in class
size, an A in academic reputation, and an A– in recreation and athletics.
A study by the National Survey of Student Engagement placed Mount
Allison at the top of fifty-seven categories, including level of academic
challenge, study satisfaction, student–faculty interaction, supportive
campus environment, and enriching educational experience. The
school was the first in the British Empire to award a bachelor's degree
to a woman and the first in Canada to grant a woman a bachelor of
arts. It was the first Canadian university to have an art gallery, the first

to teach Canadian studies, and the first to introduce a wireless campus.

Mount Allison—or "Mount A," as the school is affectionately known—has one of the most beautiful campuses in Canada, with seventy-seven finely tended acres, dozens of ivy-covered buildings, a chapel, a private pond with two resident swans, a large concert hall, a theater, and an auditorium; the school has a small student population, an award-winning teacher–student ratio, and an alumni that includes nationally known poets, artists, writers, politicians, athletes, journalists, academics, businesspeople, actors, and just about everything else. Mount Allison has graduated eight Rhodes scholars in just ten years, and fifty in its history. But the crowning jewel of achievement is the school's designation as "the best undergraduate university in the country," a position it's held fourteen times in the last twenty years and for as many as ten years consecutively. In a truly remarkable demonstration of accomplishment, Mount A never falls below second place.

Mount Allison University owes this tremendous prestige to *Maclean's*, a nationally read current affairs magazine. For twenty years, *Maclean's* has developed, administered, and scored its own test, called "Maclean's University Rankings," which rates colleges and universities across the country. The results are published in November, in time for graduating high school students to consider before applying to university. "Maclean's University Rankings" is published again the following spring, in the magazine's bestselling issue, called *Maclean's Guide to Canadian Universities*. With a circulation of 350,000, and over two million readers, *Maclean's Guide to Canadian Universities* is printed after high school students have heard back from the universities they applied to and are making the final decision about which school to attend.

More than any of its other achievements, Mount Allison's success with *Maclean's*—the school's designation as the number one undergraduate university in the country—is the very pinnacle of Mount Allison's reputation.

———————

Mount Allison University is located at the southeast end of New Brunswick, Canada's least populated mainland province.

Forestry, the principal industry, accounts for two billion dollars in yearly revenue, a third of which is derived from the sale of solid-wood products and three-quarters of which comes from pulp (used to make paper and other fibrous goods). To give a sense of how lucrative trees can be, this two-billion-dollar sum is the result of harvesting less than 2 percent of New Brunswick's total forests, which cover some fifteen million acres. Of the trees that are cut down, two-thirds grow back naturally, and of the remaining wood provincewide, about 50 percent is owned by the Crown and remains undeveloped.

Precisely because there are so many trees in New Brunswick, an excursion down its middle on the new Trans-Canada Highway from the Quebec border toward Nova Scotia can exceed even the most enthusiastic driver's patience. I was reminded of a jingle I'd heard on the radio: "The woods may be thick and the highway may be new / but that don't mean you should drive right through." The song, paid for by the New Brunswick tourist bureau, was meant to address the tendency of motorists, upon entering Atlantic Canada, to head straight for Green Gables or the Cabot Trail without stopping in New Brunswick, a geographically necessary thoroughfare. For this reason, New Brunswick is known as the "Drive-Through Province," a reputation that settled for me personally when I noticed that *Lonely Planet* had relegated my destination—the hometown of Mount Allison University—as "the right place for a pit stop ..."

By the time I reached the New Brunswick–Quebec border, I had been driving for thirteen hours straight and was not looking forward to the remaining five it would take to get to Mount Allison. Quebec is the provincial home of a town called Saint-Louis-du-Ha! Ha!, a single moment of comic relief I'd been relying on, a little too eagerly, from back in Ontario and that I savored, a little too wistfully, into New Brunswick. Aside from being the province you drive through to get to a better one, New Brunswick is known for bearing a number of large and peculiar monuments. The town of Shediac, for instance, is home of the world's biggest fake lobster, while Nackawic is home of the largest ax. Other provincial offerings include the world's biggest artificial Atlantic salmon, maple leaf, and fiddlehead. It seemed an especially cruel coincidence that in a region trying to counter the image of being a drive-through province, one could also find Hartland, New Brunswick—home of the world's longest covered bridge.

On the off chance the attractions weren't appealing, a number of provincial towns had begun making the extraordinary claim that they were, in themselves, interesting. Digby, New Brunswick, was said to be the "Scallop Capital of the World"; or there was Grand Manan, New Brunswick, the "Dulse Capital of the World." So it was with some initial skepticism that I found myself in the "French Fry Capital of the World."

Four hours from the Mount Allison campus, Florenceville-Bristol is nestled into a verdant hillside and surrounded by thousands of acres of potato fields. I would read later that 22 percent of New Brunswick's agriculture—its second most important economic sector—comes from potato sales and that New Brunswick exports fifty potato varieties to some thirty-five countries around the world. Potatoes are such a serious commodity and their harvesting such a valued endeavor that until as recently as 2012, students took a two-week holiday from school to help bring in the fall harvest. While the province has only a couple of hundred potato farms, they produce over fifty thousand acres of potatoes and do so almost entirely from one region: the Saint John River. It's this river that Florenceville-Bristol straddles and which I found myself glimpsing shortly after turning off the Trans-Canada Highway.

Though I was eager to get to Mount Allison, I had decided to make the detour in order to visit something called Potato World. An oddly shaped building with interactive displays, a theater, café, and gift shop, Potato World is a museum, information center, and homage to New Brunswick's most important crop. Because I was both too late in the day and too early in the season to be admitted, I stood for a few moments looking in through the glass door. What I had wanted to see most was what the museum's website referred to as the "Hall of Recognition," where individuals "who have made a significant contribution" to the province's potato industry are honored (though evidently not to a degree that would satisfy the presumably more stringent requirements for a "Hall of Fame"). Of the dozen or so honorees, I was interested in only two: Wallace and Harrison McCain.

Like many farmers from the British Isles, the McCains emigrated to North America during the early nineteenth century, arriving in the Saint John River Valley in 1825. According to Grant Gordon and Nigel Nicholson, the family was entrepreneurial, industrious, and creative. In 1909, the McCain-family patriarch founded a successful seed potato export company. Across the border in Maine, a different company had begun manufacturing frozen foods—a process that had only recently become technologically possible—and Andrew McCain's children saw an opportunity to combine modern conveniences with New Brunswick's premium crop.

The opportunity turned to reality when the senior McCain died in 1953 and bequeathed enough money for his sons to start McCain Foods Ltd. Harrison became the company's president and Wallace its vice-president. In a meteoric rate of growth, McCain Foods Ltd went from being a one-factory operation with 30 employees and $150,000 in first-year sales to today's multinational corporation, with products in 160 countries and operations on 6 continents. With 57 factories, 21,000 employees, and over $6 billion in sales, McCain Foods is the world's largest french fry manufacturer: one in three french fries around the world is made by McCain. The Florenceville-Bristol plant alone produces over a thousand pounds of french fries every hour.

Today, the McCain brothers are recognized as two of Canada's most successful entrepreneurs, though during the 1990s they were engaged in a bitter family feud, centered around who would succeed them as CEO. Wallace wanted to appoint his son, Michael; Harrison wanted to appoint his nephew, Allison. The court eventually ruled in Harrison's favor, with the result that Wallace McCain was ousted from his own company and Allison McCain succeeded Harrison as the head of McCain Foods. While the brothers' relationship never recovered, their professional lives are unrivaled in Canadian business. At the time of Harrison's death in 2004, he had a net worth of over a billion dollars. In 2008, three years before his own death, Wallace McCain was listed as the three-hundred-and-fifty-eighth richest man in the world, with a net worth of over three billion dollars.

In the eighteenth century, Joseph Allison was a poor Irish farmer.

He was so poor, in fact, that when the tax agent came to make his yearly collection, Allison's wife invited him in for a home-cooked meal, with the hope their debt might be forgiven. The tax agent agreed, and in an effort to make the dinner more seductive, the table was arranged with a set of silver spoons. Upon seeing the spoons, the tax collector is said to have understood at once what was happening, stood up, and demanded the overdue tax—shouting that if the family could afford a set of fine silverware, they could afford to pay their taxes. Allison shouted back, saying he would sooner emigrate than pay his taxes.

And so it was that in the fall of 1769, the Allisons left Ireland on a vessel bound for Pennsylvania. But on November 21, the *Admiral*

Hawke ran into a brutal Atlantic storm that foundered it off the coast of Nova Scotia. Rather than board another vessel to the United States, the Allisons decided to stay in Maritime Canada. Though nearly all of the ship's contents had been lost at sea, according to the *Nova Scotia Chronicle*, the Allisons somehow managed to retain their collection of silver spoons. Settling in Kings County on the Bay of Fundy, Joseph and his wife raised a son, passing their silverware to him, who in turn passed it on to his son, Charles Frederick Allison.

Charles Frederick grew up in Nova Scotia, but crossed the border into New Brunswick when he and a cousin, William Crane, started a small business. Based out of Sackville, the southernmost town in the province, Allison and Crane traded local New Brunswick commodities with imported goods. The business made them both wealthy, and as it expanded into shipbuilding and other ventures, Allison and Crane ascended through the Sackville community to become two of its best-known residents. Allison evidently felt the need to give back, and at a meeting of Methodist missionaries in 1839, he announced that he would personally fund the construction of a Wesleyan school.

Originally called the Wesleyan Academy for Boys, Mount Allison was "delightfully situated upon an elevation of ground" in what is now downtown Sackville. Partly because Allison had converted from Anglicanism to Methodism—and the spirit moved him—and partly because he had more money than he knew what to do with, Allison agreed to donate one hundred pounds to the school annually, which he did faithfully until his death ten years later. Construction began in the summer of 1840, and by 1843 the school was ready to receive students. After appointing Humphrey Pickard the first president of Wesleyan Academy, Allison continued to act as treasurer, "for I am naturally fond of money."

In addition to his yearly endowment, Allison was instrumental in petitioning and funding a second institution, the Wesleyan Academy for Girls, which opened in 1854. When the school gained degree-granting status in 1862, it was renamed Mount Allison College and for the next fifty-one years operated as three institutions. By the mid-twentieth century, the separate schools for boys and girls had been closed, and Mount Allison University stood alone and prospered.

While it was customary for post-secondary institutions to be founded by ministers and those of faith, Mount Allison was unusual in that Charles Frederick was first and foremost a capitalist and one who (in contrast to his grandfather) was good with money. From its mercantile beginnings, the school was governed as a business—one that needed a well-appointed governing board, large amounts of cash, and powerful connections within regional, provincial, and national circles.

And here, as if sent from God Himself, was the McCain family.

Mount Allison's history with the McCains began with a man named George Trueman, who started his career at the school as a student. Evidently, the experience was a positive one, and in 1923, Trueman became Mount Allison's fifth president, where he oversaw the enrollment of his niece, a homely and industrious woman named Margaret Fawcett. Almost immediately thereafter, Fawcett became part of the school's faculty and soon afterward married another Mount Allison alumnus, J. P. Norrie. Fawcett and Norrie's daughter, Margaret Norrie, would graduate from the same school decades later, as would her seven siblings, her entrepreneurial husband, Wallace McCain, and all of their children. In 1974, Margaret Norrie McCain was appointed to the school's board of regents, a position she held for twenty years, even after being appointed the school's chancellor in 1986. The year following her retirement from governance, Margaret was awarded an honorary degree, Wallace was appointed to the school's national advisory council, and their son, Scott, was placed on its board of regents. Harrison McCain's nephew, one of the few McCains not to attend Mount Allison, is named Allison.

And so it was that a tiny school, in a drive-through province, became the wealthiest and most powerful undergraduate university in Canada.

The trend began in correlation with the success of McCain Foods. It was after his graduation in 1952 that Wallace McCain, along with his brother, Harrison, incorporated McCain Foods Ltd. By the 1960s, the company was shipping as far away as Australia. In the 1970s, McCain Foods increased its product line to include frozen pizzas and throughout the following two decades opened facilities in Europe and the United States, expanding its lineup again to comprise not just potatoes but frozen vegetables, juice, and appetizers. As the business flourished and the McCains grew richer, Wallace followed the tradition of Charles Fredrick Allison and donated money to the school (which still has, by the way, the family's collection of silver spoons).

On the morning of my first full day in Sackville, I made my way over to the Mount Allison campus. I had scheduled a tour, which began in the newly constructed Wallace McCain Student Centre. Joining me was Nicole, a prospective student who was graduating from a private school in Toronto, and her father, Andy, who wore a faintly pin-striped suit and spent the next ninety minutes fiddling with a BlackBerry. Our tour guide, Fraser, had given us a bag of Mount Allison paraphernalia, and as a light rain pattered down on the atrium, I took a few moments to examine a long, narrow brochure. Like every other prospectus I'd seen, the brochure featured pictures of students confidently raising their hands in class, attending a competitive sports rally, and mingling interracially on the campus lawn.

What caught my eye was a single sentence on page three. "This view book will show you why we are consistently ranked #1 in the annual *MacLean's* [sic] university ratings edition." The sentence was of course referring to "Maclean's University Rankings": more than the

school's Rhodes Scholars, technological innovation, ivy-covered buildings, or tradition of gender equality, it's the *Maclean's* ranking that
represents the peak of Mount Allison's achievement.

Whenever the rankings are released, the school makes an official
announcement; in the press release from November 2010, President
and Vice-Chancellor Robert Campbell was quoted as saying, "At
Mount Allison, we strive to offer the most enriching and engaging
experience for our students in a sustainable fashion. We are pleased
that the *Maclean's* assessment once again validates our approach." The
bulletin noted that student awards, student–faculty ratio, awards per
full-time faculty, library expenses, and library holdings per student
were among the categories that *Maclean's* awarded to Mount Allison.
Indeed, the school thinks so highly of its *Maclean's* ranking that on
the school's website, it's featured above the *Globe and Mail* report, the
study by the National Survey of Student Engagement, and the number
of alumni Rhodes Scholars.

As I flipped through the brochure, Fraser asked Nicole and Andy
how they'd heard about the school.

"You guys read the *Maclean's* magazine?"

They nodded. "Yeah, we did."

Fraser seemed unsurprised. I had no idea what percentage of
Mount Allison students first heard about the school through *Maclean's*,
or who—like Nicole—ended up on a tour after seeing Mount Allison
at the top of a list twenty-two schools long, but given the magazine's
millions of readers, I guessed it was high.

After leaving the McCain Student Centre, Fraser led us, under
cover of umbrella, through some of the school's forty-odd buildings,
walkways, and communal areas, pausing at the rear of the Athletic
Centre so we could appreciate the sight of a rain-soaked sports
field. In every sense, Mount Allison is a competitive school, and its
athletic department is no exception. In addition to a men and women's

badminton team and men and women's swimming team, there are separate teams for men's basketball, soccer, and football, and women's volleyball, hockey, and basketball. The school is similarly fond of clubs and societies, and has 140 to choose from: There are student associations for the arts, the environment, religion, sexual orientation, academics, theater, business, world issues, and more. (Among the more memorable are the Salsa Society, Opera Lovers Anonymous, and a club dedicated to Brazilian Jiu-Jitsu.)

For most of the tour, Nicole exuded the enthusiasm one normally reserves for a coma. When asked what she liked to do with her free time, Nicole claimed to have no special interests or abilities, apart from shopping and hanging out with friends. As Fraser showed her the girls' dormitories, I asked Andy if they were going to visit any other campuses in the area. He told me they were considering tours of Acadia and King's University College. Given these three options, Nicole would almost certainly choose Mount Allison. All three schools are small, have a liberal arts curriculum, and appeal to families like Nicole's, who school privately, are used to paying tuition, and want to give their children the best education they can. But in the recruitment of Nicole, Mount Allison had an advantage.

She had read *Maclean's*.

With Mount Allison being the McCain family's alma mater, it's no surprise that—after he'd made a fortune in frozen foods—Wallace chose it as a beneficiary. But it isn't just money the McCains have brought to Mount Allison. Both Margaret and Wallace McCain have been in an executive governing capacity, as have their son and many of their business associates.

In fact, at the time of my visit, nearly every member of Mount

Allison's principal governing bodies—the national advisory council and board of regents—was an active or retired executive officer of a corporation. There was Wallace McCain, the retired CEO of McCain Foods Ltd; his son, the CEO of Maple Leaf Foods; and David Booth, the president of global sales and marketing at the McCain Institute. There was the CEO of Nestlé Canada, one of few food processors not owned by a McCain subsidiary, and the former CEO of Sobeys Canada. There was John Bragg, a director at Sobeys and co-CEO of Oxford Frozen Foods. There was the CEO of Moosehead beer. There was the CEO of an investment group in Bermuda who resigned after a public inquiry, and a CEO of a company that owned Imperial Tobacco during the decade it was criminally charged for tobacco smuggling. There were the CEOs of internet startups, telecommunications companies, and media conglomerates; there were the former executives of banks and brokerages, a number of preeminent lawyers, and a former CEO of the Year. In 2007, three of the country's fifty wealthiest executives were on the governing board at Mount Allison.

Because of its powerful governance, Mount Allison has benefited in ways that other universities have not. While Canadian universities are over three billion dollars in debt collectively, Mount Allison University is completely debt free. It may have produced the most Rhodes Scholars in the British Commonwealth, but more importantly, Mount Allison is the wealthiest school per capita in Canada. Its annual endowment exceeds eighty million dollars, which, relative to the size of the school, puts it in the same category as a private boarding school (and not a public university). By way of contrast, the University of British of Columbia has eighteen times the number of students, but only eight times the annual endowment; Queen's University has eleven times more students, but only seven times the annual endowment.

Looking at the view book Fraser had given me, it would be possible, even natural to assume that the school was ranked number one by *Maclean's* because of its inviting atmosphere, beautiful campus, arts and culture, proximity to beaches and ski hills, student clubs and sports teams, observatory, modern student center, ivy-covered buildings, international programs, and more. But none of these amenities factor into the *Maclean's* ranking. Even more sober criteria—library holdings, class size, student–faculty ratio, resources, student awards—that do factor into the ranking don't hold as much weight as the amount of money a school has, what it can afford to provide its students, and the power of its boardroom.

The ranking breaks down as follows: 20 percent goes to the academic success of a university's student population; 20 percent to the academic distinction of a university's teaching staff; and 20 percent to the school's broader reputation, including the opinions of CEOs. Of the remaining 40 percent, 12 is taken up by the school's resources, 13 by its scholarships and other support, and the final 15 percent by its library. Mount Allison University does well in all of these categories, with the probable exception of student support: as a wealthy and selective school, Mount Allison is in a separate category from the Ryersons and Carletons, the universities of British Columbia or Toronto, and doesn't have to offer competitive scholarships.

In fact, when it comes to financially supporting its students, Mount Allison is surprisingly stingy: in 2010, the school received an endowment of eighty-two million dollars, 2.5 percent of which went toward student financial aid. Upon entrance to the school, freshmen with an A average are guaranteed a scholarship of just five hundred dollars. Considering full-time Canadian students can expect to pay almost seven thousand dollars a year in tuition alone, this is more of a symbolic than practical amount. Of course, international students incur even greater expenses. A non-Canadian student with a full meal plan and a single room will pay over twenty-three thousand dollars a year, and that's without books, membership fees, communication fees, access to the gym, health insurance, and airfare for the holidays. Since 90 percent of first-year students choose to live in residence and many spend the entire duration of their degree living on campus, the school makes more money in these areas than competing institutions.

According to an unaudited financial report from 2010, Mount Allison earned $18.7 million from tuition fees, $5.5 million from residence fees, and $4.3 million from dining fees—or 41 percent of its total revenue (the remaining 59 percent came from provincial operating grants, investments, donations, and other sources). The school received over $8 million in unnamed cash donations and bequests, and ended the school year with not only a surplus, but a surplus of almost $1.5 million. To compare with Acadia University—another of the schools on Nicole's list, which often falls directly behind Mount Allison in the *Maclean's* ranking—the same fiscal year was closed with just $80,000. Whereas Mount Allison made $18.7 million from tuition fees, Acadia made $28,704; whereas Mount Allison made $18.2 million from provincial operating grants, Acadia made $28,924. In a final demonstration of Mount Allison's economic fortitude, it began construction on its most expensive building ever—the $15-million, 71,000-square-foot Wallace McCain Student Centre (a third of which was paid for by the McCain family)—before the economic recession of 2008, and nevertheless managed to finish "on time and on budget ..."

The point, of course, is that Mount Allison is a rich school. And as a rich school, it tends to promote itself as a good or successful school, as though there were no difference.

One problem with this is that it creates a socioeconomically homogeneous environment: wealthy parents like Andy are impressed by the beauty of the campus and by the feeling of a close-knit community, and nudge their children into attending. Moreover, by not offering competitive scholarships, Mount Allison effectively prohibits poor students from applying, and as is commonly known in the field of education, poor students are less likely to succeed than wealthy ones. The result is a school that has a tremendous reputation but little to back it up with. Mount Allison is all too happy to credit itself with the success of its students when, in reality, the chances are that the same students would've done just as well anywhere else.

This self-regulating system began with the McCains. Because of the McCains, Mount Allison is a school that thinks like a business: it knows how to solicit donations, manage its money, and most of all, how to advertise. This is where *Maclean's* comes in. In the school's brochures, on its website, and from the mouths of its tour guides is the mention of its number one *Maclean's* ranking. This mention is enough to draw students from the west to a province with little else to offer, save some oversized monuments and a few thousand acres of potatoes. This mention is enough to motivate parents like Andy, and students like Nicole, to fly out for a campus tour. This mention is what, in turn, *is mentioned*: more than any other of the school's achievements, the first question from Fraser was not, "Did you hear about our Rhodes Scholars?" but rather "Have you read the *Maclean's* magazine?"

When a school thinks like a business, it puts its reputation first. The question isn't whether it's a great school—everyone agrees it is—but whether it's *the number one undergraduate school in Canada*. Probably, it isn't. In a perfectly honest world, the Mount Allison motto wouldn't be "Writing, Divinity, and Knowledge," but rather "Money, Power, and French Fries." Should Mount Allison ever be renamed, Mount McCain seems an appropriate choice, since it was the McCains who went to the school, the McCains who governed the school, and the McCains who gave the school millions of dollars. In the end, it was Mount Allison's relationship with the McCains that led to its success with *Maclean's*.

In 2006, *Maclean's* received a letter from the president of the University of Alberta.

In it, Indira Samarasekera argued that the rankings were prejudicial—calibrated to favor particular provinces and schools while overlooking others. The letter was sent, but nothing happened as a result.

Shortly thereafter, Samarasekera was in a meeting with David Naylor, Peter George, and Harvey Weingarten, presidents of the universities of Toronto, McMaster, and Calgary respectively, and it turned out that they all felt the same way. "So the four of us decided to see who else was willing to join ..." The result was tectonic: more than a quarter of all universities in Canada felt similarly snubbed, and when it came time for *Maclean's* to collect the schools' information, they refused.

As part of the ranking, *Maclean's* had asked the universities to fill out a survey—this was a self-reporting survey, designed to elicit information from the school such as its class sizes, entry averages, and so on. Because the schools had to fill the surveys out themselves, it was costing taxpayer money. When the twenty-five universities boycotted *Maclean's* that year, they did so for two reasons: first, they thought the rankings were biased. And second, they asked, "Why should we use public resources to collect data so that you can sell magazines?"

A third objection might have been this: the Reputational Survey—not the self-reporting one the presidents were criticizing, but the survey that asked CEOs what they thought of the schools in question—is worth 20 percent of the overall ranking, but in 2010 it had a response rate of just 7 percent. Out of all those surveyed, only a fraction are actually responding, yet this criteria is still as dense as any other in the ranking. In other words, *Maclean's* is giving a lot of say to a very few people, who in turn are influencing thousands of students.

Ten years before, a researcher at the Department of Statistics, University of British Columbia, published a paper on the *Maclean's* ranking. At the time of its publication, *Maclean's* had been ranking Canadian universities for less than a decade, but already the authors felt that "the potential, if not actual, influence of these articles on people's perceptions and actions is far-reaching." Nancy Heckman and colleagues noted, "The high-school counsellor may use the rankings as a basis for making recommendations. The employer may use the rankings to evaluate a job applicant based on which university s/he attended," and given the gravity of the situation, pledged to give the entire system a thorough review.

What Heckman found was startling. The ranking was effectively useless, given that "some of the indicators may not reflect actual quality adequately either because there are flaws in the collection or processing of the data or the variable is not an intrinsic measure of actual quality." One indicator that represented both problems was the Reputational Survey. Since the survey was based so heavily on opinion—and since so few people seemed actually to have one—the data was skewed, which Heckman says "makes the results just total garbage."

Canada isn't the only country with a rankings obsession.

The *U.S. News & World Report's* annual "Best Colleges" guide has the same power as *Maclean's*. When the rankings were released in 2011, the company's website registered over a million hits in a single month, and of these, an undisclosed number of applicants chose their college accordingly.

Like the *Maclean's* ranking, the *U.S. News* report uses half a dozen or so weighted variables to produce a rank of the country's post-secondary schools. The final result is a number, with 100 being the best and 1 being the worst.

And like the *Maclean's* ranking, the *U.S. News* study includes a Reputational Survey worth, in this case, more than 20 percent of the final grade. As Malcolm Gladwell pointed out to readers of *The New Yorker*, this section is the most important in the whole methodology. And yet there was a serious problem. When a panel of lawyers was surveyed about the schools' reputation, it put the law school of Penn State in the middle of the pack. The problem was that Penn State had no law school.

"Those lawyers put Penn State in the middle of the pack, even though every fact they thought they knew about Penn State's law school was an illusion," Gladwell wrote, "because in their minds Penn State is a middle-of-the-pack brand." This was a supreme example of the dangers of applying the scientific method to something as dubious as an opinion. As the most significant aspect of the ranking, the Reputational Survey makes it its job to solicit the prejudices of wealthy and influential people and, in doing so, changes the lives of untold thousands. In the United States, it elbows students in the direction of wealthy, private universities—the Harvards and Yales—and away from Penn State. In Canada, it elbows them in the direction of Mount Allison and away from the University of Alberta.

I asked Samarasekera if students were being misled.

"Yes, absolutely," she said. "*Absolutely.*"

As this fact has become increasingly apparent, the ranking industry has been compelled to change its methodology. Since the 2006 boycott of *Maclean's*, dozens of Canadian universities have chosen not to participate in the self-reporting survey, which spent universities' time and money to the benefit of *Maclean's*. This has had the effect of forcing the magazine to go to third parties such as Statistics Canada, where much of the same information is available (and was from the beginning). But even so, the University of Alberta and a significant number of other universities in Canada refuse to acknowledge the rankings even after they're published. "We pay no attention to it," says Samarasekera. "When the magazine comes out, they send the results to us, and we just yawn, pretty much."

From either way you look at it—from Mount Allison's perspective or *Maclean's*—students are being given a false impression. The school advertises itself as being educationally excellent (not rich); *Maclean's* presents itself as neutral—an unbiased third party—when in fact it favors the unreliable opinions of wealthy CEOs. This arrangement has worked to the benefit of both parties, while excluding the one it was intended for. Neither Mount Allison's representation of itself as excellent nor *Maclean's* representation of itself as scientific accurately depicts the services being offered to students, and as a result, lives are being altered.

As we returned through the rain to the McCain Student Centre, I wondered how many students there were like Nicole, who waited for the March issue of *Maclean's*, flipped to the right page, and put their finger on the name at the top of the list. Plane tickets were bought, cars rented at the airport, and here they were. Fraser estimated he had given seventy-five campus tours—how many in attendance thought they were seeing the best school in the country? How many thought that its beautiful grounds, resident swans, and Brazilian Jiu-Jitsu had something to do with it? How many drove past the endless potato fields, the fake lobsters and maple leaves, to arrive at the base of Mount Allison?

THE CORPORATE EQUATION

In 1923, a professor of biochemistry made an extraordinary new discovery.

Soft-boned rats would grow stronger when they ate food exposed to ultraviolet light. Through a process known as irradiation, almost any food could become nutritionally enhanced. The reason for this, Harry Steenbock correctly observed, was that ultraviolet light contains stores of vitamin D. In his research laboratory, Steenbock had just discovered the cure for rickets (and, more memorably, ushered in an era of vitamin-enriched food).

For the first time in American history, a humble professor—at the University of Wisconsin, no less—was approached by a large corporation with an offer to buy his invention. The company was Quaker Oats, who wanted to use irradiation on their breakfast cereal in order to claim it was "the only oatmeal with Sunshine Vitamin D." For this they were willing to pay one million dollars, a sum so exorbitant in the 1920s that Steenbock was thought to be half mad when he turned the offer down.

Then, instead of selling his invention outright, Steenbock obtained a patent for "the Steenbock process" and began selling the *rights* to his invention—not the invention itself—which he did through the Wisconsin Alumni Research Foundation. In this way, the "Steenbock process" was licensed to not only Quaker Oats but hundreds of other companies as well. Instead of making one million dollars, Steenbock made many. Today the research foundation is endowed with over two billion dollars, nearly three-quarters of which continues to derive from inventions involving irradiation.

Steenbock died in 1967 having cured a deadly disease, become immensely rich, and ushered in a new era of corporate–university relations. Not bad for a humble professor from Wisconsin.

But this story begins in full with a thirty-four-year-old doctor named Judah Folkman, who, in 1967, became the youngest person ever appointed as professor of surgery at the Harvard Medical School. Folkman was a bold, risk-taking man who wanted to begin his career with a singular and revolutionary discovery. According to a writer for the journal *Science*, "Folkman postulated the existence of a chemical signal, TAF, that tumors send out to stimulate the growth of new blood vessels." To prove TAF existed, Folkman and colleagues implanted minuscule tumors in the eyes of rabbits. If TAF were real, it would elicit new blood vessels, and it would take only an inhibitor to stop the growth of the tumor, effectively cutting off its blood supply.

In 1974, Harvard was approached by the agrochemical giant Monsanto, which was interested in Folkman's research. Under the terms of the resulting agreement, Monsanto would give Harvard $23 million over the course of 12 years. Monsanto also tossed into the bargain new laboratory equipment worth $1.4 million and perhaps as much as another $12 million in ancillary support funds. Folkman and his principal colleague, a man named Bert Vallee, were given $200,000 a year, to be adjusted with inflation, for research purposes, guaranteed for the duration of the contract.

In turn, Monsanto was given the rights to design, market, and profit exclusively from every invention that came from Harvard's laboratories. If Folkman discovered the cure for cancer, Monsanto would be the only company in the world with the formula and—just as important—the only company in the world profiting from it. For a multibillion-dollar corporation such as Monsanto, a few million dollars was no big deal when what it bought was potentially the most powerful and profitable invention ever made.

Though ultimately Folkman never made his breakthrough discovery and the Harvard–Monsanto deal ended without any major inventions (at least none that have been disclosed to the public), an important thing happened. Before Monsanto arrived on the scene, Harvard, like every other university at the time, had an ethics policy that forbade it from profiting on inventions that were "concerned with therapeutics or public health ..." Post Monsanto, Harvard amended this policy to permit profit on inventions that *did* involve health, such as the discovery of TAF, the mythical—and still illusive—chemical substance that could stop the growth of tumors (though of course Harvard claims the timing was coincidental).

This was to be the new model of corporate–university relations. Or, as a Monsanto press release noted, "Committee members have expressed the hope that their activities may eventually serve as a model for others who embark on a similar industrial–academic project in the future."

A decade or so later, in the late 1980s, a Yale professor named William Prusoff created a drug that slowed the progression of AIDS.

Yale then licensed the invention to the pharmaceutical company Bristol-Myers Squibb who, in the early nineties, submitted the product for FDA approval. The drug, which came to be known as Zerit, was administered to 10,000 AIDS sufferers—predominately young white males—79 percent of whom were still alive 18 months later. Though an alarming 2,100 recipients reported experiencing a painful side effect in the nervous system, Bristol-Myers released the drug anyway—and released it into a market in which there were only three other available brands at the time (one of which, a drug known as ddI, was also owned by Bristol-Myers).

FDA approval of Zerit cost the pharmaceutical giant $15 million, or something like eight times the normal rate of prerelease testing. However, according to the director of Knowledge Ecology International, a nongovernmental organization that specializes in intellectual property, Bristol-Myers has profited more than $2 billion from the Prusoff invention alone. In just one year of administering the drug, Bristol-Myers earned $618 million and is today the eighth largest corporation in the United States, with an annual revenue of nearly $20 billion. When the company's CEO retired in 2010, he was making over $18 million a year; his replacement, Lamberto Andreotti, is expected to receive an 89 percent raise.

But none of that is particularly controversial.

The controversy erupted back in the summer of 2000 when a Yale law school student named Amy Kapczynski attended the World AIDS Conference in South Africa. There she was confronted by five thousand AIDS-afflicted protestors who were demonstrating against the high cost of available medicine, which was preventing them from receiving treatment. Kapczynski returned home to the US, where, some months later, she received an unexpected phone call from Doctors Without Borders.

Much to her surprise, the organization wanted Kapczynski's help with blowing the whistle on her own school, on what has been described as "Yale's complicity in the AIDS crisis ..." Together with other activists on campus, the group discovered that, between 1994 and the year 2000, Yale University had made $262 million in Zerit royalties. A third of Yale's new research laboratory was funded with Zerit proceeds, and Prusoff—the drug's inventor—had likewise grown rich.

And here was the thing: the overwhelming majority of people who had AIDS couldn't afford the price of Zerit, ddI, or any of the other antiretroviral medications. Ninety percent of the world's thirty million people who have AIDS live in the developing world, especially sub-Saharan Africa, and don't have the money for pills (or, as may be pointed out, the clean water to take them with). As this information began to circulate around campus, students and professors alike signed a petition calling for Yale to intervene by demanding that Bristol-Myers release a generic, nonprofit version of Zerit. Not surprisingly, Yale insisted its hands were tied; Bristol-Myers claimed it was doing everything in its power to reach more people with AIDS. Then, in a story by *The New York Times*, William Prusoff was quoted as publicly denouncing the pharmaceutical giant that bought his own invention, an action that humiliated Yale in the process.

Within days, the price of Zerit was slashed, from $2.23 a daily dose to 15 cents. Though Bristol-Myers announced the timing to be a coincidence, Prusoff's article had nevertheless affected the outcome. However, what is noteworthy about the conclusion of this particular story is the striking way in which Prusoff denounced Yale's corporate partnership. "I once helped create a drug that could enable millions of people to lead better and longer lives," he wrote. The sense of betrayal Prusoff felt was when the miraculous nature of his invention—the product of serious academic inquiry—was compromised by corporate greed. "We weren't doing this to make money," he told Yale's *School of Medicine Chronicle.* "We were interested in developing a compound that would be a benefit to society."

Then a similar story emerged at UC Berkeley.

There, in 1998, the school's Department of Plant and Microbial Biology entered into an agreement with Novartis. In exchange for twenty-five million dollars, Berkeley would give the world's largest pharmaceutical and biotech company first dibs on a third of its inventions. Novartis was even given the right to delay the results of the department's findings and to put two of its representatives in seats on Berkeley's five-chair committee (which, among other things, decided how that twenty-five million dollars was spent). To even out the deal, faculty members were given unprecedented access to the company's proprietary databases, allowing them to glimpse select "trade secrets" in the detailed (and closely guarded) world of plant genetics.

What makes the Berkeley–Novartis deal especially controversial is that it was Berkeley that approached the company and not the other way around. Though this was an unusually bold move, Berkeley had some reason to think a multibillion-dollar sponsor such as Novartis might be interested. One-third of the entire world's biotech companies were founded by faculty at the University of California—a clearly staggering proportion. After making a few adjustments to the contract, Novartis agreed to the school's conditions, and, in the memorable words of Chancellor Robert Berdahl, the "Faustian bargain" was struck.

Backlash was instantaneous. When the partnership was announced at a press conference on November 23, a university official was struck in the face by a banana-cream pie (an activist group called the Biotic Baking Brigade later claimed responsibility). Moreover, a separate organization—Students for Responsible Research—was formed specifically to investigate the Berkeley–Novartis contract. When the FDA held a series of meetings in December 1999, the student group was there—along with hundreds of others—to protest what one paper called "the largest rally in the United States against the use of genetic engineering in food."

To the general public, the principal concern in the alliance between Berkeley and Novartis was the potential for Novartis, a very much for-profit leader in plant and microbial pharmaceuticals, to skew the university's findings. Chancellor Berdahl would later compare it to "lung cancer research funded by tobacco companies." The de facto neutrality of academia—one of higher education's defining charac-teristics—was thrown seriously into question. Berkeley's own motto, "Let There Be Light," could hardly be trusted when Novartis was the one with the keys to the electrical panel. According to a poll conducted at the time, half the department's faculty thought the contract would restrict their academic freedom, service to the public good, and limit the exchange of free ideas within the school. In the end, only two academics refused to participate—the rest had no lasting moral objection.

Shortly after the Harvard–Monsanto deal, in 1981, Harvard made new arrangements with DuPont, the multibillion-dollar chemical company. (Among other things, the partnership led to the famous "Harvard mouse," a genetically modified rodent that's virtually guaranteed to get cancer—and thus makes for a better research subject.) As for Monsanto, in the same year it entered a contract with Washington University for $23.5 million. Soon, corporate–university liaisons were the norm: Columbia University partnered with Bristol-Myers in 1983; Carnegie Mellon with Westinghouse in 1997; and Cornell University with Exxon Mobil in 1998. Of the period, one journalist remarked that corporations and universities had "wooed and won each other as never before." Or, as the historian Roger Geiger has written, "Almost uniformly, universities in the 1980s made the judgment that the inducements to commercial activities outweighed the possible risks to their core academic roles."

Canada is not free from its own scandals.

In the 1990s, Nancy Olivieri was a medical researcher at the University of Toronto's Hospital for Sick Children. In 1993, she signed a deal with Canada's biggest pharmaceutical company, Apotex Inc., to conduct experimental trials of a drug called L1, which was designed to treat a hereditary blood disorder caused by malfunctioning hemoglobin. What Olivieri found was shocking: L1 produced dangerously high levels of iron, leading to toxicity of the liver and effectively poisoning the same children it was supposed to treat.

Thinking the company would tell her to stop the trials at once, Olivieri contacted her corporate sponsor. Much to her surprise, Apotex told her she was wrong. Moreover, they reminded her that she'd signed a nondisclosure agreement, "and threatened to sue her if she made her opinions public." When Olivieri publicized her opinions anyway, the University of Toronto removed her from its faculty, claiming that the research surrounding the benefits of L1 was mixed. It wasn't. After a lengthy legal dispute, Olivieri was eventually compensated for her firing on the condition she not "disparage Apotex" in the future. To this day, Olivieri remains Canada's most famous whistleblower and was even suggested to have been the inspiration behind John le Carré's *The Constant Gardener*.

In 2000, the University of Toronto was again the subject of controversy when David Healy was offered a job with the school's Centre for Addiction and Mental Health (CAMH)—before having this offer rescinded when Healey began speaking about the negative effects of Prozac. As it turned out, CAMH was receiving donations from the multibillion-dollar pharmaceutical company Eli Lilly, which manufactures, among other things, Prozac. Here was a perfect example of corporations taking control of universities, resulting in an astonishing and illegal breach of academic freedom. Fortunately, after settling out of court, Healy was able to shed light on the issue and has since become an outspoken critic of the pharmaceutical industry. (He was also invited back to the University of Toronto, though has since chosen employment elsewhere.)

Sheldon Krimsky is a professor of urban and environmental policy and planning at Tufts University in Massachusetts whose extensive commentary on corporate–university alliances includes the authorship of a chapter in *Universities at Risk: How Politics, Special Interests, and Corporatization Threaten Academic Integrity.* "I dealt with the question of what standards we should use when we look at research funds coming into the university," Krimsky says. "The important thing for me is the autonomy of the institution and of the researchers. And when you have an external company that's deciding on the research projects, that's a great loss of autonomy."

Krimsky recommended I speak with Lawrence Busch, a professor of standards and society at Michigan State University. In 2004, Busch was the principal investigator of a study that examined the Berkeley–Novartis contract. Though the report concluded that the contract produced "modest benefit and very little harm" to Berkeley's Plant and Microbial Biology Department, Busch continues to be cautious of university–corporate alliances. "It seems to me one solution is to have diversity of funding," he says. "The second thing is the question of public goods versus private goods. It's not to say that private goods are necessarily invalid, it's that if you're talking about a public institution, you have some duties to the public. And basically from the vantage point of the company, the only reason why a company would want to be involved in a relationship with a public institution is to get some sort of private benefit ... The question is, Do both sides benefit?"

University–corporate alliances also seem to rely an awful lot on luck. In the case of Harvard–Monsanto, no radical, tumor-solving invention was ever discovered—yet twenty-three million dollars was wagered on the belief that there would be. Busch agrees: "An enormous amount of what goes on consists of straining massive amounts of things and coming up with higher and higher throughput, in the hopes that one is going to find the proverbial needle in the haystack." Busch noted that this method of inquiry was radically different even from when he was an undergraduate ("back in the Dark Ages," he told me). Today's method is totally different. "It's closer, if you wish, to Thomas Edison's figuring out how to make filament for a light bulb and going through I forget how many hundreds of things before he discovered carbon was going to do it."

Yet the sheer investment on the part of corporations suggests there's more to it than plain luck. Even when not strictly involving research, corporate gift-giving to universities has bordered on the extreme. Coca-Cola's Asa Candler donated 75 acres and $1 million to the chartering of Emory University, and that was in the currency of 1914. The University of Oregon has received $230 million from Nike cofounder Phil Knight, who only stopped giving the school money when the campus athletic store refused to carry clothing made in sweatshops. Seemingly out of spite, Knight's next philanthropic donation was in 2006 to the Stanford Graduate School of Business, which received

$105 million—the largest single donation in business school history. The record was shattered just two years later, when the University of Chicago's business school received $300 million from David Booth, the cofounder of a successful investment firm. An equivalent in the annals of Canadian education would be Joseph Rotman's $36 million in gifts to the University of Toronto's business school. (As with Booth, the school was renamed in his honor.)

Today, deals between universities and corporations are almost too numerous and common to mention. While the amounts being given—$23 million to Harvard, $25 million to Berkeley—are, relative to the overall endowment of the school, a small percentage, they are nevertheless significant, considering that federal and state funding have generally been on the decrease since the economic recession of 2008. Between 2009 and 2010, the average American university endowment decreased by 18.7 percent, "the worst returns since the Great Depression …" At Queen's University in Ontario, the market value of the school's endowment fund plummeted $125 million in six months of 2008. Montreal's McGill University lost approximately 20 percent, or $185 million, of its endowment over the same year. Some schools have it even worse. State support to UC Berkeley has been dropping nearly 1 percent a year from 1980 to the end of the Novartis contract—from 60 percent of the school's overall operating budget to 34 percent. Chancellor Robert Berdahl has claimed that this kind of shrinking governmental support justifies the solicitation of large multinationals.

But Busch is not convinced by this line of reasoning. "There is no such thing as *ever* having enough money for research. You can always find something else to do research on," he says. "There's also a kind of interesting accounting fiction that goes on at universities. It's that universities are generally obsessed with how much research dollars they can bring in, and pay relatively little attention to how much things cost." In the meantime, universities are still coming up short, and instead of making do with less research—and fewer corporate partnerships—students have had to pay more for tuition. In fact, the correlation between rising tuition costs and shrinking federal funding would be more justifiable if there was some explanation— official or otherwise—as to just where the money was going. It's not as though students benefit from university–corporate alliances—more than a minor oversight, considering that, technically, universities are for them.

But universities and corporations are (perhaps unsurprisingly) not altogether forthcoming about the deals they make. If we knew what went on behind closed doors, there's a chance that fewer of us would attend certain institutions. It is worth pausing for a moment to reflect that between 1994 and 2000, Yale was effectively sponsoring death— not the death of those who were taking Zerit, but the death of those who weren't. The same could have been true with Harvard, had its contract with Monsanto produced some pharmaceutical discovery.

It's entirely possible, if not likely, that more cases such as these exist. Unfortunately, we may never know if they do. University– corporate alliances may be shrouded in secrecy, but they've become so widespread that many feel a new era has been ushered in. Berkeley's own chancellor now refers to "the privatization of public universities," and others have begun calling corporate-sponsored institutions "the university-industrial complex," while claiming that irreversible damage has been done. In her book *University, Inc.: The Corporate Corruption of Higher Education*, Jennifer Washburn argues that these alliances serve the "short-term bottom line" of the sponsor and that nonprofit univer- sities are among a country's "most unique and important economic and cultural assets, and therefore worthy of special public support."

The very mission of education—to liberate oneself from one's environment, to deepen one's understanding or enrich one's life in a way that makes one more appreciative, inquiring, and compassionate—seems antithetical to the interests of mere capital. It is perhaps telling that university–corporate alliances tend to be found in the scientific and mathematical disciplines that typically earn the most money. (We don't find Penguin Books making million-dollar donations to the classics department at the University of Toronto in exchange for first dibs on the manuscripts of all graduating students of English.) The fact that corporations go after the microbial departments and chemistry labs is a revealing indication of the value these areas have—and perhaps constitutes a greater need for their preservation and autonomy.

Despite the opinion that university–corporate alliances are harmful, evidence suggests that—at least with Berkeley–Novartis—sponsorship didn't do the damage everyone thought it would. Still, academic studies may not be the best way to determine the impact of university–corporate sponsorships—especially if the universities doing the studying are themselves receiving corporate funding. The level of subtlety in bias can be maddeningly hard to pinpoint. Even Sheldon Krimsky's *Science in the Private Interest: Has the Lure of Profits Corrupted Biomedical Research?* begins by thanking "the Rockefeller Foundation for providing financial support for this book ..."

But while virtually every public university has a corporate sponsor, there's another way in which corporations have influenced higher education—as we'll see next.

A BILLION-DOLLAR IDEA

Vincent Hale is a professor at a university in Illinois. What makes his job unusual is not his teaching style or policy on exams, but the subject of his lectures and the kind of school where he works.

Hale is employed at a degree-granting institution owned by McDonald's. With twenty full-time professors and five thousand graduates a year, Hamburger University's standard fare is a Bachelor of Hamburgerology, with a minor in french fries.

McDonald's isn't the only corporation to have its own school. Burger King has a similar academy in Massachusetts called Whopper College. Disney University, Microsoft University, and the University of Toyota are all real places designed to school the employees of their parent companies. For this reason, they're also known as "career schools," which are distinct from traditional schools in that they don't offer accreditation (save for Hamburger U, which does).

But a variation on the idea also exists. Some incorporated businesses have their own universities and *do* offer accreditation—and what's more, they make a lot of money doing it. The Apollo Group, Corinthian Colleges, and Kaplan, Inc. are private companies that own schools. Their universities and colleges work just like any other institution of higher learning, except that the money they earn from tuition and other sources they get to keep.

While historically, public universities were established as places to acquire special and privileged knowledge, today's institutions of higher learning exist as a bridge to adulthood. After three or four years at a local college, a student is no longer a student and can style him- or herself a manager or banker or artist. According to Clark Kerr, former president of the University of California and father of the modern university, "Higher education began as an effort at moral uplift. It continues as an effort to get a good or better job."

Intriguingly, private for-profit universities offer the same service as their public nonprofit forebears. When they received a write-up by the Carnegie Foundation in the 1980s, corporate universities were described as "incorporated organizations whose first purpose [is] not education." (The actual "first purpose" wasn't specified, though we may assume it had to do with making money.) Since then, corporate universities have become the fastest-growing sector of higher education.

Between 1998 and 2009, for-profit universities grew 225 percent, with the top fourteen of these schools sharing an enrollment of nearly one-and-a-half million students. Today, the US alone has more than two thousand such schools. Their popularity has risen so quickly and so amazingly that enrollment at for-profit universities has in some cases exceeded enrollment at traditional ones.

Yet for-profit universities are not without their controversies. Obviously, many people feel that business interests and education interests shouldn't be mixed. The idea of paying money in exchange for knowledge seems somehow strange, but thanks to Clark Kerr and the Carnegie Foundation, this is the condition even at traditional schools. When it comes to higher education, we have arrived at the intellectually bewildering position of objecting not to the fact that an education costs money, but that other people may profit from it. Paying for a degree is okay, so long as the school itself doesn't get to keep the money.

Founded in 1973 by the Apollo Group, Inc., the University of Phoenix is a school that makes a profit and doesn't care who knows it. With twenty thousand faculty members and half a million students, it's the biggest private university in North America. Unlike Whopper College and Motorola University, the University of Phoenix is for actual students and not just for the employees of multinational corporations. This, supposedly, is to the benefit of both students and shareholders. In 2009, the Apollo Group grossed nearly four billion dollars. In the estimation of Gary Berg, its bestselling educational institution is "the single most significant mass-education phenomenon of recent times."

But despite (or perhaps because of) its unprecedented success, the University of Phoenix is probably the most hated school in history. It's been vilified by everyone from students to the mainstream media; nick-named "Drive-Thru U" and "McUniversity"; used to coin the phrase "diploma mill"; investigated by the FBI; and sued by everyone from the federal government to its own employees. Even the normally dispassionate academic community has defaulted to attacks on the school's founder. "John Sperling's vision of education is entirely mercenary," a professor at San Jose State University has written. "When education becomes one more product, we obey the unspoken rule of business: to give consumers as little as they will accept in exchange for as much as they will pay. Sperling is a terrible influence on American education."

Part of the problem, it ought to be pointed out, is Sperling himself. A dangerous combination of smart and stubborn, Sperling is a self-proclaimed revolutionary—perhaps the only thing he's called himself that was true. After amassing a personal fortune of over a billion dollars, he spent at least some of it successfully cloning his favorite dog, a mutt named Missy. Sperling's next venture was to try to invent a formula that would prevent himself from aging. This failed, however, and Sperling has grown into a rebellious seniority.

———————

John G. Sperling was born in 1921, the sixth child of a poor Missouri family. While his mother worried about running out of food, his father didn't bother looking for work and stayed home most days in order to beat his children. Once, after a particularly violent outburst, Sperling threatened to kill his father. Luckily he didn't have to, and soon after, his father died of natural causes. As for Sperling, he went running out to the yard and rolled joyfully through the grass: "There I lay looking up into a clear blue sky, and I realized that this was the happiest day of my life."

As a student, Sperling was average at best, probably because he was mildly dyslexic. After a brief stint as a sailor, he tried out for the navy, transferred to the army, and was eventually discharged. Another couple of odd jobs and Sperling began thinking he should go back to school.

Thanks to his connections with the army, he was accepted to Reed College—a school normally outside his academic possibilities—where he despised the advantages of his wealthier, more naturally gifted peers and later professed to having learned nothing. After graduating with a BA in history, Sperling completed subsequent degrees at Berkeley and finally Cambridge, coming out with a doctorate in economic history.

Next, Sperling took a teaching post at Ohio State University. It was his first real job, but he quickly grew restless and unappreciative. The parties and functions were boring, and the hors d'oeuvres—once an unimaginable indulgence—seemed only to annoy him. "The hostess almost invariably served either a tuna or macaroni casserole and cheap red wine," Sperling writes in his memoir. "Only then did it begin to dawn on me that academic life … was a depressing affair."

So Sperling moved to San Jose, where he became a union organizer. Unfortunately, this wasn't his calling either; in 1968, a teachers' strike backfired, making him the most hated man on campus. With characteristic paradox, Sperling later claimed, "The strike was one of the most liberating experiences of my life." By his own estimate, he learned "it didn't make a goddamn bit of difference what people thought of me."

His career as a union organizer over, and now in his fifties, having been married and divorced twice, Sperling was selected to run a workshop at San Jose State University. Its purpose was to train police officers and teachers to work with troubled teens. Rather than standing at the front of the room and lecturing, Sperling broke the class into small groups and brought in teachers who were experts in their field. His adult-aged students were so pleased with the program, they told Sperling he should offer degrees to working adults who didn't want to quit their jobs.

It was a good idea. In fact, it was such a good idea that it's amazing no one had thought of it before. As Sperling explained to *The New Yorker*, "Higher education is one of the most inefficient mechanisms for the transfer of knowledge that have ever been invented." And then, with a reminder of his own genius, "I decided to go back to my economics and conceive of education as a production function, in which you specify the learning outcomes you want—they're your product—and then do a regression and figure out the most efficient way of producing them."

In 1976, the Institute of Professional Development—as the University of Phoenix was then called—moved from California to Arizona, where the laws governing the accreditation of for-profit universities were less restrictive. When the University of Phoenix became a publicly tradable company in 1994, the school became one of the greatest success stories in academia. Born into true poverty, Sperling reached retirement the richest man in the history of American education.

But there were problems.

Attacks on the University of Phoenix began to increase in what it has since characterized as an "elitist bias against nontraditional higher education." Everyone from the press to the FBI has questioned the school's practices and motives, and there have been an astonishing number of legal suits since the beginning of the millennium alone.

Following an audit in the year 2000, the school owed $6 million to the Department of Education. In 2004, another $9.8 million was issued—the largest fine in the country's scholastic history—for awarding pay incentives to recruiters based on the number of students they registered. In 2009, two former employees successfully sued the University of Phoenix for $78.5 million—$19 million of which went to them—after proving the school had defrauded the federal government of over $3 billion. (The University of Phoenix has maintained its innocence in more or less each of the charges and claims it paid only out of a desire to have the issue resolved.)

There's another problem that affects not just the University of

Phoenix and other for-profit universities, but all institutions of higher learning. To become a school that dishes out diplomas, a university must be accredited. This is where it gets a bit complicated: First, there are two kinds of accreditation—institutional and programmatic. Generally speaking, institutional is the more important of the two, since it gives accrediting power to the entire university. No matter what program you take, if the university has been institutionally accredited, the degree will hold power.

Organizations that accredit by program, however, look at specific parts or courses within the school that fulfill a specific role. Vocational colleges and technical academies mainly fall into this group, and it only makes sense: a technical institute that specializes in nursing may be accredited to do so, but very probably won't be equipped to offer degrees in classics, for example.

As far as the government is concerned, both programmatic and institutionally accredited universities are completely acceptable: schools of either type may call themselves a college or university, have a campus, library, and offer financial assistance to students. The only real difference is within the academic community: get a diploma at a programmatically accredited university and it almost certainly won't get you into an institutionally accredited one. That's why graduates of ITT Tech don't go on to Harvard—in a practical sense, they can't.

Now, private for-profit universities are mainly accredited at the programmatic level. The reason has to do with the criteria used by accrediting agencies. For-profit universities will often have a disproportionate number of part-time professors since the overwhelming majority of their clientele are adults who work during the day. Classes, out of necessity, take place at night, and so many for-profit institutions can't claim to have a full-time faculty as we would expect at a traditional university.

The University of Phoenix is the gold standard of for-profit universities in large part because it *is* institutionally accredited and has been since 1978. But unfortunately, even it and other institutionally accredited for-profit universities often have a hard time convincing people—especially prospective students—that their degrees are actually worth anything (or at least, that they're worth the same as a degree from a traditional institution). One of the most serious complaints from graduates of corporate universities is that they were lied to—that an enrollment counselor told them the school's degree would get them in the door of a traditional university, where they could continue to further their education.

Take, for instance, the story of Terry Pitts.

Pitts was a prison guard who wanted to become a lawyer. He enrolled at Florida Metropolitan University, a for-profit school owned by Corinthian Colleges. At the advice of an enrollment counselor named Dolly Brown, Pitts spent four years working toward his diploma, graduating in 2003. Degree in hand, he approached a law school only to discover he couldn't get in. "I spent four years for nothing," he told *The Wall Street Journal.* When the case went to court, Brown, the one who'd advised Pitts in the first place, claimed she'd never told him the school's diplomas would get him into law school. Meanwhile, Pitts had amassed fifty-six thousand dollars in debt, moved into a mobile home, and become a father. Brown, on the other hand, was given a promotion.

Of course, for-profit schools are quick to say that these are isolated instances of wrongdoing and don't represent the views or policy of the university. "Do we train our people to give that kind of mis-advice? Absolutely not," Bill Pepicello, president of the University of Phoenix, told an ABC News reporter. ABC had gone undercover to visit several recruiters' offices and been told the same thing each time—namely, that the university's degrees counted in the real world. (Pepicello had no direct response to the reporter, except to claim that he was looking into the matter.)

Like Terry Pitts, Beverly James-Snyder approached a guidance counselor before enrolling in Florida Metropolitan University. She wanted to eventually transfer her credits to the University of South Florida, and the counselor told her that would be fine. But when she finished her degree in 2002 and promptly went to enroll at USF, "They laughed me out of their office." James-Snyder had no choice but to enroll at another corporate university—the University of Phoenix, as it happened.

In 2008, the Apollo Group opened its first Canadian school.

At the time, Meritus University was New Brunswick's second private for-profit venture. And while it closed just three years later, this is by no means indicative of the overall trend.

The Australian-based Navitas Ltd has been deal-making with Canadian provinces since 2006, when it entered into a contract with British Columbia's Simon Fraser University. Unlike the Apollo Group—which asserts itself with the force of Sperling's personality—Navitas has a noticeably subtler presence. Rather than establishing fully operational institutions, like the University of Phoenix, Navitas piggybacks onto existing universities, often negotiating deals in private—most recently, at it moves gradually east, with the University of Manitoba.

When the subject of for-profit universities was first mentioned by Ontario's legislators, it was met with a predictable outcry from the public. The Canadian Federation of Students published an information sheet that argued an education system with both profit and non-profit schools would be "the end of accessible education in Canada." While private *non*profit universities have existed for centuries—Harvard and Yale among them—the organization was concerned that universities that were both private and profitable would fracture the education system, leading to "a high quality post-secondary system for the wealthy and an underfunded system for the rest ..."

In point of fact, corporate universities cater to poor students, not wealthy ones. One of the most shocking revelations about the University of Phoenix is the tactics it uses to accomplish the seduction of low-income students. "Students don't buy benefits," one of the school's memos proclaimed, "they buy ease or avoid pain. Finding and burrowing into that pain moves the sale to a CLOSE." Recruiters at a different for-profit school were told to identify a "pain point"—an issue prospective students found humiliating—and then turn it around and use it against them. If students mentioned they worked at McDonald's, the topic would come up later in the conversation, as a way of shaming them into registration: "Do you want to work at McDonald's for the rest of your life?" one former recruiter remembered asking.

These and other brutal tactics are common among many— perhaps even all—for-profit universities. Between 2008 and 2010, over seven hundred students and fifty former employees sought legal action against one for-profit school alone. The process uncovered practices such as paying enrollment counselors based on the number of students they signed up; instructing recruiters on how to detect and manipulate prospective students' confusion, embarrassment, uncertainty, and fear; pitting recruiters against each other in competitive teams; and giving away trips to "sunny Cancun" when weekly quotas were exceeded.

Recently, some of these policies have been restricted by the US government. The practice of tying a recruiter's pay into registering a certain number of students, for instance, has been banned. More importantly, the government has begun looking into the funding students receive at for-profit universities. Since low-income students qualify for loans and provisional gifts, an astonishing 75 percent of these schools' revenue comes from the federal government. As the students get poorer, the school gets richer. Upon graduation, for-profit students may realize that not only is their degree worth less than one from a nonprofit institution, but it cost them more to get it. Moreover, students graduating from for-profit schools typically earn less than those from nonprofit schools and account for roughly half of all defaulted student loans, meaning that in the process of making other people rich, they've impoverished and indebted themselves, ruined their job opportunities, and spent years doing something they could have done more cheaply somewhere else.

Such is the reality of an education whose first purpose, to quote from the Carnegie Foundation, is not education. Fittingly, even the heads of for-profit universities seem not to know what the first purpose is. Michael Markovitz, chairman of the for-profit Argosy University, has stated, "We are educators in the business of education, not business people selling education." But as we might expect, John Sperling has a more colorful response: "This is a corporation, not a social entity," he once snapped. "We are not trying to develop [students'] value systems or go in for that 'expand their minds' bullshit."

While for-profit universities have clearly commoditized education, is this any different from the condition at a nonprofit university? In today's world of academia, we're only comfortable with the idea of purchasing knowledge as long as other people aren't profiting from the transaction. To Sperling's credit, he had a billion-dollar idea, but as with any true genius, he got there by borrowing from the geniuses before him. The real billion-dollar idea is the university itself—which owes credit to Clark Kerr and the Carnegie Foundation.

GRATEFULLY INDEBTED

When it comes to an education, the one thing we can agree on is that it's expensive.

In the Canadian public system, schooling one student for one year costs about $8,000 in taxpayer money. In the United States, it's more like $10,000, but can soar all the way up to $27,000, depending on the state.

And this is only the least expensive route.

If one were to select the finest private institutions, from preschool to grad school, it would, of course, be possible to spend a fortune.

As of 2012, a single year of preschool can cost $30,000—and upwards of $40,000 at Riverdale County School in New York. While this figure already exceeds the tuition at Harvard, Princeton, and Yale, at the elementary level of schooling, Riverdale charges even more.

While Toronto's Upper Canada and Havergal colleges can cost between $48,000 and $52,000, Canada's most expensive private boarding school is Appleby College, which can exceed $55,000 per annum. The United States surpasses this amount only with Sarah Lawrence College, a private liberal arts school in Westchester County that costs $58,334. However, neither Canada nor the United States, nor any other country in the world, can match Institut Le Rosey, the famous Swiss academy that charges 100,000 francs—$115,000 US dollars—for a single year of high school.

And all of this is before college, when, as the Scottish *Herald* solemnly observed, "Children are at their most costly ..." For four years of tuition at a public university in Canada, students can expect to pay some $20,000, though, after housing, food, and other expenses, a more likely estimate is $80,000, and at Queen's University in Kingston, an undergraduate degree can cost well over $100,000. In Britain, most students pay more than twice the average rate for developed countries, or £123,000 by the time they graduate. And in the United States, students can expect to spend $150,000 on in-state tuition, or $500,000 for four years at a private college or university.

With any of these figures, it's clear that school is becoming increasingly burdensome. It says something about our weariness of such expenses that, when the American government estimates the cost of raising a child to adulthood, it gives the job to the Department of Agriculture. More seriously, the rising cost of tuition in the wake of a declining world economy is causing many parents to rethink how they provide for their children. In Britain, some parents are sending their children to India, where school is cheaper. And in India, some parents are liquidating their inheritance to send their children to Britain, where school is better.

Such transnational tendencies are reshaping nothing less than our collective social landscape. As one's path through school typically defines one's success in life, the gravity of the issue is difficult to over-state. This helps explain why preschools are becoming the new Ivy League: In an effort to give their children a head start, the best schools are chosen as early as possible. The fact that some three-year-olds are being treated to $40,000-a-year schools while many parents are strug-gling to buy diapers, is a testament to the sheer insanity of our times. As one mother put it, writing in *The New York Times*, getting into a private preschool is both "absurdly cutthroat and wildly expensive ..." (And this, it warrants repeating, is a school for toddlers.)

Still, for the time being anyway, post-secondary schools are the ones that count. And here, there is nothing to surpass the cost of becoming a certified human being. Consider for a moment that the average university degree is 400 percent more expensive today than it was just thirty years ago. Over the course of a single generation, post-secondary education has gone from being merely expensive to almost unthinkably so. To meet the cost of higher education, students are sinking deeper into debt. Twenty-five percent of all students who take out a loan can't afford to pay it back and are sometimes forced into extreme poverty, desperation, and even suicide. Never before has the cost of an education come at so high a price. Debt created by student loans now exceeds the debt created by credit-card holders and increases at the rate of $2,853.88 per second.

At present, American students owe an astonishing $1 trillion—more than the sum of all debt in Canada.

The SLM Corporation, better known as Sallie Mae, is the both the single largest source of student loans in the United States and one of the most successful corporations in the world.

It oversees $150 billion worth of loans from 10 million students (including their parents) and makes an absolute fortune in the process. Between 1995 and 2005, company profit rose 1,600 percent, at one point hitting an all-time high of $73 a share. In just five of those years, the company's fee-derived income jumped from $280 million to just under $1 billion, making its chief executive officers obscenely rich. When chair Tim Fitzpatrick resigned in 2007, his severance package included $4.1 million in bonuses and stock options; $3.2 million in cash; a $945,000 pro-rated bonus; $8.4 million in accelerated unvested stock options; $11.8 million in accelerated restricted stock units; a $271,400 retirement benefit; and another $8.1 million in a pending federal tax ruling. His successor, a man named Albert Lord, is one of *Forbes'* richest men in America.

What is interesting about the wealth of the company's executives is how little they do to earn it. If a student can't pay a loan back to Sallie Mae, the government will pay it back on their behalf (plus interest). But of course, then the government is out the money. So the Department of Education hires a collection agency to go after the student. But here's something not many people know: most collection agencies are in fact owned by Sallie Mae, who—acting now as the collector—adds 25 percent to the total loan amount and gets to keep

28 percent of whatever that is. This unusual arrangement allows Sallie Mae to get paid twice by students who, for one reason or another, couldn't afford to pay the first time. As Elizabeth Warren, a professor of bankruptcy law, has noted, "It's a market in which the protection goes to the lender, and the students are served up like turkeys at the Thanksgiving dinner."

Warren is referring specifically to the government's practice of offering almost no protection to students who are being pursued by a collection agency. After a loan has defaulted, agencies like Sallie Mae have the authority to withhold tax refunds, garnish social security and disability income, and suspend professional licenses. In fact, every kind of income except child support is available for the lender's taking (even though they've long since been reimbursed by the government). Moreover, as the student-loan activist Alan Collinge has noted, "Student loans are the only type of loans in our nation's history, ever, to be specially exempted from bankruptcy protection."

Fewer protections for students mean more protections for lenders. And according to Warren, American bankruptcy laws were written explicitly to favor companies like Sallie Mae. Lenders in credit-card and home industries don't get the protection of student-loan lenders, and borrowers in the student-loan industry don't get the same lack of protection of borrowers elsewhere. Declare bankruptcy on the purchase of your home, and forgiveness of that loan—in whole or in part—is at least possible. But a student who declares bankruptcy isn't afforded the same luxury. As Warren summarized for *The Wall Street Journal*: "Student-loan debt collectors have power that would make a mobster envious."

———————

As with much of the American school system, the origins of Sallie Mae can be traced back to the Carnegie Foundation.

We may recall from earlier that the foundation's board was chaired by the astronomer Henry Pritchett. Pritchett had been president during a number of significant achievements: the creation of faculty pensions in 1906; the Flexner reports on "formal discipline" in 1916; the founding of Educational Testing Service in 1947. But in 1967, the leadership of the Carnegie Foundation's Commission on Higher Education fell to another promising individual. Just five days after his dismissal from the University of California, Clark Kerr took the role of presidency for the Carnegie education empire. (On his dismissal from UC, Kerr's remark was customarily sharp: "I left the presidency just as I had entered it—fired with enthusiasm.")

Kerr's appointment to the Carnegie Foundation owed thanks to his expertise in higher education. *The Uses of the University*, which Kerr based on his famous address at Harvard's Godkin lecture, was published in 1964—three years before his appointment—and would eventually be translated into half a dozen languages. As president of the University of California, Kerr did more than any other educator before or since to make university accessible to everyone. As Arthur Levine, president of Teachers College at Columbia University, reflected in 2003, "Clark Kerr did for higher education what Henry Ford did for the automobile. He mass produced low-cost quality education and research potential for a nation that hungered deeply for both."

All this made Kerr ideal for Carnegie interests. Under Kerr's stewardship, the commission began releasing a series of influential publications. This would continue until 1980, by which time 175 documents would be published in all. The subject of each was higher education. More specifically, as Kerr wrote, "We are just now perceiving that the university's invisible product, knowledge, may be the most powerful single element in our culture, affecting the rise and fall of professions and even of social classes, of regions and even of nations." Knowledge was what the American government needed to sell, and the Carnegie Foundation was here to help them do it.

First, there needed to be a base of consumers. Here it looked like the timing was good: In the late 1960s, there were approximately eight million students of higher education in the United States; that was up 300 percent from just ten years earlier. In fact, attendance rates at college and university had been exploding since 1870, when the total number of post-secondary students was just fifty-two thousand (today's student population of the University of Ohio). Moreover, according to Francis Smith and Thomas Bender, the number of students enrolled at colleges and universities doubled between 1870 and 1890; doubled again between 1890 and 1910; quintupled between 1910 and 1945; and septupled between 1945 and 1994. The number of students who attend institutions of higher learning has slowed in recent decades; today, there are something like eighteen million students in five thousand colleges and universities.

So the Carnegie Foundation could rest assured that there were people out there who were interested in the product of knowledge. The trick, of course, was getting them to pay for it. Then Clark Kerr had an idea. In fact, he had it back in 1960 when he authored *A Master Plan for Higher Education*, his signature work. In it, Kerr guaranteed Californians a spot in the state's colleges and universities—in effect, opening their doors to as many people as possible. For a system that had been elitist by definition, this was a bold declaration indeed, and Kerr was counting on the government to help keep his promise.

Whereas before colleges and universities had been the recipients of federal money, Kerr now suggested giving it straight to the students. This would have the effect of making higher education more widely available—especially to the lower and middle classes, who had previously been excluded—not only in California but in the entire United States. In 1972, thanks to pressure from the Carnegie Foundation, Congress created the Basic Educational Opportunity Act, which established permanent programs of financial assistance, including the famous Pell grants. Suddenly, higher education was available to everyone, and with the enticement of free money, students came in droves. (An issue of *Time* magazine from October 1960 shows Kerr on the cover, a horde of students behind him squeezing through the gates of a university and into a bulging graduation cap.)

All this had the disconcerting effect of causing students to go into debt. With college and university becoming the standard precursor to a professional livelihood, a desperation arose for people who couldn't afford the tuition but still needed a degree. Between 1965 and 1973, 3 million men and women took out student loans, creating $4.5 billion in pending annuities. In 1972, the very year of the Basic Educational Opportunity Act, nearly half the students at the University of Wisconsin were borrowing money to pay for tuition. At a time when some families were earning $3,000 a year, 15.5 percent of the student population reported owing more than $2,000. Ten years later, students at the University of Iowa were paying $7,000 tuitions and were saddled with a debt of as much as $1,000 per month to a lending agency. Ten years later, students at the University of Iowa were paying $7,000 a year in tuition and as much as $1,000 per month to a lending agency.

Which brings us back to Sallie Mae.

In 1965, the US government created the Guaranteed Student Loan Program. A far cry from today's lending authorities, the program gave students money straight from the national treasury. This meant that each loan would appear as a loss in the year it was taken out (even if it was paid back by the student over time). The official story is that, for budgetary reasons, the government wanted a system with greater liquidity. The loan program had no secondary market. Additionally, loan repayments didn't commence until nine to twelve months following graduation (whereas today, some lending agencies insist on payments almost immediately).

To solve this problem, the government created the Student Loan Marketing Association—Sallie Mae—in 1972. According to a news clipping of the day, "The new corporation is designed to establish a secondary market in student loans and expects to tackle the liquidity problem in two major ways: By outright purchase of student loans and by making advances to eligible lenders using their portfolios of student loans as collateral." In other words, Sallie Mae would behave just like Fannie Mae and Freddie Mac, its cousins in the mortgage and home-lending industries. It would help people afford—and be indebted to—a service or product.

Market capitalism had just been introduced into higher education.

Larry Leslie is a professor of higher education at the University of Arizona. In 1972, he wrote a paper on behalf of the Committee for Economic Development, which he was then called on to testify about before Congress. The paper was on "The Management and Financing of Higher Education," a theme he returned to two years later with a colleague named Gary Johnson. In "The Market Model and Higher Education," Leslie and Johnson discussed the historic change that was then occurring at the very foundation of higher education. "The shift was monumental largely because it instituted the needs-based student aid program that allowed, politically, for the reduction in state support of higher education," Leslie says.

Essentially, the government got tired of paying the bills. And by making students pay them, corporations such as Sallie Mae were able to profit from massive debts, which Leslie believes to be an "inherent result" of applying the market model to higher education.

But student-loan agencies aren't the only ones profiting. In 2007, news began to break about a scandal involving both the student-loan industry and institutions of higher learning.

In 2007, Andrew Cuomo, the current governor of New York, led a public investigation into deals between universities and lending agencies. As it turned out, university officials were encouraging students to take out high-interest loans with certain "preferred lenders" (such as Sallie Mae and Citigroup Inc). In exchange, the officials were given stock options, golf trips to Pebble Beach, and other compensation. If students at Boston University took out between $1 million and $5 million in loans, a California-based lender called Education Finance Partners would give the school a kickback of .25 percent of the total loan value. Loans between $5 million and $10 million would pay half a percent, and loans over $10 million would yield three-quarters of one percent.

These may sound like small amounts, but on loans of such enormous sums, they were incredibly lucrative. Student loans represent an $85-billion-a-year industry, and 90 percent of those earnings were contracted through "preferred lender" recommendations. As Cuomo explained to the Associated Press, "That's the nature of the relationship. You trust the school. The school is in a position of authority." So too is Sallie Mae. In fact, the line between Sallie Mae and school has blurred so thoroughly, so drunkenly, that Sallie Mae has been known to staff financial aid offices with its own employees, pay advisors to appear on university boards, and even answer the telephone using the school's name.

Officially, these practices are now over. Sallie Mae and another lender were forced to pay a $2-million fine each in 2007. The universities that took the bribes have also done some repenting. Three of the highest-profile schools caught in the scandal—Syracuse University, the University of Pennsylvania, and New York University—paid $3.3

million to affected students, or an average of $60 per student. In total, $13 million was awarded from 28 participating schools, including the universities of Columbia, Southern California, Boston, Pepperdine, Clemson, Texas Christian, and Southern. Cuomo used the money to fund a 24-hour call center. "Students, graduates and their families will now have a trusted source for information about financing their higher education, as well as assistance if they are struggling to make payments," he told *The New York Times.*

But for some, of course, it's too late.

In the 1990s, a student at the University of Southern California took out $38,000 from Sallie Mae. Alan Collinge was completing three degrees in aerospace engineering. "My plan was simple: graduate with a bulletproof education, get a fine job in my field, repay my loans, and let life blossom beyond that." But Collinge shorted on a single payment and was hit with a late fee. In 2001, his loan was placed in default status. The penalties began adding up, and at the same time, Collinge's financial situation changed. The "fine job" he had envisioned fell through, and for two straight years, Collinge worked seven days a week for minimum wage.

By 2005, $38,000 had become $103,000. "I decided I basically had three options," Collinge writes in *The Student Loan Scam: The Most Oppressive Debt in U.S. History—and How We Can Fight Back.* "The first was to accept my fate and live at the poverty level while I paid off this exploded debt … The second option, I'm embarrassed to admit, was to escape the debt entirely, either by fleeing the country or by remaining here and assuming a new identity." The final option—which Collinge chose—was to start a grassroots movement and petition Congress for change.

Today, Student Loan Justice is an activist organization with some nine thousand members and a number of state chapters. "Our philosophy is that this is a simple enough problem, with an obvious enough solution ..." Collinge wants to see the return of standard consumer protections for all student loans. "Ultimately, we expect our work will return rational pricing to higher education, improve quality of education, and in general reorient the motivations of the lenders, Government, and schools to truly want the students to do well, and be rewarded accordingly." In particular, Collinge sees the return of bankruptcy protection as foundational to the cause.

"This isn't so borrowers can run off and wipe their hands of their debt," Collinge says, "[but] so that the lending side will have a financial incentive to keep the loans out of default, and to keep the schools providing high-quality educations at low costs. When you take away bankruptcy protections, well, pretty soon everyone's making, not losing, on defaults ..."

After six years of activism, Student Loan Justice has helped lodge the debate in the public discourse. Collinge has been interviewed by *60 Minutes* and *The New York Times* and was approached by Michael Moore and Ralph Nader in the same week.

Not every debtor's tale ends so optimistically. The number of student-debt horror stories is beyond counting: $38,000 turning into $70,000; $47,000 becoming $100,000; $5,000 jumping up to $50,000. Some students claim to have changed their name and even fled the country, while some outcomes are even bleaker. In 2005, Michele Guidoni committed suicide over a $100,000 student debt. Two years later, Jason Lee Yodder, a chemistry graduate from Illinois State University, killed himself in the same campus lab where he'd completed his master's research. Yodder owed $65,000, was unemployed, and was tired of the collection agency phone calls. "It made him feel lower than low to tell somebody every week, 'I don't have a job,'" Yodder's mother told a news source. Even as she was preparing the funeral arrangements for her son, the phone continued to ring.

There is an unintended consequence to all this.

In the early 1970s, as the government shifted the onus of paying for college onto students, the education for which those students took out loans turned into a product. As Francis Wilson Smith and Thomas Bender describe in *American Higher Education Transformed: 1940–2005*, writing in the past tense, "Increasingly higher education was treated as a private good, a product to be purchased for personal benefit, hence the notion of student loan programs, which amounts to a capital investment in oneself, in contrast to a scholarship signifying a collective investment in a public good."

Like credit-card and home-mortgage lenders, lenders of higher education have permitted—even encouraged—students to borrow outside their means for the product that is their education. For nearly half a century, students have had to buy their own education, using "a rather enigmatic combination of grants, initiatives designed to encourage family savings, and universal tax credits," to borrow from *The Routledge International Handbook of Higher Education*.

Moreover, in a surprising turn of events—but one not out of keeping with the rest of this book—even Clark Kerr came to regret the degree to which higher education had become commercialized. Specifically, Kerr felt that large, impersonal classrooms, the use of teachers' assistants, and the hiring of professors with research (and not educative) expertise, would alienate students from their own education. More memorably, he helped popularize the phrase "knowledge factory" to describe the kind of institution he almost single-handedly brought about.

In not an insignificant number of countries, it's worth remembering that higher education—even medical schools, law schools, and specialty colleges—doesn't cost a thing. Students in Finland, as we shall see later on, never have to worry about going into debt—at least not for the sake of their education. Such conditions can only be imagined in the United States, where Collinge's biggest piece of advice to students is to put themselves through school by saving, working, or borrowing from family—but never by taking out a loan. (And if you already have, well, to never miss a payment.)

Moreover, it could be claimed that public nonprofit universities no longer exist. Between universities' lending of labs to corporations, stacking of boardrooms with CEOs, and treatment of their only resource—education—as a consumable product, it's no wonder students consider the whole thing, in the words of Christopher J. Lucas, "required irrelevance." Describing this perspective in his history of higher education, Lucas writes:

> Universities, many further argued, had become knowledge factories. They were the principal manufacturers and retailers of knowledge as a commodity. Their buyers included students seeking credentials to guarantee themselves a prosperous future, industries in search of the skills and products of research, and governmental agencies needing an array of specialized services. In their quest for competitive advantage and prestige, such critics lamented, academic institutions had "sold themselves out" to the highest bidders.

5 | POWERFUL PEDAGOGIES

According to Anthroposophy, in considering the planetary system, we must separate the kingdom of Ahriman from that of Lucifer.

—Undisputed Fact #96, *PLANS Inc. vs. Sacramento City Unified School District, Twin Ridges Elementary School District*, Case No. CIV. S-98-0266 FCD PAN

THE WEIRD WORLD OF RUDOLF STEINER

So far, we've witnessed the end of history, the beginning of the American and Canadian public school systems, the history of the SAT (and origin of standardized testing), the birth of the modern curriculum, and the resulting rise of low literacy. We've seen how school has been used to make citizens and soldiers, used to punish and imprison, used by the government and by corporations, used to make money and used to make debt.

What we haven't seen are the alternatives. These are the educational systems that break away from the mainstream to offer a different agenda. Waldorf, Montessori, private schooling, and homeschooling are distinct in their rejection of the public school system and often distinct in their rejection of each other. Even if combined, alternatively schooled students comprise a fraction of the overall schooling population—and yet, each year, their numbers increase. Today, some of the best-known, most successful people on earth were educated by one of these powerful pedagogies.

And of these, almost none is more highly regarded than Waldorf.

Former Waldorf students have included the CEO of American Express, the prime minister of Norway, and the award-winning musician Sufjan Stevens. According to some, it is the fastest-growing education movement on the planet, with something like a thousand schools in over thirty-two countries. In contrast to other pedagogies, plenty of studies have been conducted on the effects of Waldorf schooling, and they nearly all reach the same conclusion: Waldorf students are more creative, artistic, and inspired than most.

A study by the president of the World Futures Studies Federation, Jennifer Gidley, examined the ability of educational systems to foster in students a healthy outlook on the future, which Gidley calls "preferred futures." The study found that students with a Waldorf education "develop richer and more detailed images of their 'preferred futures' than mainstream students." Moreover, about three-quarters of students polled were able to imagine positive transformations both in the environment and in human development. Waldorf students were able to envision not only a future without war but a future in which conflict resolution and dialogue were the natural stepping stones to peace. (And just imagine if all school systems could say the same thing.)

As we might expect, the success of Waldorf schooling owes considerable thanks to its founder. Rudolf Steiner has been called "one of the most original thinkers of the twentieth century." The bestselling critic of compulsory schooling, John Taylor Gatto, has called Steiner a "philosophical genius" and Waldorf schools a "revelation of what might be possible." According to Europe's *Spiegel* newspaper, many features of ordinary life are "heavily influenced" by Steiner's ideas. Since 1998, there have been over eighteen Steiner-related research papers, seventeen Steiner-related articles, fourteen Steiner-related chapters in scholarly works, and four Steiner-related academic books—and that's in Austria alone, where at least one doctoral student has completed a PhD on Steiner annually for the last fifteen years.

Unlike John Holt, the enduringly popular champion of home-schooling, or Maria Montessori, founder of the famous Montessori Method, Rudolf Steiner is the only pedagogue in modern times to have made contributions in multiple academic fields. In fact, Waldorf education is only part of Steiner's overarching philosophical system, which encompasses everything from spirituality to organic farming. Students of Steiner may come from backgrounds as disparate as architecture, philosophy, sculpture, agriculture, pedagogy, mysticism, Christianity, medicine, eurhythmy, drama, art, occultism, science, music, politics, speech, and psychology. Steiner made not just one or two scholarly observations within these fields, but delivered entire book-length lectures on each.

Toward the end of his life, Steiner moved away from public speaking and into the world of politics. World War I had left Europe with serious problems, and Steiner claimed to have a solution. To this end, he proposed a radical new theory that called for the balancing of spirituality, business, and politics. Leveraged by his popularity as an orator and disseminated by way of a hastily organized political campaign, Steiner's idea was briefly considered a legitimate proposal for the reorganization of society. This was enough cause for a young Adolf Hitler to feel threatened and publicly denounce Steiner as a Jew-loving occultist. When Hitler eventually came to power, Steiner was effectively forced into exile, and his social theory faded from memory.

But before his theory could be completely forgotten, Steiner used the basis of it to create a new model for social reorganization. Instead of changing society himself, Steiner decided he would change the way people were educated and then let his students do it for him. Waldorf schools have been engaged in this endeavor ever since—often in a highly unusual manner. Traditionally, Waldorf students learn to read only after they've lost their baby teeth, learn the art of dancing their own name, and play with dolls that don't have faces. Waldorf students may draw only in curved lines and with bright colors; sit in classrooms that have no right angles; and attend classes for which there are no textbooks. As Sufjan Stevens wrote of his experience in one Waldorf school, "Every room was designed to imitate a tree house or a bear cave or an underground den where foxes slept through the winter, nuzzling their young."

It's a testament to the peculiarity of Rudolf Steiner that he believed these practices would change society—and a testament to his prescience that they have. According to one interpretation, Steiner designed Waldorf education to be a kind of elaborate induction, in which the attendance of classes marked progressively deeper "awaken-ings" of the mind. The prescriptive use of certain materials, according to some, exists in order to guide the students into total spiritual immer-sion. The end result is a Waldorf alumni who sees the world the way Steiner intended and who becomes a spiritual exemplar for the rest of humanity. This was Steiner's final wish—and even though he didn't live to see its realization, Waldorf schools have succeeded in carrying this vision into the present.

———————

Rudolf Steiner was born in 1861 in the village of Donji Kraljevec, in what is present-day Croatia. At the time, the area belonged to Austria and was considered a halfway point between central and eastern Europe. It was a geographic happenstance to which biographers would later draw significance.

Steiner's father, Johann, had been educated by the Ordo Praemonstratensis, a group of canons regular, and tended the estate of a wealthy diplomat. Steiner's mother, Franziska, was a maid on the same estate, but the count of Hoyos, who employed both Johann and Franziska, refused to let them marry. In a surprising act of will-fulness, Johann Steiner left his job as a gamekeeper—which men of his family had done for generations—in order to marry the bride of his choice. The two moved from central Austria to Donji Kraljevec, where Johann was stationed by his new employer, the Southern Austrian Railway.

Rudolf Steiner, the first of the couple's three children, was born sickly and weak. According to one account, his parents had him baptized early—just two days after birth—so if he died, his soul would be safe in heaven. In 1862, Johann Steiner transferred to a station near Vienna and again to a station on the Semmering Railway at Pottscach the following year. It was here Steiner spent the first few years of his life attending the village school. According to Steiner's account, the schoolmaster was a deeply unpleasant man whose son was a classmate of Steiner's. When the boy vandalized the school's desks, it was Steiner who was blamed. This so irritated Steiner's father that it was decided Rudolf would be homeschooled.

For the next five years, Steiner accompanied his father to the railway station and whiled away the hours in the office by the platform. Johann was hoping to instill in his son an interest in engineering, but Steiner was preoccupied by other matters. He taught himself the alphabet and passed the time watching ink dry on scraps of paper. Then one day a woman entered the office, stayed for a moment, and disappeared into the stove. Steiner had had his first vision. The woman, a relative of the family, had committed suicide shortly before her ghost appeared in the office of the station in Pottscach. The experience was so profound that Steiner was middle-aged before he told anyone—and even then, it was in the third person. "The event made a deep impression upon the boy but he could not speak of it to anyone."

In 1868, the Steiners moved again, this time to the Hungarian town of Neudörfl. Although a tiny village, Neudörfl was close to Vienna, and there was an air of exoticism. Steiner began attending public school once more, where he discovered a strange attraction to geometry. He borrowed a book from the teacher, "and for weeks my soul was completely filled with the congruence, the similarity of triangles, quadrilaterals, and polygons." Steiner found that geometry led him to a world of spirituality. "The ability to grasp something purely through the spirit brought me an inner joy," he later wrote. "I realize that I first knew happiness through geometry."

Johann Steiner was transferred to a suburb of Vienna in 1879, and shortly thereafter, Steiner—now aged eighteen—enrolled at the Technische Hochschule. Riding on the train into school each week, Steiner encountered a herbalist named Felix Koguzki, who was on his way to Vienna to sell tincture remedies to the city's apothecaries. According to Steiner, Koguzki was a clairvoyant, and for the first time Steiner opened up about some of his own psychic experiences. Koguzki was Steiner's first spiritual teacher, and the friendship was one Steiner would cherish for the rest of his life.

At the polytechnic, Steiner made another important contact. His professor of German literature was a man named Karl Schröer, a member of Vienna's Goethe Society who had recently been asked by an editor of Goethe's scientific writing to prepare a new manuscript. In an extraordinary show of faith, Schröer decided to give the task to Rudolf Steiner, who was then just twenty-one years old and hadn't even finished college. What's more, it was a paying job. Steiner would spend the next fifteen years of his life devoted to all things Goethe.

In 1897, Steiner moved to Berlin.

His work on the Goethe manuscripts was over, and now he became editor of a small literary magazine. On the 150th anniversary of Goethe's birthday, Steiner had the journal publish a lengthy article entitled "Goethe's Secret Revelation and the Riddle of Faust." It was inspired by Goethe's *The Green Snake and the Beautiful Lily*, and in Steiner's mind "the content of the fairy-tale lived as something wholly esoteric, and it was out of an esoteric mood that the article was written."

It was Steiner's first officially esoteric work, and it attracted the attention of the Theosophical Society. Since its founding in 1875, the Theosophical Society had become the international authority on occultism. Its headquarters was located in India, where one of its members, Madame Blavatsky, was immersed in mystical Eastern philosophy. The society's core belief was that the pursuit of truth was more important than adherence to any particular doctrine or faith, an idea that held considerable appeal to the New Age movement that followed. In November 1901, Steiner gave his first theosophical lecture, "From Buddha to Christ." As he explained later, "In these lectures I tried to depict the line of development from Buddha to Christ. I sought to present Christ as the culmination of what had existed previously."

Steiner's involvement with Blavatsky had a profound impact on his own thinking. Shortly after relocating to Berlin, Steiner began lecturing on a Western counterpart to theosophy—a system of thought that combined Blavatsky's version of Eastern philosophy with predominately European ideas such as Rosicrucianism, gnosticism, freemasonry, and the like. It was this meeting of east and west that appealed to the spiritual scholar, and he called the result *anthroposophy*, "the study of human wisdom." For the next ten years, Steiner developed his hybrid system into something resembling a workable philosophy.

As with Madame Blavatsky and theosophy, Steiner used his self-proclaimed clairvoyance to construct the belief system of anthroposophy. While retaining full consciousness, Steiner professed to be able to access the sum of all knowledge, both human and cosmic, which he did via an alternate plane of reality. Blavatsky, by way of contrast, needed to be in a deep trance—"asleep," as the state is known. This seemingly slight methodological difference was deeply important to Steiner and at least initially seemed to be one of the reasons he founded anthroposophy: "waking" psychics were thought to be more credible sources of information—or as Steiner put it, they were more "scientific."

According to the eyewitness accounts of Friedrich Rittelmeyer, Steiner would sit "where he would not be obliged to look against the light," make "a certain deliberate adjustment of his being," and "pass without effort into the higher state of consciousness ..." From this higher state, Steiner's stream-of-consciousness thoughts were transcribed by followers and published by the Anthroposophic Press. Questions were often asked impromptu, and topics varied from the evolution of the cosmos to the reason why some fish have striped sides. Steiner's answers to these questions and other of the six thousand lectures he is said to have delivered constitute the bulk of anthroposophy.

Even a surface reading of Steiner's work reveals a world view that varies from esoteric to beyond. At his most obtuse, Steiner is capable of such non sequiturs as "The Beings who live in the Sun have for their subordinate organ the Spirits of Venus," and "If we could not develop in us all the secretive forces, the forces that proceed from our ductless glands, we would not be men." Even slightly more coherent phrases are bewildering. Steiner believed that "every Copernican concept is inspired by Lucifer" and that in 1604, Siddhartha Gautama was "transferred to the belligerent realm of Mars." The involvement of what Steiner calls "the Mission of Gautama Buddha on Mars" was something of an obsession, and much of his literature on the subject, to paraphrase one scholar, sounds like the lyric sheet of a Jimi Hendrix album.

Steiner is on record as believing that "strong thoughts will come when you eat radishes" but that "anyone who eats many potatoes will not have powerful thoughts ..." Steiner believed the spleen was of great spiritual significance, but relegated the brain to nothing more than "an excretion!" Steiner claimed that Einstein's theory of relativity had "no feeling for reality" and that he had personally disproved Descartes's famous saying "I think, therefore I am" by asserting that humans cease active thought during the night. When asked about reincarnation, Steiner insisted that Charles Darwin was once an eighth-century Spanish Umayyad, that the French astronomer Pierre-Simon Laplace was a Persian caliph, and that he personally was the reincarnation of Thomas Aquinas.

Taken out of context—or very often even in context—Steiner's beliefs were sometimes not only bizarre, but offensive. According to Steiner, schizophrenia and other illnesses are the result of bad karma and thus the fault of the afflicted. Steiner also believed in what he called "root races" and that "the Negro race" was a mixture of "the normal Spirits of Form and the abnormal Spirits of Form." Steiner referred to each root race by an alternate name: Africans were the "Mercury race"; Natives, the "Saturn race"; Asians, the "Venus race"; and Caucasians, the "Aryan race." Such remarks, while not categorically unusual of the period's broad and deep prejudices, have led more than one commentator to claim that Steiner and his anthroposophy are racist.

In fact, the sheer esotericism—the weirdness—of Rudolf Steiner has occasionally resulted in not just offense but serious misunderstanding. In the late 1990s, two residents of Northern California claimed that Steiner's spiritual philosophy counted as a religion. Moreover, since Waldorf schools had recently begun receiving taxpayer money—and not their usual private donations—Dan Dugan and Debra Snell argued that Waldorf schools were in violation of the First Amendment, which prohibits the spending of public money on schools of a religious nature. The resulting lawsuit hinged on a seemingly farcical contention—whether Waldorf schools were "under the guardianship of Lucifer," as Dugan and Snell's lawyer claimed they were.

Even though the case was thrown out of court in 2010, Dugan and Snell have remained adamant that anthroposophy is a religion. They've even convinced a small number of Christian fundamentalists of the same thing, based on the fact that Steiner did indeed refer to Lucifer, and that, even more incredibly, it was originally a Waldorf teacher who claimed Waldorf schools were under his guardianship. But Steiner didn't intend for a Western definition of Lucifer. Instead, he used the word as it connotes in the East, where Lucifer is described as the good guy, the "bearer of light." Because of this apparently trivial distinction, Waldorf schools are probably more fairly characterized as being influenced by Zoroastrianism (a minor spiritual practice from the East), and not Christianity (a major religion from the West)—though the case was dismissed before these finer points could be debated.*

In December 1916, as German and US governments were discussing the possibility of peace, Steiner suddenly became a political icon.

---

* The judge's reason for terminating the trial was that Dugan and Snell, who formed the basis of a 501(c) called People for Legal and Nonsectarian Schools, had consistently failed to organize their case (a somewhat perverse condition for a group that goes by the acronym PLANS). At any rate, the final ruling was that "anthroposophy is more akin to a methodology or approach to learning as opposed to a religious doctrine or organized set of beliefs." In other words, Waldorf schools may be under the guardianship of Lucifer, but he's good enough to guard them in a way that doesn't violate the First Amendment.

At the time, Steiner was lecturing to Swiss audiences of theosophists and anthroposophists. To these people, the fate of Europe was uncertain. World War I had left the continent in substantial economic turmoil, and the government—which had got everyone into this mess in the first place—couldn't be trusted to envision a better future.

The people of Switzerland wanted someone to lead the way, and Steiner appeared at precisely the right moment. According to Steiner, governments were propagandizing civilians into denying their own spiritual development, resulting in what he called "the karma of untruthfulness." The entire social order was "totally wrong" and needed to be re-created.

With this in mind, Steiner proposed the Threefold Idea, or the "New Scheme of Social Organization," as it was called by the American press. "He wants the social order completely revised and changed," wrote one reporter. "He does not want capitalism ... All talk of socialization he regards as futile ... Least of all does he want anarchism." Steiner was more dissatisfied with proposed solutions to postwar Europe than its numerous problems. An inability to rationalize spiritually was "the tragedy overshadowing all our interpretations of the social demands of the day ..." What Steiner *did* want was to incorporate anthroposophy into everyday social workings. The problem with society and warfare was simply "the impotence of spiritual life." It was called the Threefold Idea because, in Steiner's view, society was composed of three parts: economics, politics, and spirituality. In his new social vision, each would keep the other in check.

The popularity of anthroposophy and Steiner's reputation as a one-time theosophist led to a brief period in which the Threefold Idea was considered a legitimate proposal. Steiner met with a member of the Bavarian Royal Cabinet, Otto Graf Lerchenfeld, to discuss making the plan real. "Three hours with Dr. Steiner today," Lerchenfeld recorded in his journal, before announcing, "The solution to everything lies before me." Steiner's contacts even prepared a summary of the Threefold Idea to send to the emperor of Austria, members of the cabinet, and the Prince of Baden. While it was eventually rejected, Steiner's "New Scheme for Social Organization" found an unlikely champion in the form of Emil Molt.

Molt, who was born in southern Germany, had been orphaned as a teenager, spent time in the military, and gone on to work for a man named Emil Georgii. Georgii's son, Emil Georgii Jr., worked at the Waldorf-Astoria cigarette factory and hired Molt as a young man. Molt worked hard and eventually became the factory's general manager. At the same time, Molt had become interested in spirituality and signed up for membership to the Theosophical Society in 1906. Following the end of World War I, the Waldorf-Astoria factory was confronted with the problem of having its former employees, who had fought in the war, return back to the factory only to discover that their jobs had been taken by replacements.

Rather than fire one group or the other, as the story goes, Molt decided to keep both, educating them on-site in half-day rotations (the replacements worked while the veterans were educated and vice versa). For a while, the factory even paid for the workers' education. Eventually, Molt's focus shifted from the factory workers to the children of the factory workers, at which time Rudolf Steiner was summoned. According to the records, Steiner and Molt met with the minister of culture in May 1919. The minister approved the proposed education plan, provided Steiner met certain state standards. Steiner's lectures on social reorganization ceased two months later, and in the fall of 1919, the world's first Waldorf school was opened (named after the factory it was born in).

But soon afterward there were problems.

In 1921, Adolf Hitler wrote to the editor of the *Völkische Beobachter*, the official publication of what would become the Nazi Party, to register a personal attack. Steiner was called "the adherent of the Threefold Social Order, which is one of the many completely Jewish methods of destroying the people's normal state of mind ..." Steiner was so well known at the time that the article found others guilty by association, such as Germany's foreign minister, a man named Walter Simons. "And what is the driving force behind all this devilishness? The Jews, friends of Dr. Rudolf Steiner ..."

A little over a year later, Steiner was lecturing at the Four Seasons in Munich, a venue that was often used by the national, pro-Nazi occultist organization known as the Thule Society. Partway through Steiner's speech, members of the Thule Society cut the lights, plunging the room into darkness. A moment later, firecrackers sizzled through the air, and "Steiner's foes stormed the stage," according to *The New York Times*. Steiner wasn't hurt, but his life was clearly in danger. When he heard of Hitler's Beer Hall Putsch the following November, Steiner supposedly remarked, "If these people ever come to power, I will never be able to set foot in Germany again."

Which is pretty much what happened. Toward the end of his life, Steiner spent the majority of his time in Switzerland, where, in self-appointed exile, he oversaw construction of the famous Goetheanum—which an arsonist burned to the ground almost immediately thereafter. This wasn't the end of Steiner's troubles but something more like the beginning. Many of Germany's Waldorf schools were closed shortly before World War II, and by 1941, they all were. Hitler, it seems, had won. When Steiner died in 1925, the future of Waldorf education was far from being certain, and as if to signal the total collapse of his reputation, the Anthroposophical Society itself was closed in 1935.

_____

Then, slowly at first, interest in Steiner began anew.

The first postwar Waldorf school was opened in the American zone in 1945; by 1948, there were 17 Waldorf schools in Germany, 5 in Switzerland, 7 in England, 3 in Italy and Switzerland, 1 in France and Norway, and 4 in the United States.

But it wasn't until the 1970s that Waldorf schools became truly popular. Friends of Waldorf Education was founded in 1971, and has since been instrumental in supporting and funding Waldorf school ventures. According to the organization's internal statistics, Friends of Waldorf Education donates over 4 million euros annually to hundreds of Waldorf-methods schools and programs internationally.

In 2001, when the last major census appears to have been taken, there were 775 Waldorf schools, 1,400 Waldorf kindergartens, 120 Waldorf-methods remedial institutions, and 68 Waldorf-methods teacher training schools, on every continent (excluding, of course, Antarctica).* According to anthroposophy scholar Alduino Bartolo Mazzone, Waldorf education is currently "the largest non-denominational, non-sectarian, independent school movement in the world."

For Rudolf Steiner—the introverted Goethe scholar whose father had wanted him to become an engineer—this was indeed a profound accomplishment. In fact, when it comes to nontraditional peda-gogues, Steiner's legacy is difficult to match. Even excluding Waldorf schools, his influence in fields as diverse as child rearing, spirituality, and farming may be felt to this day. Parents who speak of educating "the whole child," New Ageists who believe in karma and reincarna-tion, and farmers who use organic techniques all owe thanks to Rudolf Steiner (among other assorted groups).

---

* Since the 2001 UNESCO census, less formal estimates have put the number of twelve-year Waldorf elementary schools at 1,000 and some at even 2,000.

But of course, the supreme achievement of Steiner's life and work is Waldorf schooling. Here, Steiner's intention was to give students an education—which he viewed as being synonymous with the development of their souls. According to one prominent Waldorf educator, Waldorf schools were designed to be "a path of initiation" that leads to increasingly deeper levels of spiritual attainment. At each stage, students are taught with specific objects in specific ways. This explains the censorship of black crayons, straight lines, and dolls with human faces—for archaic reasons, Steiner believed that these things (and many others) interfered with children's development at the soul level. Today's Waldorf students may use them only under certain conditions, with close supervision, and after they've acquired a sufficient level of evolution.

For better or worse, the Waldorf system of education contains many of the idiosyncrasies of its founder. Because Rudolf Steiner favored a shade of pink he called "peach blossom," some Waldorf schools have painted their classrooms this exact color; because Rudolf Steiner reserved a special antipathy toward right angles, Waldorf schools are often built with rounded corners or softened with drapes after construction; because Goethe had built himself "an altar to nature" on which he placed "plants from his father's herbarium," Waldorf schools sometimes feature their own variation, called "nature tables"; and so on. Perhaps most famously of all, Steiner pioneered a kind of interpretive dance known as *eurhythmy*, in which he advocated the discipline of dancing one's own name—which Waldorf students continue to practice even now.

For a man who wanted to change society by injecting spirituality into business and government, Steiner has arguably achieved precisely such an outcome. The Threefold Idea may have fizzled, but Waldorf education has never been stronger. Students of Steiner bring their founder's vision with them wherever they go. Today's Waldorf alumni are some of the most powerful and popular people on the planet—they've gone on to study at Harvard, Stanford, and Brown, and have become successful artists, celebrities, CEOs, heads of states, and a hundred things more. Through their work and world view, Waldorf students offer proof of the enduring—and peculiar—legacy of Rudolf Steiner.

THE MONTESSORI METHOD

The Montessori Method is considered one of the best education systems in the world, and the Dearcroft school in Oakville is a good example of why.

It's the oldest school of its kind in the region and sits on a wooded estate overlooking Lake Ontario.

I visited the school at the end of October and was led into a large kindergarten room (the best place to be introduced to everything Montessori, I reasoned). In contrast to Waldorf, with its incredible zeal for color, the room was almost ascetically bare. Tables and shelves were plain wood, and the walls a nondescript beige.

The class directress, as female teachers are called, was Alison Smith, a young woman with delicate features and a calming voice. "For Montessori of this age group, we accept children from two and a half to six," she told me. "It's a mixed group, so those three ages are all in this same classroom, which we call a *casa*." She noticed my look of surprise. "*Casa* is the Italian word for home. We use it because we see this as the children's second environment." She paused. "It stems from Maria Montessori."

Maria Montessori is the founder of the schools that bear her name. But unlike other school systems, which often grow uncontrollably away from their founder's values, Montessori the school is still an inextricable part of Montessori the woman.

"Our curriculum is broken into five areas," Smith said, as she led me to a shelf on the far side of the room. "This is Sensorial." On top of the shelf were a number of objects—pegs and cylinders and other colorful shapes. "Everything is very concrete, very hands-on," she explained, casting her hands over the items. I studied the scene appraisingly. "At this age, we're trying to encourage an exploration of the senses and teach children to discriminate by touch and sight."

We walked to a different section. "Next we have Culture." There were more objects—a small globe, a collection of miniature flags. "Culture is very unique to Montessori schools, since most kindergartens don't really address the issue." I stooped to examine the model planet while Smith continued to explain. "We start by talking about the solar system—how there are planets, how we live on one planet, how within that planet there are continents and water. And where we are within all that."

We moved down the shelf to Language, the third group of materials. Of all things Montessori, the materials are the salient feature. They were developed by Maria Montessori when she was the codirector of a facility for developmentally handicapped students. Their purpose is to show children how to teach themselves using the five senses. With this unique system, an impressive number of her students were able to write regular public-school exams—a feat that launched Montessori into near-instant celebrity.

Smith pointed to a game that reminded me of Charades. "This is one of my favorites," she said, picking up a stack of red cards. She drew one that featured the word "laugh." "We ask children, Can you go and get a laugh? No you can't—you actually have to do it. So a verb is something that happens and then it's gone, but a noun is something that you can actually get and see and hold."

We walked to the far side of the room and saw the final two sections, Number and Practical, where children learn real-life skills like how to tie shoelaces and pour tea from a pot.

We paused by the window, and I took the opportunity to ask Smith a few questions. "How faithfully would you say you follow the original system?"

"Oh, very," she said, "we're a true Montessori school." I asked her what she meant and was told that the Montessori name had never been trademarked. Anyone can open a school and call it Montessori, but only the CCMA—the Canadian Council of Montessori Administrators—can designate an authentic Montessori school. And Dearcroft, where I was, was one of the first CCMA-approved schools in the country.

"We even use the materials from a hundred years ago," Smith told me, happily. Then she paused, looking slightly guilty. "Well, there may be some things in here that aren't *true* Montessori materials, but they would stem from the original materials. Things like books and reading materials change over time."

Smith explained that the materials changed if it better suited students' development. "Our focus is to help children grow and succeed and have a positive working experience. Whatever it is they're interested in, we'll go with that, since what we're trying to do is create a love for learning." Her phrase for this was "intrinsic motivation," as in "Our goal is to allow children to actually love to work and discover."

This is the hallmark of Montessori and why in recent years the school's popularity has grown literally beyond measure.

Since the opening of the first school in 1907, tens of thousands of Montessori schools have opened worldwide. The first was in Italy, but now—with the exception of Cuba, Somalia, and North Korea—there's a Montessori school in every country of the world. In Japan, there are over 1,000 Montessori schools alone. In the US, there are 4,500 private Montessori schools, and another 500 charter and magnet (schools that are publicly funded and independently managed, and offer a specialized curriculum to a particular group of students). In Britain, Montessori methods were formally adopted by the public education system in 2005—the first time in the country's history that an alternative system received public money (not to mention 40,000 pounds of it). In 2010, the first-ever Montessori state school was planned. In India, the number of Montessori applicants at one school grew by over 60 percent between 2009 and 2010. "Wherever we have Montessori, we have a waiting list," the superintendent of a Charleston school has said, rather summarizing the schools' popularity.

Maria Montessori was born in the small town of Chiaravalle, in the Italian province of Ancona. It was 1870, and Italy had only just become a unified country. Public schools were available to boys, but it took another seven years for girls to be legally allowed to attend them. In what would become an enduring trait of personality, Montessori took this small allowance as far as it would go and at age thirteen enrolled at a technical school for boys.

After graduating with honors, she abruptly changed course and applied to become a doctor of medicine. At the time, there were only five other female doctors in the world. It just wasn't something girls were supposed to do, and her application to the University of Rome was denied. However, Montessori was nothing if not persistent and, according to her own version of the story, took her case all the way to the Pope. "Leo told me he believed medicine was a noble profession for a woman," she explained to one reporter, referring to Pope Leo XIII.

Being on a first-name basis with the Pope apparently had its advantages, and Montessori was finally admitted. Even so, it can't have been the friendliest environment. Of the school's 21,813 students that year, 132 of them were women. According to the biography by Rita Kramer, Montessori was shunned by male students, faculty, and even by her own father, Alessandro, whose disapproval compelled him to abstain from helping with tuition expenses. Sexism was so prevalent that even during autopsies, Montessori was forbidden from being in the same room as her male peers and had to come back after hours to do her own examinations.

Following graduation in 1896, Montessori worked at a psychiatric clinic adjacent to the university. Her research consisted of examining children's illnesses, and two years later she published a landmark paper. The idea was that slow learners weren't at a biological disadvantage, but rather an educational one. This was the first inkling as to what would become her signature blend of controversy and insight. Luckily, not everyone was offended. Luckier still was that the minister of education happened to find the paper completely fascinating and chose Montessori to become codirector of an institution for the mentally disabled.

The other codirector was Giuseppe Montesano, a handsome doctor who was as radical as Montessori. The two soon became lovers, and in 1898 Maria gave birth to a son, Mario, who would become instrumental to the Montessori movement. Strangely, and for reasons unknown to history, Montesano and Montessori never married and appear to have had a dramatic falling-out. Mario was placed in the care of relatives in Italy's anonymous countryside and later introduced as Montessori's nephew. As for Montesano, he married a different woman in 1901—the same year Montessori withdrew from public life.

Meanwhile, the Montesano-Montessori facility was developing quite a reputation. Eight of its twenty-two students passed the same exams as their nondisabled peers. This extraordinary feat led to Montessori being given charge of her own school. Founded in 1907, Casa dei Bambini was located in eastern Rome, not far from the university, and is considered the world's first true Montessori school.

Which is what made it so unusual. Considering the image we have of Montessori today, Children's House was curiously prescriptive.

Students were made to come to class in clean clothes, where they were sized with chairs according to their weight, sat at tables according to their height, and given Montessori's specially approved materials. Classes were built around the idea that children would learn how to correctly perform an activity, such as differentiating between a noun and verb, only after becoming self-conscious of their own mistakes. Until this critical stage was reached, they were to be left alone and only given the barest of direction.

Though Casa dei Bambini was then located in a Rome ghetto, three more schools were soon established, one of which was in a middle-class neighborhood. Soon afterward another *casa* opened in Milan, through the patronage of Società Umanitaria, Italy's Humanitarian Society, which helped to popularize Montessori education through the sponsorship of conferences and teacher training programs. By 1910, Montessori had become a national icon, and her philosophy spread rapidly to the rest of Europe and even the United States. By 1919, her work had been translated into Russian, German, Dutch, Polish, Danish, Chinese, Japanese, and Romanian. In Spain, Montessori schools were being financed with government money, and there were already four hundred Montessori schools in England (at least one of which was financed by a private donation of two thousand pounds). Jean Piaget made his first observations at a Montessori school, and even Gandhi visited the pedagogue in London.

But out of all of her admirers, one in particular stands out.

At the time, Benito Mussolini was working as a reporter for the Società Umanitaria, the same organization that funded Montessori schools. They may have had some passing contact, but it wasn't until 1924 that the two met face to face. Montessori had already been made inspector of schools under Mussolini's governance. But now the dictator was forming a new government and pledged his full support to Montessori, officially adopting her schools as Italy's own. It seems an odd match to us now: Montessori the frumpish, kindly pedagogue, Mussolini the man who once claimed to have personally "buried the putrid corpse of liberty" and meant it in a good way.

Though her life has been made public in innumerable biographies and professional works, the issue of Montessori's political and social values during the 1920s has received little in the way of scholarly attention. Rita Kramer struggles palpably with the question in *Maria Montessori: A Biography*. The definitive biography by E. M. Standing does even worse, skipping over the issue entirely. *The Encyclopedia of Educational Reform and Dissent*, a book whose first volume alone is over a thousand pages, refers to Mussolini only in passing, when Montessori left Italy in exile. The explanation for the exile that is often given is that Mussolini banished Montessori for being a pacifist, or even that it was self-appointed. One source that does acknowledge the connection took this view: "During Mussolini's regime in Italy Dr. Montessori was at first patronized by the Italian dictator; but she fully appreciated the dangers of such patronage and left Italy in 1932."

While this is at least partially true, the real story is significantly more complicated, and more interesting.

In 1923, Montessori's son, Mario, now in his mid-twenties, wrote a letter to Benito Mussolini. In it, he pointed out that the Montessori Method had become internationally popular yet remained unappreciated by the national government. Mussolini responded by inviting Maria Montessori to meet with him. Two years later, the Montessori Method had received official recognition from the government. Mussolini began financing Montessori schools with his own money, ordered Italy's factories to manufacture Montessori materials, and even became president of the Opera Nazionale Montessori, a still-existent training program for Montessori teachers.

A glimpse of the full extent of Mussolini's admiration can be gleaned from this resolution of parliament:

The Chamber, noting that solely through the personal interest of Benito Mussolini, the Montessori method, for many years widespread, appreciated, and adopted in all the countries of the world, has had solemn recognition in Italy, where the old regime had almost always ignored or misunderstood its scientific, social, and national value, votes that the School of the Montessori Method now risen in Rome under the auspices of the Fascist Government is, by the Ministry of National Education, developed so that it becomes an international centre of instruction of the Method, so that there may be restored to the land of its origin this pedagogic enterprise which for many years has honoured the name of Italy abroad.

For her part, Montessori became an honorary member of the women's Fascist organization Tessera Fascista, continued to meet with Mussolini in private, and became Italy's national school inspector. In exchange for Mussolini's financial support, Montessori represented the dictator worldwide, effectively propagandizing Italy as a place of tolerance and learning. For the better part of a decade, Maria Montessori was Mussolini's "children's ambassador to the world."

Then, suddenly, that changed.

As Montessori's fame continued to skyrocket—in addition to those in the United States, there were Montessori schools as far away as New Zealand and Thailand—Mussolini appears to have felt threatened. Because Montessori offered a rival ideology—one of child-centeredness and personal development—it had to be killed. Dictators, after all, don't compromise. As Hitler had with Rudolf Steiner, Mussolini ordered the closure of all Montessori schools. It speaks to the power of a pedagogy that two of the most brutal

dictators of the twentieth century were intimidated by such a seemingly innocuous thing as school.

After appointing himself Italy's new philosopher of education, Mussolini transformed the country's schools into institutions
of straight indoctrination. Uniforms were distributed and faculty
replaced by military officers. As one visiting professor observed,
"Pupils arrive at the 'truth' that all history and all historical
philosophy lead inevitably to the conclusion that fascism—the
rule of a purposeful élite—is the only adequate form of social-
political organization." When Mussolini joined forces with Hitler
during World War II, they were fighting with schools—as much as
bombs and armies—against the Allies (who were, of course, doing
the same).

———————

While the Montessori Method differs appreciably from Fascism, the
two have a certain amount in common.

A quote from Mussolini can sound eerily like Montessori:
"(Students) cannot be fed solely by concerts, theories, and abstract
teaching," he once proclaimed. "The truth we aim to teach them should
appeal foremost to their fantasy, to their hearts, and only then to their
minds." Likewise, a quote from Montessori can echo Mussolini: "The
first idea that the child must acquire, in order to be actively disciplined,
is that of the difference between *good* and *evil* ..."

While Montessori was exiled from Italy in 1932 and became a
respected champion of pacifism, the fact is that for much of the 1920s
the Montessori Method was Italy's official pedagogy. Montessori's
preference for order and discipline were a big part of her philosophy.
In her portrait of the pedagogue, Kramer speculates that this is what
initially interested Mussolini: "the sight of all those good, neat little

children, so busily occupied and so well behaved." While as educator and education, Montessori stands for freedom of the individual, it cannot help but be paradoxically prescriptive in its insistence that it and it alone can achieve this aim.

Of little notice to scholars today was the fact that, like Waldorf schools, Montessori schools are simply the most visible part of a larger philosophy. The real agenda was social—education being the way of achieving this grander societal outcome. "My pupils learn their three R's earlier than other children," Montessori would say in one breath, and with the next, "My larger aim is the eventual perfection of the human race." As with Rudolf Steiner, Maria Montessori wanted to educate not just the intellect but the very essence of children, with the belief that doing so would liberate or free them from the bonds of ignorance and poverty.

This formula would prove enduringly popular. Even after Mussolini closed all Montessori schools in Italy over the course of a single day, it didn't take long before they returned. When they did, Montessori schools would far exceed the number of Waldorf schools and boast alumni such as P. Diddy, Gabriel Garcia Márquez, and the founders of Google, who have specifically cited Montessori as the reason for their success. Yet for all its esteem and its reputation as one of the finest alternatives to mainstream schooling available, the Montessori Method was not without its adversaries.

One of its chief critics was a man named A. S. Neill.

A HOUSE ON SUMMER HILL

Once, in 1921, a little-known Scottish educator did something odd. He started a private boarding school where children could decide what they wanted to learn and even whether or not they felt like attending class. They had the same say as teachers and at any moment could do whatever they pleased so long as it didn't interfere with someone else's desire to do the same. It was, in other words, a school where children might actually want to go.

This was, of course, a completely radical idea. Giving equal rights to children had never been tried before, and reactions were predictably mixed. *Summerhill: For and Against*, published in 1970, gathered the opinions of fifteen scholars. John Culkin called the school "a holy place," but another educator swore he would "as soon enroll a child of [his] in a brothel ..." Though Summerhill's founder, A. S. Neill, was voted one of the twelve greatest educators of the last thousand years, his school has a history that is as disturbing as it is revolutionary.

In 1992, a Channel Four documentary caused a sensation when it showed teachers and students swimming together in the nude, wild animals running through the halls, and the decapitation of a rabbit by a student wielding a machete. The hour-long video was shot over two semesters, time during which there appeared to be nothing but bedlam and butchery. Not surprisingly, Britain's Office for Standards in Education got involved and until recently has offered a blistering critique of the school, even going so far as to threaten it with closure. The case went to court in 1999, with the general consensus being that this was the end of Summerhill. But in an astonishing upset, the school defeated the Blair government, and has since resumed being as radical—and controversial—a place as ever.

Alexander Sutherland Neill was born in Forfar, Scotland, in 1883. His father was a severe, uncommunicative man, and his mother suffered from a vague but serious illness (growing up, she had been the only of her twenty siblings not to die of tuberculosis). In the era of large families, Neill had thirteen brothers and sisters, five of whom didn't survive into adulthood. This somber, sickly upbringing appeared to have a lasting effect, and Neill would spend the rest of his life safeguarding children.

Still in his early twenties, A. S. Neill became a *dominie*, the Scots word for teacher, and followed in his father's footsteps. The job eventually led to a headmastership at a school in Gretna Green, where Neill began to write a series of thoughtful, if not especially popular, books. *A Dominie's Log, A Dominie Dismissed, A Dominie in Doubt*, and others suggested an emerging—and radical—pedagogy. "A school that makes active children sit at desks studying mostly useless subjects is a bad school," he wrote. "I am trying to form minds that will question and destroy and rebuild."

Neill was invited to coedit a journal called *Education for the New Era*. The other editor was a woman named Beatrice Ensor, a theosophist and advocate of the Montessori Method. From his office in Tavistock Square, Neill smoked incessantly and played jokes on Ensor, "the only adherent I ever met who could laugh at Theosophy and herself." Working on the *New Era*, Neill discovered he could write whatever he wanted and Ensor didn't seem to mind. In fact, as Neill grew progressively sharper in prose, Ensor only seemed to grow more pleased. "The more outrageously I attacked pedants and schools," Neill later recalled, "the more delighted she was."

In his late thirties, Neill traveled to Salzburg and then a suburb of Dresden called Hellerau. In 1921, with a few close friends, he opened his first school. Neue Schule (New School) was an international school with a broad curriculum and high number of foreign students. Though Neill claimed it was the most exciting period of his life, he detested German bureaucracy and, in contrast with the rest of the world's opinion, found the German school system to be "pedantry masquerading as progress."

Nevertheless, Neill stayed in Hellerau for another two years. Then, as the country grew politically unstable, he moved. But rather than part ways with his students, he took them with him—"to a mountaintop at the edge of the Tyrol, four hours' train time from Vienna." The New School's new schoolhouse was an old monastery, a suitably sacred location to cause outrage among the locals. As with the school in Hellerau, Neill's pupils spent their time how they pleased. One sunny day a nine-year-old German girl lay outdoors in a bathing suit, an act that so incensed the town's worshippers, they sent a policemen to accost Neill.

It was the beginning of the end. Shortly thereafter, Neill's loathing of Germans became second only to his contempt of Austrians, "the most hateful people I ever met." Once again, rather than abandon his students, he took them with him—this time to England. The location was a house on Summer Hill in the town of Lyme Regis, and for a while, things were looking up. Neill hired a staff: "good old George," "Jonesie," and Neill's wife, Lillian, and was even visited by the Earl of Sandwich, an occasion that brightened his reception within the community considerably.

For once, he was on good terms with his neighbors.

In 1924, the lease was up, and A. S. Neill bought the house in Leiston where Summerhill may be found today.

In the nearly hundred years since the move, Summerhill and its founder have garnered much praise. Henry Miller called the school "a tiny ray of light in a world of darkness" and Neill "the one true educator in all Christendom." When the actor Orson Bean and Neill were introduced in 1968, Bean claimed he was meeting "one of the warmest and wisest men in the world." Neill was visiting New York, and at age eighty-five appeared before a *Tonight Show* audience of fifteen million. His international bestseller, *Summerhill: A Radical Approach to Child-Rearing*, led to an avalanche of new students at the Suffolk school, saving it from one of many periods of near impoverishment and ruin.

But undoubtedly Summerhill's most significant accolade is its status as the world's first children's democracy. That is to say its pupils are treated as adults—they vote about what goes on in the school, are able to have relationships with each other, say and do whatever they want, and call teachers by their first names. Summerhill was not only the first school to try a children's democracy, but the first institution of any kind. It wasn't until the 1960s that a similar idea was established in the US. There, the Sudbury Valley School's ideological founder, Daniel Greenberg, has called children the "last oppressed minority," and this is precisely the group Neill is credited with liberating (before Greenburg was even born).

Yet Summerhill has also had its share of detractors. One of the disadvantages of having a democratic mandate, of course, is that people are bound to disagree. Graffiti and property damage have always been within the well-exercised rights of Summerhillians, and particularly foul swearing is observed by students and faculty alike. One visitor went so far as to describe the environment as "a Kafkaesque universe with dilapidated and sometimes vandalized buildings." Everyone from journalists to Ofsted inspectors have commented on the utter chaos, filth, and sometimes savagery that is Summerhill—associations that didn't seem to bother Neill in the slightest. "Inspection makes Summerhill insincere," he once complained. "The kids tidy up, rub out the *shits* and *fucks* on the walls; they feel self-conscious and unhappy."

But bestowing democratic rights and being willfully controversial is a distinction Summerhill hasn't been particularly clear on making. Neill's interest in Freud, for instance, translated to often senseless and outrageous behavior: students of any age were encouraged to have "a full love-life." This type of sexual freedom led to students and teachers swimming together in the nude (and this was in the 1990s—there is no telling what happened before the public began to take an interest in the school's activities). As Neill explains in his book, "The whole idea of Summerhill is release: Allowing a child to live out his natural instincts."

In the same work, advice is offered to parents who may be confused about their child's sexual development. "My daughter of twelve likes to read smutty books. What shall I do about it?" Neill's response is customarily flippant: "I should provide her with all the smutty books I could afford to buy." "Would you reprove a boy of fourteen for telling sex stories?" "Of course not. I should tell him better ones than he knew." Neill's love of irreverence carried over into admissions, and often—even if the school was facing bankruptcy—Neill would turn away the parents of prospective students if he felt they were especially pretentious.

In one scenario, a stern, military father visits Summerhill with his nine-year-old son. "The place seems all right," says the man, "but I have one fear. My boy may learn to masturbate here." Neill asks why such a thing would be a problem, to which the man responds that, of course, it would do his boy harm. "It didn't do you or me much harm, did it?" In another example, a husband and wife visit Neill in his office. After pestering him for an hour with what Neill felt to be offensively stupid questions, the wife turns to her husband. "I can't decide whether to send Marjorie here or not," she says. "Don't bother," Neill interjects. "I have decided for you. I'm not taking her." When asked why, Neill responds, "I should waste half my life explaining to you what it was all about, and in the end you wouldn't be convinced."

Interestingly, A. S. Neill's democratic approach to education arose (at least in part) out of opposition to Montessori. "The Montessori world is too scientific for me," he once wrote. "It is too orderly, too didactic. The name 'didactic apparatus' frightens me." Of the apparatuses in question—the famous Montessori materials—he complained that education was "more than matching colours and fitting cylinders into holes." It speaks to Neill's own character that he found this exercise to be oppressive and confining. In fact, his biggest complaint of the Montessori Method was Montessori herself: "She is a church woman; she has a definite idea of right and wrong. Thus, although she allows children freedom to choose their own occupations, she allows them no freedom to challenge adult morality."

This seemingly irresolvable philosophical divide helped push Neill toward a total democracy—one where children could question the choices of adults as freely as adults questioned the choices of children. For this reason, Summerhill is often called "the school with no rules," though in fact this is a total misconception. At last count, there were 179 rules—a clearly high proportion for any school. It's just that, like everything else at Summerhill, the rules are decided by both faculty *and* students (in fact students, by virtue of there being more of them, hold more sway than faculty). Meetings are held two or three times a week, during which voting takes place on everything from the fine for smoking to a reasonable time to turn out the lights. In fact, as Heather Piper and Ian Stronach have observed, the school has "invisible boundaries, powerful inspections, binding agreements and redemptive rituals, as well as a set of public punishments that prompt and enact acceptable ways to live together."

Because students board at Summerhill and often come from places as far away as Japan and California, it's imperative that everyone get along. Conflicts have to be dealt with swiftly, or else the entire community may be plunged into chaos. The school's 179 democratically established rules are the only thing standing between a genuine learning environment and the decapitation of rabbits. With this in mind, we can better understand a number of select regulations: Law 85, for example, designates everywhere that isn't the woods a machete-free zone, while Law 80 forbids students from walking into town while brandishing a dagger (other weapons are apparently all right).

But what is most interesting about the laws at Summerhill is that they carry over into life outside the school as well. For instance, by their own volition, students are prevented from swearing in town. As Stronach and Piper have written, this actually means that rules are more restrictive on public property than they are on school property. Why children would voluntarily decide to make their lives less free is anyone's guess, but one thing is certain: Given the opportunity, Summerhillians create more laws for themselves than adults impose on them in the public system. Take Law 48, which states that "Freddy can have a stick bigger than him." Or, as part of the same law, that "Len can have a lighter that doesn't light but sparkles."

With such restrictions governing their every move (sometimes literally), Summerhillians have often been compared to the children from *Lord of the Flies*. When BBC turned Summerhill into a dramatic series in 2008, director Jon East tried to dispel the association once and for all. "That single book did more than anything else to damage people's faith in the essential decency of children," he told *The Telegraph*. "If repressed public schoolboys who are used to being caned are suddenly left unrestricted on a desert island, it's not surprising that these terrible instincts are unleashed. However, I think that if Summerhill pupils crashed on to the same island, they'd soon have a meeting, set up a committee, find wood, make food and be basking in the sun, entirely happy."

Still, Summerhill is only recently emerging from a long period of substantial criticism. The famously crabby Ofsted inspector Chris Woodhead, who began his forty-year career by capturing the headline "Sack the 15,000 Useless Teachers," was especially villainous and may have even written the equally famous sentence—"Summerhill is not providing an adequate education for its pupils"—that landed the school in court in the year 2000. Since the Summerhill victory, however, government officials have softened their complaints considerably. In fact, they've even begun to offer faint praise. In a 2007 Ofsted report, the school is credited with providing a "satisfactory" quality of education and for allowing "freedom for the individual, each child being able to choose their own path in life and find, through experience, the things that they want to do and the person they want to be."

Stronach is a professor of education at Liverpool John Moores University. In 1999, he was selected by Summerhill to become its official inspector and was present during the investigation. I asked Stronach—a thoughtful, soft-spoken man of middle years—why the opinion of Summerhill is changing. He told me that while the school's policies and agenda have remained largely the same, the political climate in Britain is becoming more tolerant of progressive schooling. "If you look over the inspectorial history of the school since 1921, it's a long and enduring vendetta between the ideas of A. S. Neill and the government agency. There's something about school democracy that really gets up the nose of democratic politicians."

One particular objection that Ofsted continues to have is the Summerhill policy (or non-policy) regarding the attendance of class. Because classes are structured according to desire and not compulsion, many students choose not to follow the national curriculum and so graduate without the General Certificate of Secondary Education.

For this reason, when Summerhill students are compared with other pupils in Britain's league tables, they register poorly. Considering tuition is twelve thousand pounds a year, the investment for parents is considerable for something that doesn't necessarily produce a certificate. Zoë Readhead, the school's headmaster and daughter of A. S. Neill, doesn't place too much importance on the piece of paper (as we might expect): "If you look at a league table we're always at the bottom, but who gives a shit," she told one inquiring journalist. "What kids learn here is so much more important—things like independence and taking responsibility."

And in these areas, Summerhill appears to do rather well. Many of the school's alumni are grateful for not having been forced to attend classes, follow the national curriculum, and write standardized tests—at least this is the indication they give in interviews and select testimonials. No formal studies have been conducted that measure student satisfaction or success. Though some graduates have gone on to become actors and professors, others have become truck drivers and hairdressers. Whether the proportion of successful alumni is greater or lesser than any another school is, so far, a total mystery. Neill's own comment here is as good a summary as any: "I would rather Summerhill produced a happy street sweeper than a neurotic prime minister."*

While no studies have been carried out, Stronach and colleagues received a grant from the Nuffield Foundation to do an evaluation of the Ofsted reports prior to Summerhill's legal victory. "We found that they'd been completely dishonest and inaccurate in drawing comparisons. When we did it ourselves, we found that in fact the kids at [Summerhill] perform at roughly the same level as the average for the county they're in ... So the actual results, if you measure them by assessment outcomes, are about average." Stronach also mentioned that study results could be misleading, since the majority of Summerhillians are non-native speakers of English, on top of arriving at the school with behavioral problems or special needs. "So throw that into the mix and I'd say they do a pretty good job."

When asked if public perception of the school in Britain was favorable, Stronach chuckled wearily, "No, no, no." Stronach says that most people still think the school is a scandalous place where anything

---

* As an aside, it's interesting to note how Neill, who claimed to be "forming minds," seemed uncertain about how precisely he was doing this. For a school that rejects all other schools, the actual point of Summerhill is less clear. If happy street sweepers are preferred over unhappy prime ministers, why the need for Summerhill at all?

can—and probably does—happen. "A perfectly respectable Scottish newspaper three or four years ago started saying that somebody was thinking of starting up a Summerhill school in Scotland. The actual text was fair enough reporting, but the photograph that they used to illustrate the school was of nude bathing in the swimming pool." In fact, even when it isn't being deliberately controversial, Summerhill seems to attract conflict. At one time, Summerhill received so much negative press that reporters began to visit the school with the intention of witnessing some disaster: a child throwing a rock through a window or hammering nails into the grand piano. When these events were found not to be ongoing, the reporters grew disappointed and bribed students to pose with hammers in hand.

Despite all it's been through, Summerhill is enduringly—and now it seems indefatigably—popular. The BBC show of the same name has been nominated for a number of British Academy Television Awards, and—in contrast to most of the attention awarded by the media—has even been praised by the school itself. Zoë Readhead travels often as the keynote speaker at education conferences around the globe, and educators continue to be intrigued by the school's highly unique character. Summerhill-like schools have been the inspiration for authors from Enid Blyton to Ira Levin, and Neill himself maintained friendships with everyone from Wilhelm Reich to Henry Miller.

More importantly, Neill's impact on education is extensive. In fact, it's so far-reaching that the parameters of his influence may have yet to be determined. It's no wonder the *Times Educational Supplement* has called A. S. Neill one of the most important educators of the twentieth century. To a degree that rivals even the achievements of Rudolf Steiner and Maria Montessori, A. S. Neill's life and works appear to be growing more relevant with each day. For a man so far in advance of his time, it's as good a legacy as could be hoped for.

A PRIVATE ELITE

When it comes to a mainstream education, there is only one official alternative.

Private schools offer what public schools cannot: they turn privileged students into privileged people. From George Bush to George Orwell, Margaret Thatcher to Margaret Atwood, private schools' distinguished alumni are too numerous to name. Notable graduates from just one of the Ivy Leagues are sure to include a litany of Nobel laureates, Pulitzer Prize winners, heads of government, Supreme Court justices, billionaires, and other of the world's most influential and important people.

It says something about them that private schools are the preferred choice of presidents, even if it contradicts their politics. While campaigning on a promise to fix all that was wrong with the public school system, Bill Clinton sent his daughter Chelsea to Sidwell Friends, an elite, thirty-thousand-dollar-a-year private school in Washington, DC. Before George W. Bush pledged to reform public education with No Child Left Behind, he sent his twin daughters to some of the most expensive private schools in Texas. And when Barack Obama assumed office in 2008 and began implementing the most dramatic changes in public school history, his daughters were sent to the same private school as Chelsea Clinton, which has been the favored choice of presidents since Teddy Roosevelt gave the school's commencement speech in 1907.

The paradox is not limited to presidents. Bill Gates, a graduate of the private Lakeside School in Seattle, has personally donated billions to public school reform. (While Gates promotes large teacher–student ratios in the public system, the private school he attended "promotes relationships between teachers and students through small class sizes.") Chester E. Finn Jr., who attended the prestigious Phillips Exeter Academy, spent much of his adult life trying to reform the public school system before reaching the seemingly inevitable conclusion that we should "Blow it up and start over." Steven Brill, a journalist and author critical of traditional public schooling, was himself schooled at the elite Deerfield Academy in Massachusetts. And Davis Guggenheim, the critically acclaimed director of the 2010 documentary *Waiting for Superman*, followed the presidential path to Sidwell Friends.

Clearly, reforming the public school system is too important a job to be left in the hands of its own students. Private schools are institutions that make the makers: by design, this group of people is small, important, and powerful—in a word, elite.

What is interesting about private schools is that elitism is not their byproduct but their blueprint. Private school mottos often reflect this idea: "Let he who merited the palm bear it" is the slogan of Upper Canada College. At California's Claremont McKenna College, it's "Civilization prospers with commerce." And in the United Kingdom, "May the fortune of the house stand" is the motto of the John Lyon School, where another private school likes to claim its students "pass on the torch of life." Such themes of wealth, inheritance, and privilege speak to the very essence of a private education.

Private school students typically account for between 5 and 10 percent of the total schooling population (and this is the case in Canada, the United States, and Britain). It is evidently no coincidence that the percentage of those who attend private schools is equal to those who can afford the tuition: in many places in the world, the wealthiest 5 or 10 percent of the population controls over half the total wealth. Considering that private schools of any category and variety— preschool, university, Waldorf, Montessori—are funded independently of (though often in addition to) the government, have their own board of directors, create their own agenda, hire their own faculty, and teach whatever they want, the power they have is extraordinary.

Yet when it comes to actually delivering an education, the

superiority of private schools has been disputed. The controversy began in the 1980s, when a mercurial sociologist named James Coleman asked which was better, public or private. This seemingly obvious question has boggled academia ever since, with a never-ending number of follow-up studies repeating some variation of Coleman's experiment. As so often happens in the field of education, the pursuit of the answer has exceeded the value of the question. It turns out that *Which is better, public or private*, is something of a false dichotomy: the answer is neither—or rather, both.

That's because, while it is the most significant alternative to the public system—indeed, the only real alternative there is—the private school system isn't really an alternative at all. Public and private schools are separate and distinct things, and offer routes to two different destinations: while public school students end up in the middle class, private school students end up in the upper class. Like all other pedagogies, private schools are on a mission, and that is to prepare their students to become the social, political, and business leaders of tomorrow. In this regard, the real job is not to educate but to teach privilege, and here, of course, they excel. From crest to curriculum, private schools attest to a system that was designed for and is managed by some of the most powerful people on the planet.

———————

John Strachan was born in Aberdeen, Scotland, in 1778.

As head of a middle-class family, his father was a supervisor at the local quarry. One day, a routine blast was taking longer than expected, and thinking the explosive had been safely disarmed, he went to check the fuse. The mistake cost him his life.

John Junior chose an education over the quarry.

After graduating from Aberdeen Grammar School and then

Aberdeen University, he fell in love with a woman named Margaret England. Strachan didn't have enough money to marry, and so the love remained unrequited. This seems to have been at least partly a factor in his decision, in 1799, to accept a teaching post in Canada, then just a meager outcropping of the British Empire. The invitation had come from one of Strachan's teachers who had a connection to a prominent businessman named Richard Cartwright. For eighty pounds a year, Strachan was invited to tutor the Cartwright children as well as other children of the region.

After settling into his employer's home in an eastern Ontario town, Strachan began gaining recognition as a fine classroom teacher. Discontent with the common, uncultured citizens of Cornwall, he set about with the deliberate intention of turning his students into an elite ruling class. In a newly established private academy, Strachan wanted students to infiltrate Canadian politics because, he said, "then I shall have more in my power."

Strachan's own ambition was to become a bishop, a position he would eventually obtain. In the meantime, he first had to convert from Presbyterianism to Anglicanism, since there was already a head of the Presbyterian church. Despite his willingness to convert in order to advance his own career, Strachan would remain a staunch (and increasingly unpopular) supporter of the Old World.

At his private school in Cornwall, Strachan made sure his students received the best education possible—setting something of a precedent for the private schooling of today. When it came to providing his students with the latest technology, he spared no expense, including the purchase of four hundred pounds in scientific equipment. These children would later be known as the "Family Compact," a group of powerful businessmen, clergymen, and politicians who—according to the plan—began taking control of the country. In particular, Strachan wanted the Family Compact to penetrate the House of Assembly, one of the country's chief governing bodies, which he considered to be "composed of ignorant clowns ..." As teacher, his job was to "arm the Government" with privately schooled students, ensuring that power would stay in the Family and so with the Crown.

With this in mind, Strachan made it his mission to change the way education was organized. One historian summarized his view as one in which "The educational system must be strengthened to encourage loyalty and social order." So in 1815, Strachan proposed what would become the colony's first board of education, legislated the following year. Strachan's influence was such that when he proposed "an Inspector or Superintendent of Schools in order to produce uniformity of (the) System" in 1817, he was given that very job. But Strachan's greatest achievement, in education anyway, was in the founding of the University of King's College.

Like its namesake in Aberdeen, Strachan wanted the university to be a feeder for the Crown, and in 1827 he sailed to England to personally oversee its chartering. Even so, it wasn't until years later that the foundation stone was laid, an honor that fell to Sir Charles Bagot, the newly appointed governor-general who, later that same year, would be commissioned by the government to find a solution to the country's Indian troubles (and thus was one of the architects of the residential school system). The University of King's College admitted its first students the following year and in 1849 was renamed the University of Toronto.

But Strachan wasn't happy.

Over the preceding decades, the Canadian colonies had been engaged in a bitter ideological dispute. On one side was the Family Compact, who wanted society to be run by a private elite, as epitomized by loyalty to the Church of England. On the other side, it seemed, was everyone else—everyone who wasn't an Anglican—whom Strachan viewed with undisguised contempt.

When this second group of Protestants, led by William Lyon Mackenzie, began shifting the country's political direction toward a democracy and away from the nepotism of the Family Compact, Strachan unleashed his students like attack dogs. The reformer Robert Gourlay found himself the object of one such assault. As Strachan wrote, "All of my pupils now the leading characters in many parts of the Province opposed him sternly." Inversely correlated with Strachan's ascension to power was his popularity. One particularly wounded victim called him "the most dangerous and spiteful man in Upper Canada," a characterization that was not uncommon.

But Strachan's most noteworthy opponent was Egerton Ryerson, the Methodist missionary and founder of Canada's public school system. In Ryerson, Strachan found someone whose personality was as cantankerous as his own, and it annoyed him greatly. Ryerson was known as the "Pope of Methodism," and Strachan, who had then risen to the level of Anglican bishop, was styling himself "John Toronto." What followed was a legendary showdown of egos, with Ryerson advocating the separation of Church and State, and Strachan advocating their union.

At least, this is what's recorded by history. Though Ryerson is often described as an early champion of secularization, in reality he wasn't nearly so progressive. Ryerson only wanted religion separated from education when the religion in question was Anglicanism; Strachan, for his part, only wanted religion and education to be unified if the religion in question wasn't Methodism. The result of this epic personality clash was that, eventually, two distinct systems emerged: one in which wealth and religion—and their resulting power—would be the product of a private education, and one in which sectarianism and bureaucracy—and their resulting impotence—would be the product of a public education. Public schools would be for the middle class, private schools for the one above it.

Before this distinction, Strachan still hoped that the ruling class would be shaped at all levels of education, from grammar school to university. In Europe, a university education was the final phase in becoming a religious authority, and Strachan's hope was that the University of King's College would fulfill that same goal—namely, that it would arm the government with soldiers for the Church. This was what made it particularly excruciating when, the year following his retirement, the school was made sectarian and rechristened the University of Toronto. In fact, Strachan was so incensed that, at the age of seventy-two, he made the four-month trip back to England, returning later that year with a new charter, this time for the University of Trinity College.

There were now two schools: one for the everyday Protestant, and the other for a private elite.

———

Ontario's first private boarding school, and among the first in Canada, was founded by John Colborne.

Colborne, who had been privately schooled in Europe, spent his youth serving the British army. At the Battle of Corunna in 1809, his superior's dying wish was that Colborne be promoted to lieutenant-colonel. With his new position, Colborne served under the Duke of Wellington, who had risen to prominence during the Napoleonic Wars and was now commander-in-chief of the allied army.

At the Battle of Waterloo, Napoleon had issued his soldiers to charge the Allies when Colborne—acting out of rank—suddenly decided to maneuver his troops to face them, in a daring counter-strike. As Napoleon's army fell back in surprise, the Allies moved in for the kill. According to the late historian Alan Wilson, "Colborne's bold stroke has been credited with assuring victory at Waterloo ..." (In retrospect, this is something of an overstatement, considering that the allied forces also had Gerhard von Scharnhorst, the brilliant general who had educated the Prussian military at the same time as Johann Fichte militarized education.)

But Colborne had not escaped unscathed: one of his arms had been "half shot away," while the other was injured at a the siege of Ciudad Rodrigo. Disfigured and disabled, Colborne was sent to Canada where, in 1828, he arrived as the newly minted lieutenant governor. With the same willfulness he exerted at Waterloo, Colborne began making friends with the leading social men of the day, including John Strachan and the Family Compact. A lifelong Anglican, Colborne agreed with Strachan's vision of an elite society and that school was the way to do it. To this end, he proposed a private boarding school, where "only the sons of the wealthiest inhabitants" would receive their education.

Established the following year, Upper Canada College was "a privileged school" that appealed to the interests of the Family Compact. It would function as a "stepping-stone and ultimate feeder to the University." Thus would complete a two-step process: graduates of Upper Canada College would study at Strachan's Anglican university—the pre-secularized University of Toronto—and would then graduate into a society that they owned. In *A History of Upper Canada College, 1829–1892*, this is phrased as "the training of opulence for the administrative offices and positions of public trust."

This would be the school's mandate going forward. Today, UCC is considered one of the finest private schools in the country. Its trained opulence have gone on to become the country's business, social, and political leaders, from Ted Rogers to Michael Ignatieff. As *The Globe and Mail* noted in 2010, Canada is not governed by politicians on Parliament Hill, but by the students "of approximately three acres of finely tended lawn" in Toronto.

Michaele Robertson and Barry Wansbrough are a powerful team.

Wansbrough—"the Wonz," as his wife refers to him—was head-master of Hillfield Strathallan, an elite day school in west Hamilton, Ontario, and is the founder of a tutor training certificate program called Licensed to Learn. Robertson—or "Mike," as her husband calls her—was Hillfield Strathallan's academic director before becoming head of UCC's Upper School and, finally, principal at University of Toronto Schools. Together, Mike and the Wonz are a singular force in academia, often speaking as if one person.

On the role private schools play in the formation of a social hierarchy, Robertson defends the need for a private elite, pointing out the difference between leaders and followers. "Schools right now teach leadership without acknowledging that leaders in our society actually know more than the people they lead," she said. "If Canada doesn't have an elite among its young people, it should fold its tent right now and we should just become part of the States or something."

"Which definitely does have an elite," Wansbrough noted.

For Robertson, the job of private schools is to nurture elitism: "Everywhere there's a stream for kids to demonstrate a particular talent in something. What I mean by 'elite' is having that talent nurtured and brought to fruition, instead of having that flame tamped out in favor of the more factory model of education ..."

At University of Toronto Schools, where Robertson ended her forty-year career in private education, students arrive with a feeling of privilege. "It's an academically elite school," she said. "There's no question about it. Those kids are going to do well no matter where they are." But Robertson said the faculty is able to cater specifically to their students' needs, which has the result of giving them an advantage over others. "Those kids aren't just like any other kid, like kids who are talented in the arts are not just like any other kid. I'm a great believer that people who know how to deal with those particular talents and skills move the kids ahead hugely."

"And that's actually what an independent school can do better than a public school," Wansbrough added.

While there's little doubt that private schools graduate successful students, the question is how exactly they go about doing this. Do they *create* billionaires and politicians, or through a careful screening and admissions process, do they simply know how to *select* them? This was the question that eluded James Coleman in his 1981 landmark *Public and Private Schools*. Coleman, along with colleagues Thomas Hoffer and Sally Kilgore, had made a large-scale study of public and privately schooled students and concluded, "the selection of superior students into private schools cannot explain the higher levels of achievement in private schools." In other words, private school students were being *created*, not selected.

But the Coleman study soon came under fire. Coleman had used questionable data methods, and critics pointed out that the willingness of parents to spend the money, time, and energy giving their children the best education possible would affect the outcome, which Coleman hadn't factored into his reasoning. Added to this was Coleman's own personality. Already a controversial figure, Coleman had developed the disconcerting habit of renouncing his own work almost immediately after it came out. Two weeks following the publication of *Public and Private Schools*, Coleman told one reporter his data was flawed and that he would do it differently if he were "writing the report again …"

Meanwhile, the Coleman Report had ignited a firestorm.

One of those singed by the blaze was Judith Kleinfeld, a professor at the University of Alaska. Kleinfeld herself had studied at a remote private school on the Andreafsky River. Now defunct, St. Mary's was a Catholic elementary school for Inuit children, "a school whose graduates were noted both for their college success and for their leadership within their home villages." After years on the frozen Alaskan tundra, Kleinfeld had had enough time to ponder the same question as Coleman. Did private schools create exceptionality, or reject mediocrity?

And here was the thing: if answered definitively, the question would have the power to disprove the validity of the private school system. From Summerhill to Harvard, private schools bill themselves as being places where an exceptional education is provided—and not just a babysitting service for the rich and powerful. But if private schools don't actually deliver a superior education—and in fact, if public schools do the same job for free—then the whole foundation of the private system would collapse. This is the debate Coleman ignited, the debate that the academic community has struggled to extinguish ever since.

When asked which was better, public or private, Robertson and Wansbrough said there were three factors that contribute to a student's success, no matter which system they're in: The first is socio-economic—wealthy students do better than poor students. The second is the education level of the parents—the better educated the parent, the more likely the student is to succeed. And third, strange as it may seem, is the student's ability to contain impulsive behavior. (This final factor is famously depicted in the "Marshmallow Test," where children are given a simple choice: they can either have one marshmallow now, or they can wait a few minutes and have two. After presenting these options, the administrator leaves the room while the child agonizes over his or her predicament. One now, or two later? The children who wait for the second marshmallow have learned to *delay gratification*, an indicator of future success.)

According to the rationale, private schools excel in all three areas: they attract families with money, families where the parents are often the alumni of private schools, and families who've taught their children to eat their marshmallows later (or something like that). If one subscribes to this theory, private schools really do what they say they do: they produce highly successful people.

At least, that's the thinking.

But while it's true that private schools may do better in these three categories, at least two of them—the socioeconomic factor, and the level of the parents' education—seem to have nothing to do with the schools themselves and everything to do with forces entirely out of the school's jurisdiction (namely, having the good fortune of being born into a rich family, where education is seen as the key to a prosperous life). Just because private schools graduate successful people, in other words, doesn't mean they deserve the credit.

Which puts us back at the start.

After living in a remote corner of Alaska, Judith Kleinfeld seemed to appreciate just how maddening a problem it was becoming. But unlike Coleman and colleagues, Kleinfeld relied on the power of her own observation: she had seen Inuit children graduate into positions of leadership and esteem, and in the small community of St. Mary's, she guessed that the reason for the private school's success "was to be found neither in the students alone nor in the school alone but in their combination." That is, private schools *select* privileged students and, with them, *create* privileged people.

In the United States, the story of private schools begins in 1645, when John Eliot founded the Roxbury Latin School.

At the time, Latin schools were becoming increasingly common, and initially Roxbury was no different: it was financed by the community, regulated by a board of trustees, and facilitated by teachers who taught Latin and Greek (among other classical subjects). But unlike other grammar schools of its day, the Roxbury Latin School was never closed down or re-chartered and so has become—according to some, anyway—the oldest continuously run independent school on the continent.* As Cotton Mather put it in his celebratory biography of John Eliot, "From the spring of the school at Roxbury, there have run a large number of 'streams which have made glad the whole city of God.'"

To teach at the Roxbury Latin School, Eliot selected men of learning and distinction, including the patriot Joseph Warren, who had attended Roxbury as a pupil soon after its opening. Despite the considerable wealth of its board of trustees, the Roxbury Latin School wasn't particularly generous when it came to paying its teachers. Warren had been promised a salary of forty-four pounds, sixteen shillings, but by the start of his second semester, he had spent most of that sum on heating and repairing the schoolhouse, work he did himself. When

---

* I've decided to call Roxbury Latin the first independently managed school in North America, although it should be known that this is not a general or even especially popular opinion. Some academics feel that the Collegiate School in New York was the first private school, owing to the fact that one of its teachers, Massimo Maglione, discovered documents that put the school's founding at 1628, which would make it older than even Boston Latin, the first American public school, founded in 1635. But Maglione's documentation appeared to prove only that the Collegiate School's founder, someone named Jonas Michaëlius, was active in the teaching profession, and that the school's actual founding wasn't until ten years later, in 1638, which would make it younger than the Boston Latin School but still older than the Roxbury Latin School. The reason I've cited Roxbury Latin as the first independently managed, privately funded school is that, since its inception, its charter has never been revoked or come under government control, which makes it the oldest *continuously run*, independently managed, privately funded school in North America. (Whether it was founded in 1628 or 1638, the Collegiate School closed during the American Revolution and therefore probably doesn't technically qualify as the "first," though at that point, the debate gets pretty silly.)

Warren asked to be reimbursed for his own out-of-pocket expenses, the trustees refused, and Warren resigned.

By 1764, the Roxbury Latin School had found a replacement teacher, but he was treated to even greater frugality. John Prudden received the equivalent of only twenty-five pounds annually, "to be paid three quarters in Indian Corn or peas, and the other fourth part in barley, and good and merchantable, at price current in the country rate." Though everyone was in favor of the Roxbury Latin School, getting people to pay for it was another thing. Even Cotton Mather seemed to notice: "I persuade myself that the good people of Roxbury will for ever scorn to begrudge the cost, or to permit the death of a school which God has made such an honor to them ..."

After establishing Roxbury Latin, Eliot—who was first and foremost a Puritan missionary—spent the remainder of his life reading and writing. *A Further Account of the Progress of the Gospel Amongst the Indians in New England, and of the Means Used Effectually to Advance the Same, Set Forth in Certain Letters Sent from thence Declaring a Purpose of Printing the Scriptures in the Indian Tongue, into which They Are Already Translated*, published in 1639, reflected both Eliot's devotion to missionary work and to the writing of books with exhausting titles. Never one to overlook his own private study, Eliot spent the remaining thirty years of his life translating the Old Testament into Algonquian, the language of Massachusetts' native population because, as he put it, "If they were able to read our Bible, they should most clearly see what Jesus Christ was."

Meanwhile, after leaving his teaching post at Roxbury, Joseph Warren had joined the American Revolution, where he was killed by a musket ball. A year after Warren's death, John Hancock famously and flamboyantly signed the Declaration of Independence and two years later, in 1779, also put his name to the incorporation papers of the first private academy chartered under the new American government.

Like Roxbury, the Phillips Academy, better known as Andover, "was designed by the Founders to be rather a private establishment ..." The Phillipses were a wealthy New England family of Puritans and patriots, possibly (or perhaps just hopefully) descended from the poet John Milton. John and Samuel Phillips were leading social and intellectual pillars of their day; the family had provided munitions to patriots in the Revolution, and to return the favor, George Washington sent eight of his nephews and grandnephews to Andover. Thus began a long tradition of notable Phillips alumni and enduring Phillips prestige. (A passage from *The Catcher in the Rye* pays tribute when Holden forgets the name of someone he's just met—"George or something"—but remembers "he went to Andover," and that it was a "Big, big deal.")

Its powerful connections, large trust fund, and private governance made the Phillips Academy similar to the schools of John Strachan. Its purpose was to prepare high school students for university—hence, of course, the name "prep school"— where they would graduate into positions of religious, social, and political importance. When President Coolidge visited the school for its 150th anniversary, in 1928, he remarked on the importance of Andover, "because there the character of the youths of the land is molded." Younger and "more plastic" minds could be shaped into tomorrow's leaders, a theme that was revisited at a commencement speech in 2009, where graduating students were reminded "You will be leaders, the question is why: To wield power or to serve?"*

The real test of a private school's character, though, is its alumni, and here Andover succeeds in its aim of creating powerful leaders, including a plethora of presidents and priests, judges and justices,

---

* This quote comes from an official transcript, hence the underlining.

lawyers and legislators, brokers and billionaires. The tradition began with the school's founder, Samuel Phillips Jr., who was "shaped by excellent family and school training." Born into a wealthy Massachusetts family, Phillips was the only one of seven children to survive infancy. A sickly, pious, and highly strung youth, Phillips was enrolled at college by the age of fifteen. Shortly following graduation, Phillips is said to have written Andover's legal charter, based "strongly on the ideas of Locke and Milton."

Together with his father and uncle, Phillips created an educational model that had not been tried yet. As *The New York Times* observed, "The administration from the beginning has been left in the hands of a body of trustees who were wisely left free to meet new conditions and to adjust the curriculum to the demands of changing generations." Under such an arrangement, the school could admit whoever it wanted, teach whatever it felt like, and spend its money however it pleased. In 1928, ten members of its faculty were earning more than the average college professor (a more pleasing arrangement than the tradition established at Roxbury).

With its administrative freedom, one of the first things the Phillips Academy trustees did was open another school: Phillips Exeter Academy was established in 1781. Like the rest of the Phillips clan, its founder, John Phillips, was an industrious learner, entering Harvard at the age of twelve. Later he became a successful merchant with an estate valued at seventy-five thousand pounds after starting out, as legend has it, with only four shillings to his name. Perhaps owing to his ambitious nature, Phillips was a famously unpleasant person. Even his biographer, Charles Bell, acknowledged Phillips "has sometimes been represented as belonging to the sourest sect of puritans ..." A colleague at Exeter once recalled "he would not give a boy a cherry from his trees, unless the favor were asked with a low bow, and in the most reverent tone."

The temperament of its founder aside, Phillips Exeter swiftly became as successful as Phillips Andover. Yet despite their reputation in the wider world, a curious rivalry has developed between the schools beginning, according to sources, in 1878, when Andover and Exeter met on the baseball field. Exeter defeated Andover, but later that year, when it came to football, Andover trounced Exeter, a pattern that has more or less continued to this day and now includes administrative and academic rivalry. Where one year Andover received an endowment of about $800 million, Exeter received $850 million. Where Exeter considers students in the ninetieth percentile of the SAT, Andover considers students in the ninety-fourth. The scholastic jostling is often compared to that of Yale and Harvard, an unwittingly apt comparison considering Yale receives the majority of its students from Andover, and Harvard from Exeter.

"The essential difference between Exeter and Andover and the big (private) schools in Canada is they have endowments in the hundreds of millions of dollars," Wansbrough told me, one early morning in December. "They're much wealthier."

And this is indeed true: On any given year, Exeter and Andover might be twenty times richer than Upper Canada College. But while, among private schools, there is a gap between rich and unbelievably rich, there is an even wider gap between private and public. In fact, at a time when the private school system has probably never been wealthier, the public school system has probably never been poorer.

In response to continued economic hardships, thousands of school districts across the United States are taking radical steps to reduce the cost of public education: In California, the school year was shortened by five days. In Florida, tuition increased by 15 percent for the fourth consecutive year, while in Texas, funding for pre-kindergarten programs—serving about 100,000 children—was cut altogether. New Mexico resorted to four-day school weeks, and Detroit announced that it would close half its public schools "and send layoff notices to every teacher in the system." And that was all in one year. By the following year, in 2012, a Pennsylvania district was $20 million in debt, in the middle of a lawsuit, and too broke to pay its own teachers.

In Canada, the economic slump has carved a similar path across the landscape. Facing a shortage of $17 million, the Vancouver School Board announced that it would cut 10 days out of the school year and fire over 150 faculty including teachers, guidance counselors, librarians, and specialty staff for children who are learning disabled. Farther east, the provincial government of Alberta announced its education budget had shrunk by $80 million. At the beginning of 2012, a single Ontario school district lost 800 students, closed all of its libraries, and faced $10 million in budget cuts. In the same year, Nova Scotia announced that its public school boards would reduce spending by $13.4 million in 2013, and that, like the rest of the country, further cuts could be expected.

But perhaps most notably, 2012 was the publication year of an anticipated new report.

In "Commission on the Reform of Ontario's Public Services," the economist Don Drummond made an extensive study of the province's schools, hospitals, infrastructure, real estate, and virtually every other aspect of its public works. What he discovered shocked the country. Ontario was destined for an economic cataclysm if it didn't adhere to his 362 carefully noted recommendations, such as—when it comes to education—selling abandoned school buildings, increasing already bulging class sizes, and firing 70 percent of the province's guidance counselors. As Drummond observed in the introduction, "Our message will strike many as profoundly gloomy."

But the Drummond Commission was more than just a piece of pessimistic prose. If taken up by legislators, the reforms would reorganize nearly every public service in the province, "from how health care is provided to the way students are taught," leading to a virtual transformation of society. Indeed, the Drummond Commission is one of the most controversial pieces of reform proposals in recent history, and not least among its controversies is the commission itself: while recommending that everyone else tighten their belts, Drummond's fees cost $1,500 a day in taxpayer money (which the government insisted was "the going rate for someone of Drummond's skills").

As the public school system faces some of the most extreme cutbacks ever, the private school system is only getting richer.

In 2011, Andover's endowment grew some 20 percent, totaling just over $800 million, while Exeter's grew by almost 14 percent, to reach a total of $969.1 million. The 2011 value of Harvard's portfolio was $32 billion, a 21.4 percent gain over the previous year, with similar results among other private colleges of the Ivy League variety. In fact, during the same 2011 fiscal year, American universities received over $30 billion collectively; of this amount, the wealthiest handful were given a whopping 27 percent, thus "widening an already yawning wealth gap at the top of higher education." In a revealing correlation between wealth and perceived greatness, the richest 1 percent of American colleges is often the same as the "best" 1 percent of colleges ranked by the *U.S. News & World Report*. In 2012, the top-ten-ranked liberal arts colleges and the top-ten-ranked national universities were all privately owned.

While Canada has almost no private universities, it has many private high schools. And here the story is the same. It speaks to the disparity of the times that, while public schools are categorically strapped for cash, students at the private St. George's School are given "a fictitious sum of $10,000 to invest in North American equity markets." Elsewhere, public schools are reducing phys ed programs to save money, while Upper Canada College has its own Olympic- and NHL-sized skating rinks. While the Toronto District School Board might spend about $2.5 million on 250,000 students—or $10,000 per student—the private Appleby College spends $10 million on about 250 students, or $40,000 per student. (Also at Appleby College: five sports fields, four residences, three tennis courts, three squash courts, two basketball courts, a beach volleyball court, climbing wall, full-sized hockey arena, heated indoor swimming pool, athletic center, recital hall, dance studio, theater, gymnasium, art studios, practice rooms, library, and chapel—all on a pleasant piece of real estate overlooking Lake Ontario.)

And these aren't even the really expensive private schools. At the Kamehameha Schools in Hawaii or the Institut Le Rosey in Switzerland assets exceed the total endowment of entire school board districts. At last count, Kamehameha had billions more dollars than the Los Angeles Unified School District, the second-largest public school district in the United States. Put in another context, Harvard has more money than Zimbabwe, Liberia, Burundi, Somalia, Eritrea, the Central African Republic, and Sierra Leone combined. The isolation and encapsulation of private schools within the economy is such that, when the 2008 recession occurred, the head of a private school in New York claimed not to be "experiencing any signs of impact from the economic downturn." In fact, enrollment at private schools in New York City hit a record high, with "no significant decline in donations."

Today, in both the public and private system, wealth is becoming the single most important criteria in a student's success: the students who have it go on to become even richer, while the students who don't, don't. The result is a closed system, where it takes money to get money. Public school is for people with limited resources who end up in the working class; private school is for people with unlimited resources who end up in the ruling class. Such rampant inequality has left the overwhelming majority of students in debt and menial servitude, while a tiny minority rules the political and social spheres.

Just as John Strachan and the Family Compact envisioned, private schools are for the training of opulence. Their success lies first in their ability to select students who have wealthy parents and come from educated families, and second in their ability to mold a private elite. While they are hugely successful socially, politically, and economically, the degree to which they are successful *educationally* is less knowable. But after all, this isn't the point: from preschool to Princeton, private schools provide passage to prosperity, prestige, and privilege. In turn, their students are charged with managing society. This explains why everyone from Bill Gates to Bill Clinton are privately schooled reformers of the public system: it takes a private elite to reform the public majority.

GOD'S ARMY

Before there were Waldorf and Montessori, private and public schooling, there was education at home.

Homeschooling is the original transfer of knowledge: the idea of passing on ideas—of dialogue with a trusted mentor—was how Socrates taught Plato, Plato taught Aristotle, and Aristotle taught Alexander the Great.

Before Prussia invented compulsory education, homeschooling was how Mozart became Mozart, how Beethoven became Beethoven. For centuries, homeschooling was the dominant model in the New World as well. Puritans saw it as a way of transmitting a whole culture and even convinced the colonial governments to support them. This they did at least partly because men like Washington, Jefferson, and Franklin were homeschooled themselves (or at least, what passed for it at the time). It wasn't until Horace Mann and Egerton Ryerson imported Prussian schooling that parents were replaced by teachers, children became students, and homeschooling was suddenly deemed illegal—a status it has only recently begun to renounce.

Today, homeschoolers outnumber Waldorf and Montessori schoolers combined. In the US alone, over two million children and teenagers, or some 2.9 percent of the total schooling population, receive their education at home. Since the beginning of the new millennium, the number of homeschooled Americans has risen by an astonishing 74 percent. The story is similar in Canada, Britain, Australia, and South Africa, where—once an unthinkable taboo—homeschooling has gained something resembling mainstream appeal. As one historian observed, "By the 21st century, homeschooling was becoming cool."

And for good reason: homeschooling's illustrious alumni intervene at every interval of the alphabet, from Ansel Adams to Woodrow Wilson, Charlie Chaplin to Malcolm X. Along the way, homeschoolers occupy the whole spectrum of professional endeavor: Homeschooled minds invented the telephone, lightbulb, lighting rod, and airplane. Homeschooled hearts composed "Moonlight Sonata" and the Requiem in D Minor. Homeschooled hands drew the Vitruvian Man and *Woman with a Parasol*. A homeschooled foot trod the road not taken.

At the outer boundaries of achievement, homeschooling has been said to have almost supernatural powers. It's been alleged to lessen "the harmful effect of low parental education levels," and even recommended as a remedy to autism. Its supporters would appear to include Gandhi ("There is no school equal to a decent home and no teacher equal to a virtuous parent"), Einstein ("Education is what remains after one has forgotten what one has learned in school"), and Mark Twain ("I never let my schooling interfere with my education"). It says something about its power that homeschooling is the method of choice for parents with children who are exceptionally intelligent, creative, athletic, or driven, as though putting them in the public or even private system would squander their talent.

Yet homeschooling is clearly not without its controversies.*

Despite the fact that it was once ubiquitous, homeschooling has become the villain, the antagonist to the public and private school systems, and remains illegal in many places in the world. Though precise ruling is often a nebulous (as well as contentious) issue, in Asia and parts of Europe homeschooling is either frowned upon or forbidden. As recently as 2010, both Spain and Sweden made homeschooling against the law. More notable still is Germany, where persecution is so severe that—in the case of at least one couple—political asylum has been sought in North America. But that continent is far from a safe haven. It wasn't until 1993 that homeschooling became legal in all fifty United States. In 2008, California declared that "parents do not have a constitutional right to homeschool their children." Homeschooling may happen only under certain conditions, as is the case in many parts of both Canada and the United States.

Most damaging to the homeschooling movement is not its legal status but its association with religious extremism. Three-quarters of all homeschooled Americans are Christian fundamentalists. In fact,

---

* And lest controversy arise here, a brief disclaimer is in order: for the rest of this chapter, homeschooling will be defined as the education of children by their parents, though so far I've stretched the meaning to include education by tutor, self-education, and other means. The reasoning here is twofold: one, to make things as simple as possible, and two, to reflect the tendency of the homeschooling community to list former students who were only briefly homeschooled or were schooled by a variety of means. And actually, I've done this myself: while listing Margaret Atwood as a private school alumni in the previous chapter, she was first and foremost homeschooled. Such is the difficulty in listing alumni. Still, the kinds of people a system graduates is often a revealing indicator of its true nature, so I've included them with this notice.

according to the Fraser Institute, the number one reason parents in North America decide to homeschool their children is "the opportunity to impart a particular set of values and beliefs"—what we might call indoctrination in fewer words. When one realizes these opportunities may include biblical literalism, creationism, homophobia, xenophobia, gender inequality, opposition to birth control, skepticism of global warming, and it seems a special dislike of Shakespeare, one begins to sense homeschooling's perverse dedication to providing its pupils with everything *but* an education. (In other words, it's just like any of the other school models we've seen.)

Intriguingly, the association between homeschooling and religious fundamentalism owes credit to homeschool's best-known champion. John Caldwell Holt actively solicited the help of Seventh-day Adventists, Mormons, and other denominations, despite being secular himself. His motive was to bring together "a new Underground Railroad" of children and parents who were the indentured servants of the mainstream system. With numbers to rival public school, homeschoolers would be the new frontier in alternative education—a prediction that appears to be coming truer every day.

The fact that Holt almost single-handedly launched the Christian homeschool movement while being himself atheistic is one of many interesting anomalies of character. While he often likened public schooling to enslavement—and coined the term "unschooling" as a way to describe the need for liberation—Holt himself was educated in some of the finest schools in the world and was a private school teacher for over a decade.

Though homeschoolers owe unending thanks to John Holt, who tirelessly campaigned on their behalf at a time when parents in many states could be sent to jail for educating their own children, Holt didn't know what homeschooling was until 1976 or '77, by which time he had already had a successful career as a bestselling author—and then managed to squander it through the espousal of increasingly radical ideas. It is one of this story's many curiosities that Holt is credited as being the father of homeschooling when in fact his only real achievement was to unite homeschooling with Christian fundamentalism—a partnership that may well lead to its own undoing.

———————

John Caldwell Holt was born in 1923. His father was a wealthy insurance broker, and the family divided their time between New York and Massachusetts. By Holt's later remembering, his childhood was both oppressive and joyless. At the age of twelve, he was sent to Switzerland to study at Le Rosey, the school of choice for the sons of monarchs, dynasts, and billionaire tycoons. The fact that Holt—the de facto father of the largest anti-school movement in history—began his own education at the world's most expensive school has been all but lost in the record. (This is at least partially due to Holt himself, who, much later in life, pointedly avoided questions concerning his own education. "I no longer believe in degrees," he once told a reporter, "and if I could get rid of mine I would.")

After a year at Le Rosey, Holt returned home to enter the ninth grade at Phillips Andover. Boarding school made him unhappy, and though his mind was keen, his introversion and sense of apartness made him a social failure. Holt's perception of his own brilliance was such that he believed he knew more about his subjects than his teachers, but they of course didn't take kindly to being told as much. Bored, confused, and fearful—the very same qualities he would later ascribe to all schoolchildren—Holt reluctantly entered university. In keeping with the tradition of Andover students, he went to Yale, where he graduated in 1943 with a degree in industrial engineering.

Still uncertain about what he wanted to do and now aged

twenty-one, Holt left on the USS *Barbero* for the South Pacific. A year into its tour, a bomb exploded near enough to the vessel that it was permanently decommissioned. After being relieved of duty, Holt returned to New York. (The *Barbero*, on the other hand, eventually fell under the control of the United States Post Office Department in their short-lived experiment of delivering mail by torpedo.) The experience of World War II left a deep impression on Holt, who spent the next six years lecturing on the necessity of a one-world government—the only force he felt could stop the proliferation of nuclear weapons. But Holt soon grew restless and, in 1952, set off to backpack Europe. There is no record of where he went or what he did—no biography of Holt has ever been written—only that when he returned the following year, it was on an old patrol boat.

Holt then traveled to Taos, New Mexico, where he visited his sister—who suddenly and forever changed the course of his life. As he later recalled, "My sister suggested that, since I enjoyed children and they liked me, I might want to become a teacher." So Holt went to the newly founded Colorado Rocky Mountain School in the very small town of Carbondale and made himself available. "I sat in on some classes, answered students' questions, kicked a soccer ball around, and by the end of the day decided that the institution was a good place for me to work."

Holt lasted four years before transferring to another private school, this time in Boston. According to *Yankee Magazine*, "The school hired Holt but within a year grew disenchanted by, among other things, his insistence that testing was probably harmful to learning ..." Holt was fired, hired at a new school, and fired again. The process was to repeat itself several times before finally—and it seems rather late in the game—Holt got an idea. Together with a colleague named Bill Hull, he began a longitudinal study. For seven years, Holt observed Hull's students and vice versa, each making extensive notes.

Holt's notes from these sessions formed the basis of *How Children Fail*, which he began working on in the late 1950s, as well as a number of other books that followed. While Holt initially had difficulty finding a publisher, he eventually settled with a small company based out of the UK. In 1964, *How Children Fail* was finally published and almost instantly transformed its author into a celebrity. Notably, however, the book doesn't once mention homeschooling. Between 1964 and Holt's death in 1985, *How Children Fail* would be translated into fourteen languages and sell over a million copies. While *How Children Fail* would be used by homeschooling parents the world over, neither it nor any other book for years to come would have anything to do with education at home.

Then something strange happened.

According to the homeschool scholar Milton Gaither, Holt gradually fell out of favor. "As the 1960s became the 1970s, Holt became an outspoken critic of the Vietnam War and refused to pay taxes." Holt also refused an honorary degree from Wesleyan University, but only after showing up at the reception to criticize the entire school system, comparing it—as he increasingly began to do—with the slave trade.

In Gaither's estimate, Holt was a "fringe figure" by the mid-1970s. As his focus shifted from education to radical politics, he lost the majority of his readership. Holt's rejection of *all* schools isolated him from the political left—even from the likes of his friend A. S. Neill, who believed in the value of *some* schools (such as his own Summerhill). In this way, Holt began to resemble Ivan Illich, who advocated the complete abolishment of institutional education in his short but enduringly influential *Deschooling Society*.

During the 1970s, Holt wrote a new book every other year, but none were remotely as popular as his first two. In fact, they attracted almost no notice from mainstream readers at all. But intriguingly, the few readers who did notice couldn't have been more thrilled and began writing Holt to extend their gratitude—and to inform him about a subject they felt he'd missed. Homeschooling was suggested to Holt by his own readers and, in 1977, became the author's new cause. *Growing Without Schooling* was the first exclusively homeschool periodical and soon came to define the entire movement. In 1981, Holt also wrote *Teach Your Own*, his first and only work that explicitly endorses homeshooling as an alternative to the mainstream.

As *Growing Without Schooling* became the voice of the homeschool movement worldwide, Holt began to build partnerships with people in America who could advance the cause even further. In this area, his most powerful ally came in the form of Raymond Moore.

Moore was a psychologist and professor at Stanford University who, in 1972, had written an influential work himself. In an article for *Harper's Magazine*, Moore argued that children shouldn't begin schooling until the age of ten. Moore's article prompted *Reader's Digest* to carry the story to an even wider readership, which in turn led to Moore's writing a popular full-length book with his wife, Dorothy, called *Better Late Than Early*.

Because of *Better Late Than Early*, the Moores, who were Seventh-day Adventists, appeared on a 1982 radio broadcast of "Focus on the Family," a roundtable discussion hosted by the influential evangelist James Dobson. On two separate occasions, Dobson and the Moores discussed homeschooling—the first time a national audience had heard the idea. According to Moore's account, Dobson received three times the normal feedback volume, and literally overnight, homeschooling entered the modern era.

Of the millions who heard the broadcast, one was Michael Farris.

At the time, Farris was a Washington-based attorney and lobbyist for a number of right-wing organizations. (These included Jerry

Falwell's Moral Majority and the antifeminist group named, somewhat paradoxically, Concerned Women for America.) In 1982, Farris and his wife, Vickie, had the first of ten children. Upon hearing Raymond Moore on the radio some months later, the Farrises decided to home-school each of them, beginning with Christy. The following year, Michael Farris went one step further, and with an endorsement from Raymond Moore himself, founded the Homeschool Legal Defense Association (HSLDA).

For a hundred dollars a year, Farris offered his legal expertise to homeschooling families, should they run into trouble with the govern-ment. At the time, homeschooling was still illegal in a number of American states, notably Michigan, Iowa, and North Dakota, and one thing that naturally made parents hesitant to homeschool was the fear that they would go to jail for doing so.

But soon Farris was doing more than just defending the movement in courts of law—he was assailing what he calls the "godless monstrosity" of public education. In 1986, the HSLDA was involved in a highly controversial case involving seven evangelical families. The families had sent their children to private Christian schools in order to avoid exposing them to the pagan horrors of *Macbeth* and *The Diary of Anne Frank*, and wanted the government to pay the fifty-thousand-dollar bill. Two years after the victory, Farris won a similar case when a federal judge ruled that fundamentalist parents could demand special textbooks from public school board districts, as well as sue those same districts for "damages" already incurred.

Dozens of similar battles were fought throughout the 1980s, '90s, and 2000s. As more cases were won, membership to the HSLDA grew appreciably; today the organization exceeds some eight thousand subscribers. Farris's startup is the largest of its kind anywhere. After essentially nullifying its central purpose through its own success, HSLDA has more recently turned to other endeavors. In the United

States, homeschooling is legal thanks largely to the efforts of just three people—Michael Farris, Raymond Moore, and John Holt. Since Holt died in 1985 and Moore in 2007, Michael Farris has become the primary leader of the American homeschool cause.

In the year 2000, Farris founded an institution known (at least unofficially) as "God's Harvard." Located just outside of Washington, DC, Patrick Henry College has the singular distinction of being a university *for* homeschoolers. More importantly, according to the founder's own admission, Patrick Henry College is designed to train an army of Christian soldiers whose purpose is to "take back America for God." While some might interpret this as a kind of metaphor, Farris—as might be expected of a fundamentalist—has a more literal notion in mind.

Patrick Henry College was created in order to send its graduates into elite political, judicial, and federal professions—in effect, swaying the course of America onto the righteous path. By all accounts, it's been successful at doing just this. In 2004, the school's sixty-one graduates went on to fill a high number of influential positions: two secured jobs in the White House, and two at the FBI; six became members of Congress, eight joined various federal agencies, and one was hired by the Coalition Provisional Authority in Iraq.

Like many other fundamentalist Christian colleges, Patrick Henry College interprets the Bible literally. As Farris told NPR's Terry Gross, "We're engaged in the search of truth, and we believe that the Bible *is* truth." Inbound students must sign a Statement of Faith, which declares that Jesus Christ was "born of a virgin"; that "Man is by nature sinful and is inherently in need of salvation"; and that "Satan exists as a personal, malevolent being who acts as tempter and accuser, for whom Hell, the place of eternal punishment, was prepared, where all who die outside of Christ shall be confined in conscious torment for eternity." Professors and other faculty members sign an even more extensive document that forbids them from teaching anything other than fundamentalist doctrines.

Unlike other Bible colleges, which have a strictly Christian curriculum, Patrick Henry calls itself a liberal arts college. It teaches courses in philosophy, history, and even science. But as Farris himself admits, students are meant to learn these subjects not for their knowledge or wisdom, but as "oppositional research." In other words, Nietzsche and the evolutionary sciences may be taught, but they're only taught to reinforce the Bible, as a way of knowing what the enemy is up to. As it turns out, even the school's professors find this an unbelievable breach of academic freedom, and in 2006 nearly a third of them quit.

Then, at the same time, an article appeared in *The Walrus*.

In it, journalist Marci McDonald showed that the Canadian government was trying to place more evangelicals into positions of political importance. (The accompanying photograph showed a picture of a cross being superimposed atop Parliament's most recognizable spire.)

The article caused a stir and led to McDonald's writing a full-length book called *The Armageddon Factor: The Rise of Christian Nationalism in Canada*. As part of her research, McDonald traveled to British Columbia and visited the campus of Trinity Western University.

Located an hour east of Vancouver, Trinity Western University is a private Christian liberal arts college. At least, that's how it describes itself. McDonald calls it a training camp "not unlike Patrick Henry College: to put more evangelicals on the fast track to jobs in the civil service and the country's political power structure."

Trinity Western University began as Trinity Junior College. It was founded in 1962 by the Evangelical Free Church, which decided on the rules of attendance. In a thirteen-page contract, students were forbidden from smoking, drinking, doing drugs, fornicating, swearing, and abortion (in presumably something close to that order). As at Patrick Henry, faculty had to sign a statement of belief, "acknowledging the biblical account of creation."

These provisions prevented the college from granting degrees—and prevented its students from infiltrating Canadian politics. So in 1979, a private member's bill was pushed through in the last few minutes of the final day of a legislative session, resulting in what has since been called "one of the most significant religious events of the century." Until then, provincial universities couldn't be both religious *and* degree-granting. Now they could.

After it became a full-fledged university, the school began a period of rapid expansion, including the establishment of an education program. Students who wanted to become teachers spent the first few years at Trinity Western University and the final year at Simon Fraser University, closer to Vancouver. Because it wanted to be able to graduate its own teachers, the school needed to win approval from the provincial College of Teachers, and in 1995 it looked like it was going to. Then, at the last minute, one of the examiners noticed something odd.

In the contract signed by the school's faculty, homosexuality was on the list of "Practices That Are Biblically Condemned." Trinity's application was immediately revoked, and as a result, it filed a lawsuit claiming religious discrimination. The school took its case all the way to the Supreme Court, where it was assisted by Michael Farris and the Homeschool Legal Defense Association. In 2001, the Court ruled in favor of Trinity Western, and the school won the right to train its own teachers.

As a result, Trinity Western University has begun to steer current and future generations of students in the direction of politics. In 2002, the school opened a satellite campus just down the street from Parliament Hill, to be "a light within the city of Ottawa." The

Laurentian Leadership Centre features a number of internships designed to put its students directly into positions of power. Since its opening, graduates have filled dozens of political offices in the city. As one of the school's faculty members told McDonald, "Our students are already influencing the thinking of government."

John Holt may have been a lifelong pacifist, but the pedagogy he popularized is training students for war. As Michael Farris likes to remind his pupils, "You are the tip of the spear."

As a systemless system, homeschooling is powerful in ways that other methods are not. It offers a direct link between one generation and the next, with no regulation or interference from the government: the ideology of the parent becomes the ideology of the child. This allows for education and religion to be soldered, fused together in the molding of a mind.

The result is the formation of an army, not unlike the one Prussia organized in secret violation of the Treaty of Tilsit. At the time, public school was harnessed to produce soldiers for war; today, homeschooling is being harnessed to produce soldiers for its own battle. But who is the enemy?

Pagans, certainly. In Farris's view, public schools are "values-indoctrination centers." Yet even as he trains homeschooled Christians to be thrust into the heart of the "multibillion-dollar inculcation machine," another group has begun to pose a threat—and they're using the same weapon as him.

In recent years, Muslim homeschooling has become the fastest-growing trend within the movement (which is itself the fastest-growing trend within education). Christianity and Islam may differ on the ends—the Bible says "children are an heritage of the Lord: and the fruit of the womb is his reward," while the Qur'an says "Your progeny are but a trial; And that it is God with Whom lies your highest reward"—but they agree when it comes to the means: namely, that homeschooling is the best way to train the next generation.

Farris calls this "Generation Joshua," since it was Joshua who led the Israelites into the Promised Land. For extreme Christians, the Promised Land is a Christian nation—one where evolutionism is replaced by creationism, science by scripture. For extreme Muslims, of course, it's an Islamic nation. Such dark visions appear already to be coming true, with homeschooling being the favored choice among members of al-Qaeda. As for the Christian side, consider the following: during the eight years of the Bush administration, seven out of a hundred interns were graduates of Patrick Henry College. When Mike Huckabee ran for the Republican nomination in 2008, one of his key support groups was "his grassroots network of fellow evangelicals in the homeschool movement." Four years later, when Rick Santorum announced his own candidacy, he became "the most prominent home-schooler in America."

At this rate, one wonders when we will have a homeschooled head of government—and what will happen when we do.

6 | A MODERN AGENDA

*I work in a technical institution, so that's what we produce
is people to fit into essentially those widgets. To be widgets in
those holes. To be productive.*

—Margaret Dagenais, program planning consultant,
Saskatchewan Institute of Applied Science and Technology

STANDARDIZED STUDENTS

Recently, education scholars have attempted to answer a seemingly
simple question: Should everyone learn the same thing? Yet, as so often
happens in education, this question has snowballed into a three-decade-
long debate, cost billions of dollars worldwide, and utterly transformed
the lives of millions of students—and still not been answered.

Today, the standards-based reform movement is the prevailing
pedagogy of developed countries: it consists of standardized tests,
which, as we may remember, evolved out of Carl Brigham's interpretation of Yerkes's administration of Terman's revision of Goddard's
translation of the Binet-Simon Scale of Measuring Intelligence.
These days, standardized tests are usually multiple-choice, computer-
scored exams taken at entry and exit levels, from kindergarten to grad
school. Some standardized tests, like the SAT and *gao kao*, are also

characterized as "high stakes," since their outcomes often determine the very lives of the people who write them.

But tests aren't the only thing that are standardized. In more recent years, the process for becoming a teacher has become increasingly standardized, as have the subjects teachers are expected to deliver to their students. In fact, public education in North America, Europe, and Asia has moved toward a more standardized system overall, particularly when it comes to the creation, administration, and measurement of math, science, and reading. The reasons for this is that these are the subjects most vital to the economy.

Through a process known as benchmarking, countries that have a standardized school system compete against each other economically. After students' tests have been collected, their scores are graded en masse, with the final result representing (supposedly) the country's overall level of education. This number is then contrasted with another country's number in the governmental equivalent of comparing marks at the end of the semester. The countries that do poorly want to know the secrets of the countries that do well—and then take these secrets and implement them domestically.

The desire, of course, is to be a country with an A+. In a revealing indicator of what this means, standardized tests are often administered by economic organizations. For instance, the Programme for International Student Assessment (PISA) is administered by the Organisation for Economic Co-operation and Development (OECD). In both the micro- and macrocosm, at the level of individual students all the way up to the federal government, the idea is that educational success is synonymous with economic success—that a top-scoring student, or a top-scoring country, is the one that makes the most money.

In North America, supporters of the standards-based reform movement include Liberals and Conservatives, Republicans and

Democrats, presidents and prime ministers. Standards-based reforms have been endorsed by the Gates Foundation, the Carnegie Corporation, Educational Testing Service, and the College Board. The argument is that a standardized scholastic experience will give everyone the same opportunities, particularly students who don't normally do well in school. While advocates say this is to benefit students, the real reason is that it benefits the country, since underperforming students bring down the national average. If all students have the same knowledge, fewer students will end up working menial jobs and the economy will thrive.

But not everyone agrees with this vision. The Finnish education ambassador Pasi Sahlberg refers to a "global education reform movement," in which an increasingly standardized school experience is creating a profound lack of originality. (Finland, as will be discussed later, has no reforms to speak of.) Other critics see the standards-based reform movement as nothing more than a large-scale effort to turn a country's citizenry into a productive working class. As one critic put it, "The biggest fans of standardizing education are those who look at our children and see only future employees." Even people who don't share this view precisely have criticized the research behind standardized testing and an increasingly standardized curriculum. To them, there is an evidentiary dearth in the science behind the movement and in the association between scholastic uniformity and economic attainment.

In 1983, American scholars published a report called *A Nation at Risk*. "*A Nation at Risk* was a landmark of education reform literature," writes Diane Ravitch, the respected education scholar and former assistant secretary of education. "Countless previous reports by prestigious national commissions had been ignored by the national press and the general public. *A Nation at Risk* was different."

To start with, the authors were unabashedly direct: "Each generation of Americans has outstripped its parents in education, in literacy, and in economic attainment," they wrote. "For the first time in the history of our country, the educational skills of one generation will not surpass, will not equal, will not even approach, those of their parents." The eighteen scholars spent eighteen months in deliberation and concluded that the public education system suffered "from weakness of purpose, confusion of vision, underuse of talent, and lack of leadership." In a sentence repeated often since, they added, "If an unfriendly foreign power had attempted to impose on America the mediocre educational performance that exists today, we might well have viewed it as an act of war."

The authors urged the federal government to focus on general standards of education rather than individual student performances, which had been the prevailing reform philosophy. They recommended "that schools, colleges, and universities adopt more rigorous and measurable standards," including standard measures of achievement, standard curricular content, and standard teacher qualifications. Though its provocative prose caused an outcry, *A Nation at Risk* didn't achieve any of these goals.

Then something happened that did.

As governor of Texas and Republican presidential candidate, George W. Bush had campaigned on the need for standards in education—inadvertently reinforcing this message by posing the immortal question "Is our children learning?" After being sworn in, Bush followed the course of presidents by trying to appear as though he actually intended to follow up on any of his promises, starting with his signature on a piece of legislation called the No Child Left Behind Act (NCLB). The centerpiece of NCLB was its startling declaration that it would make every student in the country proficient in both reading and math by 2014. To this end, school districts ceded power to the government, which began to introduce standardized measures for both teachers and students. Because this was a federal act, states that failed to comply were punishable by law.

Even though NCLB was technically a reauthorization of an earlier bill and contained little in the way of originality, it was touted as the Bush administration's supreme domestic achievement (or as Bush himself put it, "Childrens do learn when standards are high and results are measured"). Never before had so much authority been given to the Department of Education and never before had this power enabled it to realize the recommendations of *A Nation at Risk*. Overnight, the standards-based reform movement was born, and with it an estimated 762 years of administrative paperwork. More importantly, classrooms were turned into "work sheet distribution centers," where students began writing standardized tests in the third grade.

By 2008, the No Child Left Behind Act had become deeply unpopular. One politician called it "the most negative brand in America." At a carefully choreographed event, Bush had been photo-graphed signing the bill into law, forging an inextricable link between his presidency and NCLB. As his popularity declined, this became a problem. "There's a grassroots backlash against this law," summarized a Democratic strategist at the time. "And attacking it is a convenient way to communicate that you're attacking Bush." Senator Hillary Clinton pledged to put an end to the whole thing. Senator Barack Obama called for a complete overhaul.

But then, after taking Bush's place, President Obama created a new program that built on the foundation of No Child Left Behind. "Race to the Top" gives money only to the states that comply with standards-based reforms, creating a situation, writes Jonathan Alter, "right out of *The Untouchables*." As an incentive, the amount of money being given away—$4.3 billion—is "by far the largest pot of discretionary funding for K–12 education reform in the history of the United States," as

Obama's secretary of education wrote in *The Washington Post*. Given the health of the economy, states would have to be crazy not to take the bait.

And here was the thing: What the states were actually signing up for was something called the Common Core State Standards Initiative (CCSSI). Officially a program that is both "voluntary" and "state-led"—meaning that it isn't enforced by the federal government—the CCSSI describes its mission as being "to provide a consistent, clear understanding of what students are expected to learn," in order to "prepare our children for college and the workforce."

Shortly after the publication of *A Nation at Risk*, the Council of Ministers of Education, Canada (CMEC), was charged with the task of bringing national standards to the north.

To do so, power was taken away from local school board districts and put in the hands of the federal government—an unprecedented move in Canadian history. With it, CMEC created the first standards-based initiative, called the Student Achievement Indicators Program (SAIP). The SAIP was launched in 1993, and by the following year, Canadian authors Maude Barlow and Heather-jane Robertson had produced a scathing critique.

In *Class Warfare: The Assault on Canada's Schools*, Barlow and Robertson contended that assessment protocols such as SAIP are non-neutral: they're designed by people who want something from the students who write them. In this case, the designer was ultimately capitalist society, since it was organizations such as the Business Council on National Issues, the Canadian Manufacturers' Association, and the Canadian Chambers of Commerce who lobbied the federal government to increase its funding of CMEC. Corporate Canada wanted to "profit from children's futures" through the administration of standardized tests.

In her doctoral dissertation for the University of Regina, Margaret Dagenais explored the question further: "Currently, education serves the economic paradigm by providing educational services that respond to nations' demand for skilled, creative and imaginative workforces that are able to compete in a global marketplace. In the globalized economy of today, intelligence is the raw material just as iron ore was the raw material of the steel industry of the industrial age." Standardized tests are how "intelligence" is measured. They are "the quality control mechanisms and customer assurance for the production of Human Capital."

In the decades leading up to the formation of CMEC, the Canadian economy had changed dramatically. No longer were resources shipped elsewhere for processing—that was now done at home. To handle the machines that refined the resources, skilled laborers were needed. Yet to find a large number of skilled laborers, there had to be some regulatory system. CMEC had been created to be such a system and to filter the output generated by schools. Standardized tests sorted the managers from the laborers, the plumbers from the prime ministers. This is the foundation of the standards-based reform movement: it's motivated not by educational interests but by economic ones.

Shortly after the SAIS was implemented, the Canadian government began spending millions on national standards, including the introduction of a more math-and-science-based curriculum (to be discussed next). This constituted the first attempt at "official knowledge"—standardized curricular content intended for every student in the country. Tests sorted smart from stupid, but with the introduction of a standardized curriculum, all students were now being treated in the same way—or rather, as the same thing. The idea was that standardized students equaled a standardized workforce. According to Dagenais, the result "is the production of useful citizens for our national and the global economy."

While Canada has no laws that force provinces to adopt standards-based reforms, businesses have exerted enough pressure on organizations like CMEC and the Canadian Council on Learning to have nevertheless instilled a climate of standardization. When SAIP was shelved in 2004, it was replaced by the Pan-Canadian Assessment Program (PCAP). When SAIP was first administered in the early 1990s, a few thousand students took the test. Next year, PCAP "will be administered to approximately 35,000 students from over 1,600 schools across Canada ..."

Chester E. Finn Jr.—known to some as Checker—is the president of the Thomas B. Fordham Institute, a Washington, DC–based conservative think tank. For most of his forty-year career, Finn has been an unwavering supporter of standards.

Like most who champion the cause, Finn believes that educational standards create equal opportunities for schoolchildren of all backgrounds. (His photo on the Fordham website features a graying policy analyst in front of a poster that bears the inscription "Everyone needs standards.") As he explained to the National Conference of State Legislators, fifth-graders in Portland, Oregon, and fifth graders in Waco, Texas, "ought to be learning the same math."

In agreement with this view is Thomas H. B. Symons, founding president of Trent University and a Knight of the Order of St. Sylvester. "There has to be some degree of equal opportunity in the experience available," he says. "I think it's important that a person doing an arts degree in a big city should have a similar opportunity to a person doing such a degree in Thunder Bay."

This same reasoning has motivated legislators and philanthropists alike: In Canada, the Harper administration has supported education standards and been backed by business magnates Lynton Wilson and Seymour Schulich. In the United States, the Obama administration has had substantial backing from the Gates Foundation. The idea is that these reforms will lead to scientific breakthroughs and innovative technological developments, which will in turn improve the country's standing economically. As Bill Gates writes in his endorsement of the Common Core State Standards Initiative, "The more states that adopt these college- and career-based standards, the closer we will be to sharing innovation across state borders and becoming more competitive as a country."

To build legitimacy for the idea that standards-based reforms are economically effective, supporters look to the results from standardized tests. According to CMEC, Canadian students "are among the best in the world" on the Programme for International Student Assessment. But Dagenais says that Canada is overrepresented on PISA: "We test about 25,000 students and most countries test about 5,000." The problem is that data from the PISA scores is used by Human Resources and Skills Development Canada to implement reforms. With circularity of reasoning, standardized tests are being used to justify standardized tests.

Neal McCluskey, an associate director at the Cato Institute's Center for Educational Freedom, has found a similar flaw in the logic. On PISA, the United States ranks poorly compared to other developed countries. This is often cited by the Department of Education, the Fordham Institute, and policymakers as a reason to adopt more rigorous standards: the countries that score well on PISA already have these standards in place. "It is true that most nations that have outperformed the United States on such tests as the Trends in International Mathematics and Science Study and the Program for International Student Assessment have national standards," McCluskey writes, "*but so do most nations that have done worse.*"

In other words, even excluding the fact that standards-based reforms are designed to benefit the economy and not to give students an education, they're not even particularly good at doing that. Like other libertarians, McCluskey believes that national standards are detrimental to the free market since they undermine self-governance and ingenuity. "I believe the best way to run any system is to have autonomy—then you can have competition that leads to innovation."

Yong Zhao, presidential chair and associate dean for global education at the University of Oregon's College of Education, agrees. "As a result of adopting national standards, schools will produce a homogenous group of individuals with the same abilities, skills, and knowledge," Zhao writes in *Catching Up or Leading the Way: American Education in the Age of Globalization*. "Such a result will be disastrous …" Zhao's articles, essays, and popular blog entries discuss the need for students to create their own jobs and fulfill their own roles in a new economic paradigm. "Any national approach is basically trying to impose what I would call a very arrogant invasion of government thinking."

Renowned author and speaker Ken Robinson has discussed similar themes. "The fact is that given the challenges we face, education doesn't need to be reformed—it needs to be transformed," Robinson writes in *The Element: How Finding Your Passion Changes Everything*. "The key to this transformation is not to standardize education, but to personalize it, to build achievement on discovering the individual talents of each child, to put students in an environment where they want to learn and where they can naturally discover their true passions."

In 2012, Michael Winerip, a Pulitzer Prize–winning reporter for *The New York Times*, pointed out that if standardization was actually improving the quality of education, it would be possible to see the effects in the English Regents exam, a standardized test administered in New York. Instead, Winerip noted that it was possible to pass the test with sentences like "*In the poem, the poets use of language was very depth into it*" and "*Even though there is no physical conflict withen each other. There are jealousy problems between each other that each one wish could have.*" As Winerip noted, "Theoretically, passing the English Regents would mean that a student could read and write."

In the same year and in the same state, thirteen-year-old students were baffled by one of the questions on a similar exam. After reading a short story, students were asked to identify the moral. The only problem was that the story made no sense—it was about a pine-apple that challenged a hare to a race—and the moral, if it could be called that at all, was fittingly absurd: Pineapples don't have sleeves. Understandably, students objected to being asked to select the logical moral to an illogical story, and critics of standardized testing seized it as an opportunity to illustrate the greater issue: that the people who make the tests wield incredible power over the people who take them.

Yet even in the face of such criticism by scholars and parents alike and from every region of the globe, standards-based reforms have already transformed education as we know it. Since *A Nation at Risk*, the Global Education Reform Movement—or "GERM," as the Finns like to call it—has infected school systems around the world. In North America, an increasingly centralized system is now charged with the task of schooling millions of students. Corporations have successfully lobbied the government to change the system to suit their own needs. Philanthropists have supported the cause based on questionable data. And even as the reforms were being legislated, it was clear that educa-tion was finally, and perversely, at risk.

AN ARMY OF NERDS

Through millions of years of adaptation, thousands of years of formal-ized learning, and two hundred years of compulsory study, education has boiled down to one thing: today's public schools exist to produce labor.

National governments, backed by scholars and philanthrop-ists, have transformed the public school system to suit their own benefit.

It's been this way since Carnegie and Rockefeller, since the tran-sition of resource-based economies to ones based on human capital. People needed skills, and school was the place to get them. But over the years the breadth of these skills has diminished, and the scope of school has narrowed. After the standards-based reform movement, all that was known—all that was worth knowing—was what could be measured.

The short-term effect was clear: students who hated school now had a good reason. Standardized tests were the gatekeepers of the future, letting in some students while prohibiting the rest. Even after these kinks were ironed out, the tests themselves remained, as did the climate of standardization. Under such conditions, wisdom was treated as knowledge, which through schooling became mere information. The only reason to go to school was to get a job, and the only reason to get a job was to make money.

In the place of what we might call genuine learning, there is school. Every few years, school is reformed by a new educational philosophy designed to remake its purpose and engineer different outcomes for its students. It wasn't that long ago that people like Rudolf Steiner and Maria Montessori wanted schools to focus on the "whole child," mind, body, and soul. That gave way to a pedagogy of pragmatism, championed by the philosopher John Dewey, in which learning is acceptable only if it benefits society. Out of this idea grew the standards-based reform movement, which introduced standardized tests and an increasingly standardized curriculum. Now it's another pedagogical paradigm.

At the center of this new reform movement is the economy. In most of the developed countries of the world, the economy is what ultimately dictates education reform. And not the whole economy, but just a piece of it. Jobs involving science, technology, engineering, and math are seen as the vital elements of all economic growth. While they currently employ a small percentage of the overall workforce, these four sectors are said to be growing rapidly. In Canada, 20 percent of all new degrees are awarded in just two of these fields (science and technology). In the United States, more than half of the country's sustained economic growth is generated by just 5 percent of the workforce (those employed in the science, technology, engineering, and math sectors).

These are the most important areas of the economy, and recently— and by now we should expect no coincidences—they've become the most important subjects in school.

In 2005, a group of scientists published a startling new report.

In *Rising Above the Gathering Storm: Energizing and Employing America for a Brighter Future*, the United States was warned its "privileged position" as the world's number one superpower was in jeopardy. Somehow, in the last few years, China and India had begun to outcompete the United States in science, technology, engineering, and math. If it didn't do something soon, the US would lose supremacy to China, which in turn would cede the title to India. "Decisive action is needed now," wrote the scientists.

The panel had been convened by the country's leading science advisory group, the National Academies, and chaired by Norman R. Augustine. As one-time acting secretary of the US Army and former

CEO of the military defense company Lockheed Martin, Augustine's solution was simple: if the country was facing an affront from China, what it needed was an army.

To this end, the National Academies advised the implementation of a program called "10,000 Teachers, 10 Million Minds." Every year, the United States would train ten thousand math and science teachers, who would instruct ten thousand math and science students; at the end of ten years, there would be ten million new recruits. Not since the Russians launched *Sputnik* into orbit had American public school students been used in such an upfront manner.

Immediately following its publication, *Rising Above the Gathering Storm* sent fissures into the foundation of American identity. Americans, it seems, didn't like the idea of being second to anyone, least of all the Chinese. Thomas L. Friedman launched something of a personal campaign, likening the group who had written the report to heroes and urging people to heed their proposed reforms. Even Bill Gates got involved. As he told the National Governors Association, "When I compare our high schools to what I see when I'm traveling abroad, I'm terrified for our workforce of tomorrow."

All of this had the effect of stirring the Bush administration into action. In 2006, Bush announced the American Competitiveness Initiative, which became the America COMPETES Act in 2007. This was the second step in changing the fundamentals of public education to suit the economy (the first being the shift to a standards-based reform movement caused by *A Nation at Risk*). To help grasp the new changes, the world was introduced to the acronym "STEM," for science, technology, engineering, and math.*

---

* The first choice had actually been science, mathematics, engineering, and technology—until one government employee realized that "SMET" sounded too similar to "smut."

STEM was the new mantra in public schooling. There were suddenly STEM scholarships, STEM workshops, STEM products, software, and for-profit resources. Advance placement or international baccalaureate STEM students—the best of the best—received a hundred dollars every time they finished an exam. STEM students were invited to the White House, given green cards, and made eligible for half a million dollars in grant money. Schools suddenly had funding for STEM-based renovations, and an annual science fair was held in the State Dining Room.

Shortly after assuming office in 2008, President Obama built on the STEM-based reform movement begun by his predecessor. Educate to Innovate is a program that spreads the STEM message through a number of influential channels, including everyone from corporate executives to *Sesame Street* (not that it's always easy to tell the difference). STEM wasn't just being promoted, it was being marketed. There were meetings about how to "make STEM cool," how to appeal to underrepresented "markets" like women and minorities. Then there was Race to the Top, which gave extra points to students who scored well in STEM subjects.

Overall, STEM students were being fast-tracked through the system—the "educational pipeline," as it's called—and into the workforce. The National Academies had urged the government to "begin in the 6th grade," based on the realization that "The competitiveness of US knowledge industries will be purchased largely in the K-12 classroom." With the legislation that followed the standards-based reform movement and now the legislation that resulted from STEM-based initiatives, the infrastructure was in place, and Augustine's army was on its way.

A year after *Gathering Storm*, Canada published its own report.

Advantage Canada: Building a Strong Economy for Canadians, published by the Department of Finance and introduced by Finance Minister Jim Flaherty, quickly became the blueprint for the country's economic future.

Like *Gathering Storm*, Flaherty's report warned that Canada was becoming less competitive in the areas that would propel the future economy. "Fewer Canadians complete science and engineering degrees than in other leading OECD countries." Among the new policy proposals, Flaherty pledged more support for students of science and engineering.

This was not the first time money had flowed into STEM disciplines. The Russia/United States space race had caused the Diefenbaker administration to sign an agreement with NASA leading to the development of *Alouette I*, Canada's first satellite. More memorably, or at least more enduringly, the government began a series of programs aimed at enhancing math-and-science-based education in Canada—programs that were continued by the Lester B. Pearson administration and the others that followed.

As the Canadian economy changed from one in which resources were shipped to one in which they were refined domestically, there was a profound need for skilled labor. Since school was already the natural feeder of human capital into society, all it took was "the scientization of education" to transform schools into laboratories. According to Margaret Dagenais, "It was no longer acceptable to offer 'data-free assertions about the relative merits of various educational systems'; data was now required." Under the new model, how well students learned became their "output." Teachers' personality or teaching style became their "methodology." Entire school systems were suddenly turned into economic engines, designed to bolster GDP. Thus began national comparisons: "'What are they doing that we're not doing, and how can we be there?,' and 'We don't want to be beat out by a bunch of people from southeast Asia.'"

But it wasn't until the publication of *Advantage Canada* that serious money began to flow. Via an offshoot of Canada's Economic Action Plan, the government authorized one of its agencies to award up to twenty million dollars to organizations with a STEM mandate, among other initiatives. Philanthropists followed, including the Canadian business tycoon Lynton Wilson, who chaired a policy review panel that produced a 2007 study called *Sharpening Canada's Competitive Edge*. Again it was concluded that Canada was being out-competed by other countries and that this was in "large part" because of its poor showing in science, technology, engineering, and math.

The message was repeated again in 2008 and again three years later, at which point the Government of Canada announced it had a full-on "human resource crisis." In response, the billionaire Seymour Schulich created the second-largest university scholarship endowment in Canadian history, "for STEM students only."

In 2010, the National Academies amended their original report. In *Rising Above the Gathering Storm, Revisited: Rapidly Approaching Category 5*, Augustine and colleagues upgraded the severity of their initial assessment.

China and India were said to be gaining ground, and a list of new facts were rolled out that showed the United States was slipping further behind. "The *Gathering Storm* Committee's overall conclusion is that in spite of the efforts of both those in government and the private sector, the outlook for America to compete for quality jobs has further deteriorated over the past five years."

Thomas L. Friedman went back to writing op-ed columns, and the media blasted a new round of missives imbued with the same panicky vernacular. "STEM crisis" became a popular phrase, and the public was told that if it didn't pump millions more into STEM-based reforms, the country was doomed.

All of this caught the attention of two scholars.

Hal Salzman, a professor and senior faculty fellow at Rutgers University's John J. Heldrich Center for Workforce Development, and B. Lindsay Lowell, a director of policy studies at Georgetown University's Institute for the Study of International Migration, had been interested in STEM since 2007, when the two had written a paper for the Urban Institute entitled "Into the Eye of the Storm: Assessing the Evidence on Science and Engineering Education, Quality, and Workforce Demand."

For the first time, scholars had taken a critical look at STEM-based reforms. Was there really a critical shortage of STEM graduates? Did North America really risk losing economic supremacy to Asia? "Our review of the data fails to find support for those presumptions," the authors wrote. Looking at the same numbers as the National Academies, Salzman and Lowell had drawn the exact opposite conclusion. But there was more.

In 2009, Salzman and Lowell performed another study, which they presented in Washington, DC, at the Annual Meetings of the Association for Public Policy Analysis and Management. In their new report, the authors looked at multiple longitudinal data sets in order to understand the relationship between education and the economy. Augustine's committee had pointed to a recent decline in the number of STEM graduates, but Salzman and Lowell's findings indicated that this wasn't the case. The United States was producing about the same number of scientists and engineers as it had in the 1970s.

And so it was with considerable bafflement that, in 2010, Salzman and Lowell read that the "gathering storm" had been upgraded to a "category 5." What was going on here? How was there such an enormous discrepancy of opinion? In the authors' view, the federal government had got it backwards. There's wasn't a shortage of STEM students, there was a basic economic principle in effect: American tech companies, such as Apple Inc., were offshoring their supply chains to Asia, where labor was cheaper and there were fewer human rights regulations. This had the effect of making it look like there was a dearth of specialized labor, when it was simply the forces of a capitalist economy. As the authors had written back in 2007, "Rather, the available data indicate *increases* in the absolute numbers of secondary school graduates and *increases* in their math and science performance levels."

In 2011, Salzman was joined by Leonard Lynn, a professor and department chair at a private research university in Cleveland. In a jointly published article, it was pointed out that building an army of STEM students wouldn't change the fact that the market is already saturated with them. Supply has to follow demand, and "Simply producing more engineers won't create technology and jobs" any more than building more cars will increase the number of people who buy them. Salzman and Lynn pointed out that already "around one-third of U.S. engineering graduates have not found engineering jobs." During the previous year, "only about 60 percent of graduates found jobs in engineering. So, where would additional 10,000 engineers a year find jobs?"

Salzman, Lynn, and Lowell aren't the only ones critical of STEM. Even when not viewed through a labor perspective, the STEM-based reform movement has received verbal lashings from educators the world over. At the Saskatchewan Institute of Applied Science and Technology, Dagenais thinks both that the STEM demand is being met and, more importantly, that the fear of a shrinking economy is used to implement sweeping reforms, the intent being to bolster a country's competitive standing and increase the bottom line—from *Sputnik* to standards to STEM. "I think if you consciously read back (through the literature), you'll find that same panic. And it will escalate and web in response to the economy. Some writers will say it's the economic engine looking for a target. Are schools really not putting out the product that industry wants?"

At the University of Oregon, Yong Zhao chalks the whole thing up to naïvety on the part of policymakers. "The misunderstanding is that all great scientists come out of STEM education. Some scientists do, but not all." Zhao, who speaks often about the need for a more creative society, believes that the STEM-based reform movement—and its governmental and philanthropic backers—miss the whole point. "With STEM, they're just talking about training technicians. They're not talking about great people, great independence, people who are self-driven and curious. Most great scientists actually have a much more humanistic perspective."

Thomas H. B. Symons, founding president of Trent University, agrees. "I've been lucky in knowing some men and women I would say are great scientists. And they were all tremendously interested in the humanities, in history and philosophy, and they brought that perspective to their science." One of Symons's friends won the Nobel Prize for chemistry, another invented the cathode ray tube, and another invented penicillin. None, he said, lost sight of the bigger picture. "Makes you think a bit … It's what you bring to it that will really make for great scientists. And have you an inquiring mind?"

Dagenais's father was a scientist who taught her the value of practical investigation. "My best opportunities to learn science didn't come in the classroom. I had access to laboratories when I was a kid. So I got to play with hypotheses and test them out and determine if they would work." Years later, Dagenais and a colleague discovered a solution that would kill the *Fusarium* that was preventing the growth of winter wheat in central Alberta. This wasn't in a laboratory, but literally in the field. "That's not a hypothesis, that's creative thought … it was the capacity to say *What if?*" Dagenais says that the teaching of science has replaced the scientific spirit of inquiry. "When people think creatively, they play."

Yet in today's STEM-based reform movement, students are being recruited in unprecedented numbers, transforming the country's social landscape into a sea of scientists and engineers.

Augustine's vision of recruiting students in the sixth grade has been ignored in favor of targeting even younger markets. Students in kindergarten, even junior kindergarten and preschool, are "Studying Engineering Before They Can Spell It." Children are funneled through the "educational pipeline" and into the high-stakes world of competitive engineering, innovation, and technological development designed to bolster a country's overall economic standing.

In every war, there are casualties. Recent studies suggest that STEM students are less likely to graduate than students in other areas and end up switching into different programs or dropping out altogether. One professor has termed it "the math–science death march."

In Canada and the United States—as in Britain, Europe, and Asia—a very small percentage of the population drives an increasingly large percentage of the economy. By expanding the number of STEM professions, the idea is that the economy—and a country's international standing—will prevail. Even if there are no moral objections to schools being used as training camps, an admittedly small number of scholars point to flaws in the science. According to Lowell and Salzman, the number of people with STEM degrees is twice the number of those with STEM jobs. Producing millions more is "like herding cattle into a chute." The problem, Lowell says, is that education is being driven by the economy. "The academic community is in the pipeline business, and STEM departments not only require tuition, they require workers and a rationale to support their self-replicating system."

Since *Sputnik*, "education" has become a synonym for the words *economic growth.* In the governments of the world's developed countries, ministries of commerce and ministries of education interface, with the recognition that the students of today will be tomorrow's executives, engineers, and employees. But governments seem to have it wrong. School and work shouldn't be unified, but separated. If students are recruited to be soldiers of capitalism, they won't perform in the way they're supposed to. But if students are left to develop an education—a world view that may or may not involve becoming a scientist, engineer, or whatever else—they'll not only perform but innovate, inquire, and create for the sake of creation.

There is, at least, one country that seems to understand this principle.

THE FINNISH MODEL

Since the beginning of the new millennium, Finland has been able to claim the world's greatest education system. Its students are said to be the happiest and smartest, its teachers the most helpful, its classrooms places of learning and growth.

In 2000, 2003, and 2006, Finnish students placed first in reading, math, and science on the Programme for International Student Assessment, beating every other country in the developed world (in some cases, by almost thirty points). This caused a stampede of foreign delegates to visit the country, eager to know Finland's secret. What they discovered was astonishing.

In Finland, the government pays for all levels of education, from kindergarten to university, including medical and law school, and even throws in a monthly allowance. Finnish children don't begin school until the age of seven, where, compared to most other countries on the planet, class sizes are smaller, the school day is shorter, and there are fewer school years in total.

Finland has no league tables, no private or charter schools, no

Ofsted or inspection system, no performance targets, no literacy or numeracy hours, no standards-based reforms—no reforms at all. Socks are worn instead of shoes, students call their teachers by their first names, and every forty-five minutes everyone bundles up to go skiing. Though the whole country excels at standardized tests, they don't value the results or encourage comparisons with other countries.

But perhaps most important of all, teachers in Finland are revered, outranking both doctor and lawyer in the spectrum of esteemed professionals. While one in four Finns wants to become a teacher, only one in ten do, at which point they're trained at one of eight universities. By the time they enter the classroom, all Finnish teachers have a master's degree, even if they're teaching at the kindergarten level. And all this for roughly the same pay as teachers anywhere else.

At somewhere between 99 and 100 percent, Finland's literacy rate is as high as can be expected, but its dropout rate is among the lowest in the world, at less than 1 percent (versus roughly 8 percent in North America). Preschool is noncompulsory but has an enrollment rate of 98 percent; high school is noncompulsory but has an enrollment rate of 93 percent (versus 76 percent in Canada, and 77 percent in the United States, where it is compulsory). Total time spent in the classroom is about six hundred hours per year; in North America, it's over a thousand. Finland has no accelerated programs for quick learners, though slow learners are always given extra help. Teachers are not held accountable for their students' success, students are encouraged to think freely, and the last time the government interfered was 1985.

Yet equal to the Finnish education system's majesty is its mystery. How do Finnish students, despite having almost no experience with standardized tests, do so well on the PISA, a very much standardized test? Why do students still go to school even if they don't have to? Why are Finnish teachers valued so highly (or more importantly, why aren't teachers valued as highly everywhere else)? How did Finland—land of reindeer and saunas—develop the world's best education system? "There is no short answer to your questions," says Jussi Välimaa, a professor at the Finnish Institute for Educational Research at the University of Jyväskylä. I had been told the same thing by another professor, George Malaty, at the University of Joensuu. "Your questions are not easy. They could be the core of a book." Still, Malaty gave me a clue as to where I should begin looking: he alluded to the country's dark past and its comparatively recent sovereignty, claiming that education was the only way to, as he put it, "bring Finland to light."

In other words, to understand Finland's system of education, it's important to understand Finland's history.

––––––––––––––

It wasn't until 1917 that Finland became its own country. Before then it was known as the Grand Duchy of Finland and was part of Russia, and before then it was owned by Sweden. Unlike many colonial empires which might last a couple of hundred years, the Swedish period alone accounts for over half a millennium. Because of the country's small population and hostile conditions (*Finland*, in a revealing derivation, means "marshland") this arrangement might actually have worked in Finland's favor, had Sweden not converted to Christianity in the eleventh century and wanted to share the religious spirit with its neighbor to the east.

The initial crusades into Finland predate historical records, and it's difficult, even impossible, to be precise about what happened. However, later crusades were both led and documented by Eric Magnusson, Duke of Södermanland, and are known to have occurred around 1239. The duke was reputed to be "peaceful, just and kind"—at least according to the Swedish historian Victor Alfred Nilsson, in the book *Sweden.* In reality, as Finland was Christianized from the bottom up, its people were subjected to unimaginable cruelty. A famine at the end of the 1600s obliterated a third of the population. By 1721, only 250,000 people remained, as it seems the Swedish military was in the habit of claiming Finland's food for themselves.

In 1808, Russian troops began moving west to occupy Finland. Their target was actually Sweden, but Finland was both in and on the way—or as one historian put it, Finland was "an incidental byproduct of wars between Sweden and Russia." After a year-long war, parts of Sweden were claimed by Russia, and Finland came completely under Russian authority. When governance officially changed hands in 1809, Finns gleaned a sense of their new ruler's personality when Czar Alexander I made the new colony pay the costs of removing his own artillery from Finnish soil.

Under Alexander's rule, Finland was plunged into a hundred-year-long tyranny during which Finnish identity, language, and culture were suppressed. One spectator described it as "the complete destruction of our existence as a nation," and even the more sober accounts liken Russia's intent to genocide. "Russia evidently intends to stamp out, if possible, any idea of freedom that still lingers in the hearts of the people," one article from the period proclaimed.

But perhaps the worst blow was the betrayal Finns felt as four successive leaders, two Swedish and two Russian, promised to uphold the Finnish constitution, and then decided, actually, they wouldn't. Finland was subjected to such extraordinary prejudice that when at last the country petitioned Russia for independence, a tax was levied just for bringing up the subject. (Russia had already impoverished the Bank of Finland by overvaluing the ruble and left the country twenty-four million dollars' debt.) Then, finally, in 1917, Finland broke free. Amazingly, they didn't hold a grudge against their former ruler. "We are not opposed to Russia," a leader of Finland's Socialist Party told the American press. "But we do not want to entrust our fate to anyone but ourselves."

For much of the twentieth century, there were still problems.

In 1918, Finns fought Finns in a civil war that eventually led to a republican model of governance. Meanwhile, 30,000 people had died in 108 days. World War II had a similarly devastating effect. For a country that then had a population of about four million, 150,000 either died or were critically injured, leaving 50,000 children orphaned. As a consequence of the war, Finland was forced to give 12 percent of its land to the Soviet Union, resulting in the displacement of nearly half a million people.

Then, miraculously, things started to improve.

At the beginning of the 1950s, there were 34,000 people attending grammar schools; 10 years later, there were 270,000. When Juho Kusti Paasikivi left office in 1956, the country didn't elect another conservative president until half a century later. Finland made grammar school compulsory in 1921, but it wasn't until 1972 that it began legislating a national system of education. Unlike Canada and the United States, which left the implementation of a public school system to Egerton Ryerson and Horace Mann, the first Finnish school system was a matter of discourse and debate, and took years to decide.

What the people of Finland invented was different from anything that had come before. At a time when the rest of the world was testing, sorting, and funneling students through an educational pipeline, Finland decided to keep all students together from the age of seven to sixteen, without discriminating based on ability or aptitude. Upon reaching high school at the age of sixteen, school became voluntary, and beyond that, it was free even for medical and law school students, and even for foreigners. Along the way there would be no expensive, private alternatives. In contrast to the North American model, Finns weren't concerned with the production of social classes, of human capital, of skilled labor. They were concerned with giving their children an education.

When Finland entered the European Union in 1995, it probably had the best education system on the planet. But it wasn't until the turn of the century that this was confirmed. On the PISA—the international test of reading, math, and science—Finns stunned the world by beating the high-stakes, test-driven contenders from Asia and every other country in the OECD. The pattern repeated itself for the next nine years, resulting in an inrush of foreign educators, desperate to learn the key to Finland's success. Among the many things that amazed them were that Finns don't like talking about the PISA, don't agree with the idea of competitive rankings, and don't believe in tests in the first place. "We want to be better than the Swedes," one Finnish educator told a reporter. "That's enough for us."

———————

To understand the Finnish education system, it's important to understand not only Finland's history, but its present.

In a landmass of about 1 million square miles, there are roughly 5 million people. To put that in perspective, it would be as if metropolitan Toronto moved into a vacated Newfoundland and Labrador (not that this would be desirable for either party). For every 1 mile squared, there is an average of just 44 people. Even at its most dense, along the country's southern coastline, Finland manages only 121 people per square mile, compared to a European average of 439.

But what's really remarkable about Finnish people is how little they differ statistically. There are almost no differences in ethnicity and culture. Ninety-six percent of the population was born in Finland, where Finnish accounts for 94 percent of languages spoken. Finns are

84 percent Lutheran and 13 percent nonreligious, meaning that only 3 percent of the population has a different faith. Even socially and economically, Finns are strikingly homogeneous. Every major political party supports a welfare state and the tax system that makes it possible. The Finnish government takes almost half an average worker's salary, and even speeding tickets are calculated by personal income. (In one legendary case, the heir to a local sausage fortune was fined over two hundred thousand dollars for a single ticket.)

The question, of course, is whether any of this can be singled out as contributing to Finland's educational success. Finland's homogeneity—second only to Iceland in terms of totality—is often cited as a primary factor, though this view has recently come into question. The number of foreign-born Finnish residents doubled between 2000 and 2010, yet student results on the PISA didn't change until 2009 (and then, from first place to second). Immigrants have settled in certain regions only, mixing some student populations more than others, yet there are still almost no between-school differences. Students in a suburb of Helsinki get the same education as students in rural Oulu.

Jaana Palojärvi, a director at the Ministry of Education and Culture, says that Finland values its educational equality above its international ranking. "Although Finland has gained a reputation because of the good qualitative results in PISA, we regard the small variance between the results of low performers and high performers as a more remarkable achievement." This is in stark contrast with North America, where social and especially economic criteria are the most defining attributes of students' success, regardless of where they go to school, how good their teachers are, and how well they do on standardized tests.

In the quest to define more precisely the reasons for Finland's excellence in education, Dennis M. McInerney and Arief Darmanegara Liem sought the advice of thirty educators from around the world and compiled a volume entitled *Teaching and Learning: International Best*

Practices. The chapter on Finland features an extensive list of possible causes, including the quality of teachers, favorable public libraries, cooperative government, small class size, superior scholastic resources, pleasant working environment, attention to academic learning, support for education across party lines, well-appointed schools—even the country's policy of free hot meals is considered a factor in Finnish fortitude. Of these, a general consensus has begun to emerge: Finland's teachers are the reason for its educational success.

The 10 percent of applicants who get to become teachers in Finland have had six years of training and at entry level have the credentials of a professor at a typical North American liberal arts college. More than this, teachers are given full responsibility for the students in their care, but are not held accountable for their students' exam scores (as is increasingly popular in the West). "The schools do not only educate pupils; the schools raise them as well," Palojärvi says. Despite being given such an extraordinary privilege, Finnish teachers go completely unevaluated over the course of their careers.

In a move reminiscent of the Common Core State Standards Initiative, Finland has developed a national curriculum. The National Core Curricula is designed at the National Board of Education, a Helsinki-based agency that works with the Ministry of Education. The board regulates many school policies, including the number of hours each subject should be studied. However, schools are free to interpret the curriculum in unique ways: where the board says "science," a local school can divide the number of allotted hours into chemistry, physics, and biology. Every ten years, the curriculum is revised and remade, with the latest version due in 2021.

During their apprenticeship, Finnish teachers get one hundred hours of paid training each year and are paid to spend two hours a day on "professional development" on top of the four hours they spend in a classroom. As trained teachers, their wages resemble that of their counterparts across the OECD, though in some ways it's impossible to compare. Finnish society isn't set up to venerate the rich, and the respect commanded by its teachers speaks more to their esteem than mere remuneration. The value of the profession is best judged by the freedom Finnish teachers are given in the classroom, where they're encouraged to follow their instincts and develop their own methods and materials. Instead of handing out standardized tests developed by multinational corporations—as happens in Canada and the United States—Finnish teachers make their own tests, though testing itself is deemphasized and doesn't carry the same connotation it does elsewhere.

One of the best perks about their job, it seems, is that Finnish teachers are happy. Almost none leave their profession at any point throughout their careers, whereas, in some parts of North America, teachers are dropping out of school faster than students. In Canada, teachers' physical and mental health is said to be at risk across the country, with fifty-hour workweeks, a stifling administration, banal curriculum, and frequent standardized testing being among the leading causes of attrition. In the United States, nearly half of all new teachers leave their jobs within five years, at a cost of over seven billion dollars to the federal government. The burnout rate of teachers in Britain is called a national epidemic, and, around the world, the story is the same: teachers can't stand the system (and who can blame them?).

But if Finnish teachers are what make the system great, why don't other countries adopt a similar training process? Or if it's Finland's welfare state that makes the difference, why don't other highly taxed, culturally homogeneous Scandinavian countries also deliver an exceptional education? It's not that they aren't close—it's that they aren't even *remotely* close. On the PISA, Finland's fifteen-year-olds score first in reading, math, and science; Sweden's, ninth, fourteenth, and sixteenth respectively; Denmark's, sixteenth, twelfth, and eighteenth respectively.

One answer might be found by way of Hannele Niemi, a professor of education at the University of Helsinki. On her frequent travels to international seminars, one of Niemi's keynote subjects is what she calls "learning as a continuous process throughout life," or *lifelong learning*. A term that used to apply exclusively to adult education now encompasses a much broader value system. Finland believes its people are lifelong learners, or, as she puts it, "Life without learning would be impossible."

The idea could be the principle that unites all the factors associated with Finnish education. More than just a pleasant-sounding concept, lifelong learning is an actual policy, written by the Ministry of Education and built into virtually all levels of school, from general education to vocational training. The overall aim is to "guarantee basic educational rights for every pupil and student according to their abilities and special needs."

Somewhat perversely, at least to Western sensibilities, is that education in Finland doesn't need to take place in school. As Niemi writes, "Learning is understood to take place in many other connections than just at educational institutions." Strangely, most of the countries in the world don't seem to acknowledge this, but equally as strange, once you do, school suddenly seems to make more sense: teachers help facilitate a process that would happen with or without them; students begin learning things not because they have to, but because they want to, and because it's as natural as life itself.

By the early twenty-first century, whenever they traveled abroad, Finnish educators were treated as celebrities. At conferences and meetings, other teachers approached them wanting to know the key to successful schooling.

And while the answers vary, most believe Finland came to value education after being prohibited from having it. It's a tempting story, but one that may not hold up to scrutiny.

Records show that other countries revered Finland even before it gained independence. In 1898, still almost twenty years from sovereignty and twenty-three years from compulsory education, *The New York Times* wrote that Finns are "one of the most highly educated peoples in Europe," clearly suggesting their reputation was even then something of a legend. But still earlier accounts may be found. Tapani Ruokanen, the editor of a popular Finnish magazine, claims the country was put on the fast track to success in the 1700s, when marriage was forbidden unless both parties could read the Bible. In the political uprisings of the following century, a large number of publications were circulated, which could have increased the number of literate Finns even further.

Still other explanations abound.

Jussi Välimaa suggests that successful Finnish education really began with the Royal Academy of Turku (now called the University of Turku), Finland's oldest institution of higher education. It was built in 1640 while still under Swedish rule. Like all universities from the period, the Royal Academy's aim was to serve the Church—in this case, the Lutheran one—by training students for the clergy. Only these particular students appear to have been especially spirited. After it burned down in 1827, Czar Alexander I had the school rebuilt closer to his palace "in order to keep an eye on its students, who were known to have contrarian opinions."

And these are just a few opinions. The truth is that we don't know when or how Finnish education got to be so great, let alone why.

At a time when education is failing in every region of the globe, Finland is intriguing just for being Finland: for having learned students, dedicated teachers, and a government that supports rather than interferes; and for not having standardized tests, standards-based reforms, and a desire to treat students as human capital. The greatest thing about the Finnish school system, in other words, may be simply that it isn't based on the Prussian one—possibly the only system in the world that isn't. The Finnish model is an example of something that was created by the people of a country and shaped by their own unique history, their own specific values, and by the intention they have for their children.

7 | THE SYSTEM

It all comes back to the Prussian military model. That is at the foundation of our education system.

—Sean O'Toole, teacher and department head at Bracebridge and Muskoka Lakes Secondary School

AN EDUCATED GUESS

From the beginning, education has been at the center of everything: it has determined the survival of species, the development of tools, the acquisition of knowledge.

Education is in the very fabric of history, holding together our lives, our worlds, by a thread. Education is how oppressed groups are liberated, and how, in its absence, liberated groups are oppressed. Peace and prosperity prevail in an enlightened society, while disease and warfare are spread by ignorance. Education can be both weapon and tool and is revealed by the choice of either.

Education has separated black from white, male from female, rich from poor—and then brought these groups together again. Education is a factor in the Human Development Index and is used in the measurement of both economic development and quality of life. Live to the age of eighty-two with a high school diploma or, without one, live to the age of seventy-five. Elections have been won and lost based on a candidate's position on education. Educated armies, such as Gerhard von Scharnhorst's, have helped defeat less educated armies, such as Napoleon's, and altered the course of history.

Like a riddle, education is completely invisible, desired by everyone, and without it, we would die. It is our first luxury, greatest refuge, and last hope.

But lately, we haven't appeared to have one.

When Ipsos Reid surveyed a thousand Canadian adults, only 53 percent could remember the first line of their own national anthem (which begins with the helpful reminder, "O Canada"). Thirty-nine percent of the same group didn't know the year in which Canada became a country (1867), or who its first prime minister was (Sir John A. Macdonald). And these were the questions people answered the best.

This is a country whose prime minister once misspelled the capital city of Nunavut, transforming its meaning from "place of many fish" to "people with unwiped bottoms." Unfortunately for Stephen Harper, this incident only added to the fallout from an earlier one in which the Prime Minister's Office made the simple yet profound error of referring to Canadian Indians as Indo-Canadians.

This is a country where almost three-quarters of southern residents think northern residents live in igloos; where six in ten don't know their rights and freedoms are protected by the Charter of Rights and Freedoms; where a percentage of the population believes the War of 1812 "preserved them from American politics, gun laws and shared citizenship with Snooki of the *Jersey Shore*."

Similarly, when the Intercollegiate Studies Institute surveyed twenty-eight thousand American students from eighty-five colleges and universities—including a number of Ivy Leagues—it found that some 50 percent couldn't name the three branches of federal government (executive, legislative, and judicial). Nearly three thousand students believed "We hold these truths to be self-evident" was a line from *The Communist Manifesto*. As a member of the institute pointed out, with evident shock, "And this was a multiple-choice test, with the answers staring them right in the face."

In fact, in the words of one deputy secretary of education, the United States is "really only a generation or two away from a republic in pretty big trouble." This is because, compared to other countries of the world—even ones that are less advantaged—the United States is completely, almost breathtakingly, mediocre. An assessment from 2010 shows the country in fourteenth place in reading, seventeenth in science, and twenty-fifth in math. By contrast, South Korea is first in reading and math, and third in science; Finland is second in reading and math, and first in science; and Canada is third in reading, and fifth in math and science. The United States is just slightly ahead of Estonia, Slovenia, and Poland (countries that, judging by the above surveys, most American schoolchildren wouldn't be able to locate on a map).

Even without these facts, it's possible to determine a decline in specific kinds of ability. Before Horace Mann and Egerton Ryerson instituted compulsory education; before Carnegie and Rockefeller financed Georg Kerschensteiner's industrial school model; before Abraham Flexner and the rise of low literacy—before there were teachers and tests, buses and bells, students and syllabi; before there was an education system, there was an education.

It wasn't that long ago that a prime minister would not only spell an Inuit word correctly, but perhaps be able to speak a few words of the language. Sir John A. Macdonald could speak Gaelic and Latin as well as English and French. It wasn't that long ago people knew "We hold these truths to be self-evident" came from *The Declaration of Independence*, because it wasn't that long ago that *The Declaration of*

Independence was written. Its primary author, Thomas Jefferson, knew, in varying degrees of fluency, Greek, Latin, French, Spanish, Italian, German, and a handful of Native dialects, in addition to being an accomplished architect, naturalist, musician, and more.

Patricians of the seventeenth and eighteenth centuries were routinely polyglots and polymaths, personalities that border on the extinct today. Even moderately diverse intelligence is a rarity. It doesn't take studies and surveys to sense the world is approaching an epidemic of ignorance. A casual glance at any number of the planet's problems reveals a critical lack of knowledge, and worse, of *understanding*. In a testament of the jadedness of our times, it is no longer a controversial assertion to claim that schools are failing to provide even a basic level of education. Indeed, this has been the refrain for decades.

And here's the thing: mediocrity is costing a fortune. With the exception of Switzerland, the United States spends more money on education than any other country on earth. The cost of educating one American student from kindergarten to the twelfth grade is $149,000. Even after adjusting for inflation, this sum is three times what it was just forty years ago. In the middle of the previous century, the government spent exactly $1,214 on the education of one child for one year (in today's money). Ten years later that number had doubled. Twenty years later it doubled again, and after thirty years it doubled once more. Since 1970, the federal government has spent no less than $1.8 trillion on education—a figure it will undoubtedly repeat and surpass, in an even shorter period of time, in the future.

While Canada is by no means a world-class education provider, it is said to have a better system than its neighbor to the south. More importantly, Canada, as well as Japan, Australia, and the Netherlands, spends less on education than the United States, but gets more in return. From this it is hard not to deduce that in America, the quality and cost of education are inversely correlated. On a plotted graph from 1970 to 2010, US reading, math, and science scores are flat lines, while per-pupil spending is almost literally off the charts. The question is, why?

While the longest-standing and firmest-held explanation is that schools perform badly because of insufficient funding, this is probably not the case.

According to Jay P. Greene, a professor and Century Chair in Education Reform at the University of Arkansas, the idea that more money equals better schools is wrong. "The assertion that schools need more money is so omnipresent that most Americans simply accept the truth of the claim unconsciously," Greene writes in *Education Myths: What Special-Interest Groups Want You to Believe about Our Schools—and Why It Isn't So*. "It is simultaneously the most widely held idea about education in America and the one that is most directly at odds with the available evidence." According to Greene, the American experience of the past three decades "has shown that a lack of resources is not one of the major problems affecting our schools' performance."

But if money isn't the problem, what is?

The question has perplexed and alluded educators for decades. Proposed explanations include bad parenting; lack of moral instruction; outdated textbooks; immigration; an unpleasant learning environment; a curriculum that is either too easy or too difficult; poverty; class size; failure to teach "the whole child"; technology; "the achievement gap"; society itself; too much or too little homework; standardized testing; not enough math and science; not enough theater and music; the political left; the political right; misallocation of funding; religion; and more. In the paradoxically uneducated world of education, every possible proposition has been proposed, from an inherently stupid country to an insufficient number of houseplants in the classroom.

In 1857, the National Education Association was founded.

Initially, the NEA was designed to protect female teachers from unfair and unjust treatment, which ranged from salary and promotional inequality to being forced to take an unpaid two-year leave of absence in the event of a pregnancy. The NEA also protected secretaries from completing a variety of chores for their boss, including "submitting to his amorous advances, fetching his lunch, brewing his coffee and buying gifts for his wife, children and mistresses." Before unions existed, working women could be fired for virtually any reason. A Boston secretary was fired "because she picked up a corned-beef sandwich on white bread instead of the rye her boss had ordered when he dispatched her for his lunch." Another teacher was fired "for refusing to make coffee."

But gradually, the NEA became less of a teachers' union and more—to adapt a quote from William E. Borah—an "insatiable maw of bureaucracy." In 1875, just eighteen years after its founding, the NEA was already being called "a Gigantic Educational Ganglion," and by its hundredth birthday, the organization had 700,000 members, "ranging from kindergarten teachers to college presidents ..." Just before the new millennium, the NEA consisted of a nine-member executive committee, nine-member board of review, 164-member board of directors, 9,044-member representative assembly, 50-person government relations staff, and 550-member staff in Washington, DC. There was 1 executive office with 42 subordinate offices, 19 standing and special committees, and 13,000 local affiliates.

Today, the NEA is the largest professional union in the United States. It is responsible for most of the country's 4 million teachers—including their tenure.

Back in 1887, when the NEA held its first conference, it was decided that the core role of the new union would be ensuring a teacher's job security.

Tenure would be awarded to professors following a number of short-term contracts and via a review of the teacher's competency and effectiveness. Once granted, tenure would guarantee the academic freedom professors needed in order to do their jobs without worry of being fired.

But by the beginning of the twentieth century, tenure had been extended to public schools and almost simultaneously transformed into a political issue. At a Democratic Party convention in New York, it was one of the headlining themes:

> We recognize in the existing process of appointment
> and removal of the teachers in the public schools of the
> State a constant menace to the well-being and effective
> service of instructors of our youth, and a detriment and
> obstacle to the progress of their pupils, and we pledge
> ourselves to the enactment of a tenure of office law that
> shall correct the present conditions, and we deprecate
> the tendency manifested by the Republican Party of
> dragging the public school system of the State into
> politics.

In the words of William Bennett, the NEA became "the absolute heart and center" of the Democratic political platform. In fact, it was allegedly the NEA that petitioned Jimmy Carter to establish the Department of Education in 1979. Since then, the NEA and the American Federation of Teachers (AFT)—the second-largest teacher union in the United States—have been the largest campaign contributors in the country. Together, the organizations have donated fifty-five million dollars in the last twenty years, 90 percent of which has gone to the Democratic Party.

Next to abortion, same-sex marriage, and the role of government, few issues are more politically divisive than teachers' tenure. While Republicans oppose the bureaucratic protectionism of teacher unions, which makes it virtually impossible to fire bad teachers, Democrats feel the need to safeguard what is generally perceived as an endangered, difficult, and underappreciated profession. Resolving this seemingly unresolvable dispute appears to be an important step in the remaking of public education.

Today, tenure is granted without much (if any) discretion. In the United States, over 98 percent of teachers are awarded tenure within two years of being hired. The criteria for awarding tenure are apparently not all that challenging. In school board districts that use simple evaluation ratings, over 99 percent of teachers are "satisfactory." Districts that use a slightly broader range still judge 94 percent of their teachers to be in the top two rating categories, and less than 1 percent "unsatisfactory."

As has been pointed out elsewhere, doctors and lawyers are far more likely to lose their licenses than teachers. Cases of teacher incompetence resolve more slowly than cases of people facing the death penalty. Teaching is clouded by some of the thickest bureaucracy of any profession on the planet, and it's easy to see why: tenure is "academic freedom plus job security all rolled nicely into one union contract," according to *Time*, which called due process "the holy grail" of the teaching profession.

Because unions have made it exceedingly hard to fire bad teachers, local school officials often devise creative ways of getting rid of their worst professionals. Teachers, staff, and even principals may be transferred from school to school, in what is variously called "passing the trash," "the turkey trot," or—perhaps most memorably—"the dance of the lemons." Rather than attempting to fire bad staff, ineffective teachers and other tenured officials of untold thousands are danced out of one school and into another. As Brendan Menuey, an assistant principal in Virginia, summarized for *Maclean's*, "I believe passionately that we need to get rid of these folks, but I'll be honest, because of the time and difficulty in getting what you need, I'm inclined, when [another] principal calls me, to just say, 'She's a fabulous teacher.'"

In 2007, Menuey asked teachers to rank nineteen administrative strategies that "deal with incompetence." The top choice was "voluntary transfer to another school," while actual, legal dismissal was fifth from the bottom. The study concluded, "There is a significant discrepancy between estimated rates of incompetent teachers and the number of teachers actually dismissed on grounds of incompetence." While 5 percent of the total workforce is professionally incompetent, tenured American teachers are—officially—one-tenth of 1 percent incompetent.

The problem is not unique to the States. In Canada, just 27 of Ontario's 200,000 licensed teachers, or .002 percent, have been terminated due to incompetence since 2004. In the same time period, no full-time teachers have been let go in Montreal and Winnipeg; in Saskatoon, only one has. In Britain, a public investigation into the teaching profession found that 300 of the country's 500,000 teachers— or .07 percent—were professionally incompetent. In New Zealand, an organization called the Secondary Principals' Association discovered teachers "so lacking in literacy and numeracy they can't write adequate reports or do primary-school maths." Nevertheless, of the 174 cases brought before the association, only one resulted in deregistration of a teacher.

Between 2007 and 2010, 88 of New York City's 80,000 schoolteachers, or .1 percent, lost their jobs due to incompetent performance. A fraction of this fraction was summoned to a number of nondescript office buildings in the five boroughs. The offices are known as "rubber rooms"—suggestive of the padded walls of a mental asylum—and at their peak held over 600 of the city's teachers, who were awaiting disciplinary hearings for offenses that ranged from general incompetence to sexual misconduct. The average length of stay was three years—or eight times longer than the average criminal case—during which teachers did the same thing each day, "which is pretty much nothing at all," according to Steven Brill.

While rubber rooms were officially closed in 2010, they were during their heyday "as boring and unpleasant as possible." Because of union bureaucracy that forbids the state from firing these teachers, the hope was simply that they would be bored into quitting.

They weren't.

While continuing to receive full salaries, rubber room teachers slept, played cards, watched TV—whatever they felt like—from 8:15 in the morning until 3:15 in the afternoon. The cost of continuing to employ these teachers, many of whom had seniority and were earning close to maximum salary, was $65 million a year. While she spent three years awaiting her verdict, one kindergarten teacher from Manhattan was paid over $300,000. But the longest-serving occupant was a math teacher from Queen's who was in a rubber room for seven years, cost the government an estimated $659,078, and had been accused of sexually molesting two students, after allegedly impregnating and then marrying a third.

———————

In 2008, a professor at Stanford University asked a question that no one had bothered to ask before. As Eric Hanushek phrased it at the time, "How much progress in student achievement could be accomplished by instituting a program of removing, or deselecting, the least effective teachers?"

The answer, it turns out, is a lot.

In the chorus of discourse—the endless list of solutions to the endless list of problems—Hanushek had found a simple truth: that if the bottom 6 to 10 percent of teachers were eliminated, "we could bring the average US student up to the level of Finland, which is at the top of the world today." In a school of thirty average teachers, getting rid of even two or three could "boost student achievement up to the Canadian level."

But Hanushek made another discovery. Good teachers have an economic as well as educative effect on their students. As he told the organization StudentsFirst, "If you take a teacher in the top quarter of effectiveness and compare that with an average teacher, a teacher in the top quarter generated $400,000 more income for her students over the course of their lifetime." Hanushek found that if the United States replaced 5 percent of the worst teachers with teachers who were merely average, "achievement would rise to somewhere between Canada and Finland."

Politicians have started listening to Hanushek and to the growing number of educators who are unhappy with the difficulty of getting rid of incompetent teachers.

Beginning in 2010, states have begun reforming public school tenure. In March of that year, the Senate proposed a bill "that would make Florida the first state to abolish tenure ..." Other states soon followed. By the first two months of 2012, similar bills had been proposed in Tennessee, New Jersey, New York, Connecticut, Minnesota, Virginia, and half a dozen other states. Instead of a system in which pay is defined by teachers' seniority (how long they've been working), the country is moving toward a system in which pay is defined by teachers' merit (how good they are in the classroom). While each state has a different interpretation of what this new approach will look like, the main idea is that bad teachers will be funneled out of the system and that this will be to the benefit of everyone.

In Canada, Kevin Falcon, the deputy premier of British Columbia, became the first politician to propose the idea of merit pay. While reforms have yet to make it through the legislative process, the country is not far behind the United States in moving toward a merit-based system. But even as the new approach was gaining momentum, critics were already pointing out a problem: until the merit system has been implemented, we won't know for certain that it's effective. In other words, like every other hypothesis—from the idea that we need more houseplants in the classroom to the idea that we're somehow not spending enough on education as it is—Hanushek's hunch is just that: an educated guess.

HOMEWORK

Sean O'Toole is an exceptional teacher.

With over twenty years' experience at a public high school in Ontario, he has been recognized by the Trillium Lakelands District School Board for his handpicked curriculum, and by the wider community for his down-to-earth teaching style.

While yearbooks attest to his popularity with students, and the respect he commands from other teachers is palpable, O'Toole's tendency to cut through the fog of pedagogical bureaucracy has led to the occasional dispute with administrators, who don't appreciate his taking things into his own hands.

After discovering that students' academic records were kept in an office cabinet, O'Toole carted them back to his classroom, where he gave the files to students to read at their leisure. These were the

Ontario Student Records, containing every educational document from junior kindergarten forward. O'Toole felt that since the information in the files technically belonged to the students, the files should be theirs for the reading. Upon learning what he'd done, however, the school's secretaries felt otherwise.

When I visited O'Toole on a cold night in the new year, we sat around his kitchen table talking about some of the obstacles of his profession.

"What you have for a chunk of time is all these kids looking to you to take them on some kind of a journey, to explore some neat ideas and get them excited about something, whether it's the Louisiana Purchase or the reason why boiling water turns to steam." O'Toole says that sometimes a school's managers can make it hard for teachers to excite their students because they don't see the teaching profession in abstract terms. "Education is an art, not a measurable science. How do you measure this stuff? How do you measure matters of the heart?"

At the elementary and secondary levels, administrators both create and regulate the public school curriculum. They tell teachers what they're going to teach, and how they're going to teach it. This can have the effect of making teachers feel like education dispensers, rather than artists or craftspeople who have a unique personality and skills honed by years of hard work. O'Toole describes the ideal teacher as someone who's "gone down that road and discovered some cool stuff and wants to throw it your way. It's foolish for a teacher, and dangerous, to put it all on a SMART Board—Lesson 1, Lesson 2, Lesson 3—and do it for twenty-five years straight."

Anyone who's ever been in a room with a teacher like O'Toole can feel the electricity, the energetic charge that takes place as teacher and students interact. But like students who actually get an education from school, teachers who succeed at their jobs are often doing so in spite of the system, and not because of it.

At the core of any school system in the world, public or private, kindergarten or university, is its administration. Undergirding Ontario's 4,931 public elementary and secondary schools are 72 school boards. Each board has a director who talks to the Ministry of Education, which employs a small army of bureaucrats in a hierarchy that is bewildering to comprehend on paper, let alone in practice: at the top is the minister of education, who has a deputy minister, who communicates with eight primary divisions, each of which has at least three subdivisions, with names like the "Ontario Internal Audit Education Audit Service Team," and the "Student Success/Learning to 18 Implementation, Training & Evaluation Branch." In 2011, there were over 1,700 people working in such offices.

While education is technically decentralized in both Canada and the United States—meaning that it's up to provinces and states to manage their own school districts—the chief educational entities in either country are intimately connected with the federal government. As a product of the cabinet, which is composed of executive-branch officers of the federal government, the United States Department of Education has 28 offices beneath the Office of the Secretary. In total, the department employs some 5,000 people whose job is to create the programs used by almost 16,000 school districts, for some 49 million students attending 98,000 public schools (and 28,000 private ones).

With both countries moving toward increased federalization, the number of administrative offices between the top and bottom can only increase, making the work done by teachers even more difficult.

O'Toole says that at the 150 staff meetings he's attended in two decades of teaching, not once has anyone mentioned "getting good material." Instead, the meetings focus on short-term programs designed by data-minded administrators who don't understand the artistry of teaching, and who only want to increase the district's reading, math, and science scores. "If you've got someone breathing down your neck trying to push a flavor-of-the-day agenda, and if all you've got is your eye on the end game, which is the literacy test scores, that's the tail wagging the dog."

So what if it were the other way around?

In 1974, Ray Budde presented a paper to the Society of General Systems Research.

Until that year, Budde had led a seemingly uneventful life. He was a recently retired assistant professor at the University of Massachusetts. Before that he was an assistant principal in Michigan, and before that, a seventh-grade English teacher. He was educated at state schools, had few professional accomplishments, and lived the quiet life of an academic. But Budde had evidently spent great periods of time in contemplation.

In his paper, "Education by Charter," Budde put forward a simple idea: schools would work better if they had less interference from the state and union, and emphasized quality of teaching. The word *charter* was chosen because it conjured the idea of a temporary, specific arrangement between two parties, and not the longstanding partnerships of regular public schools, which tended to get in the way of genuine learning. "Under a charter system," Budde wrote, "no program, course, or service can continue year after year without being judged for its effectiveness in meeting its stated objectives."

This was a radical idea.

For the first time in the history of North American academia, Budde was implying not only that there was a distinction between school and education, but that there didn't have to be. What's more, he personally had the answer: charter schools would work based on the direct appeal of teachers to school boards, removing "the two or three layers of 'administration' that have evolved between teachers and school boards over the last 150 years ..." The charter would be signed by both parties; then teachers would have a limited number of years to carry it out. Since the schools would be operated independently of government and union, money could be spent wherever the teachers saw fit, and since their own jobs were constantly at risk, it was in their best interest to be good at what they did.

Not surprisingly, when Budde first presented his paper, no one paid it the slightest bit of attention. Here was an unknown educator from Michigan calling for an entirely new school model, simply because he thought it was a good idea. Then one day, in 1988, something strange happened. As the story goes, Budde's wife opened the morning paper and gasped. In a column called "Where We Stand," Albert Shanker, then president of the American Federation of Teachers, had not only mentioned charter schools but proposed their legislation at the National Press Club earlier that year. Shanker had even paid homage to Budde for coming up with the name.

And so it was that with Shanker's support, the charter school model began to be taken seriously. This was, and is, an irony few commentators have failed to mention: at the time, Shanker was the head of the second-biggest union in the country, with nearly a million tenured teachers. The AFT, and even Shanker himself, embodied precisely the bureaucracy Budde was calling on legislators to eliminate. But Shanker was an unusually radical leader. "One of the things that discourages people from bringing about change in schools is the experience of having that effort stopped for no good reason," he has been quoted as saying. His endorsement of Budde's idea represented his way of effecting change.

There was only one problem.

Soon after Shanker saw the potential of charter schools, so did a number of other people. A Minnesota think tank began tinkering with the charter model's specifics, as did Joe Nathan and Ted Kolderie, two senior fellows at the University of Minnesota's Humphrey School of Public Affairs. Where Budde and Shanker had envisioned a vastly decentralized school run by teachers—in effect, a public private school—Nathan and Kolderie wanted outside agencies to come in and handle the school's affairs, essentially outsourcing the role of upper management to the highest bidder. According to Paul E. Peterson, "That opened charter doors not only to teachers but also to outside entrepreneurs."

This alteration of the original idea was so displeasing to Shanker and Budde that they independently renounced the Nathan-Kolderie model. Unfortunately, in 1991, the revised charter school proposal was legislated into being. Nevertheless, as was noted at the time of Budde's death, for a seventh-grade public school teacher to have come up with the idea of charter schools was a profound accomplishment. As Ted Kolderie himself put it, Budde had changed the face of education, "just on his own, thinking about it."

Today, charter schooling has become the fastest-growing segment of public education in America.

Since 2002, the number of charter school students has tripled, from over half a million to almost two million. At the present time, California alone has 941 charter schools, 114 of which opened in 2011. The Nathan-Kolderie model has won wide acceptance and praise from everyone from parents to the federal government. It's been called "a cornerstone of the Obama administration's education strategy," and said to bring bipartisanship to a divided political climate.

While Canada has been slower to accept a charter school model, recent history indicates that may be changing. Since 2009, Toronto has gone from being a city full of traditionally funded, traditionally managed schools to one in which dozens of alternatives are available. And in 2011, the District School Board of Niagara opened the DSBN Academy, a school for low-income students whose parents don't have a post-secondary education. While some praised the idea as providing an opportunity for disadvantaged students, others saw it as another splinter in the already fractured public school system.

In fact, despite the popularity of the Nathan-Kolderie model, critics are pointing to more serious flaws: namely that charter schooling, as it's presently manifest, has little in the way of scientific value. Taking a particular group of students—typically low-income, ethnic minorities from uneducated, working-class families—and putting them in a specialty school, where teachers can cater to their demographic, has been shown to have a minimal or even negative effect more often than a positive one. Charter schools, it seems, don't work.

The research began in 2003, when Jay P. Greene, Greg Forster, and Marcus A. Winters wrote a paper for the Center for Civic Innovation at the Manhattan Institute. "Assessing the academic performance of charter schools is difficult," wrote the authors, "because many charter schools are targeted toward specific populations such as at-risk students, disabled students, and juvenile delinquents." Comparing charter and regular public schools is "like comparing apples and zebras." The two systems comprise different demographics, and represent separate and opposing pedagogical approaches.

Eventually, in what became the first national study of its kind, the authors were able to remove these differences by comparing charter schools that had general student populations with the nearest traditional neighborhood school, and thus compare "apples to apples." What they found was surprising. While charter school students' performance was measurably higher, it was so by only a fraction of one standard deviation in both reading and math, equivalent to just a couple of percentile points. In conclusion, they found "positive effects from charter schools serving general populations, but for the most part these effects were modest in size."

Another major study was conducted in 2009 and published by Stanford University's Center for Research on Education Outcomes. The researchers observed almost three-quarters of all charter school students in the US and, like Greene and colleagues, found negligible improvement. While a small percentage of students surveyed outperformed their traditionally schooled peers, the report noted, "Nearly half of the charter schools nationwide have results that are no different from the local public school options and over a third, 37 percent, deliver learning results that are significantly worse ..." Overall, the researchers concluded that charter schools had "a slightly negative" impact on their students.

Yet despite these findings, educators have been reluctant to disregard the possibility that charter schools are the solution to the problems of North American education.

In the documentary film *Waiting for Superman*, director Davis Guggenheim celebrates Geoffrey Canada's "Harlem Children's Zone," and the successful KIPP schools of David Levin and Michael Feinberg, both of which represent experimental forays into chartered education. Guggenheim was clearly in favor of charter schools, even after acknowledging that only one in five get truly "amazing results." This apparent paradox prompted Diane Ravitch—once a charter school advocate—to all but rant to *The New York Times*, in an article that calls the Guggenheim film "propagandistic."

In fact, following the release of *Waiting for Superman*, education discourse seemed to settle on a negative view of charter schooling overall. When *The New York Times* invited Geoffrey Canada and Michael Goldstein, who founded the Match Charter Public School in Boston, to defend themselves in front of a national audience, they pointed out that, while charter schooling may not be a universally successful model, "For parents in devastated neighborhoods such as Harlem, the decision to send their child to the local failure factory or a successful charter school is no choice." In other words, in certain instances, for certain families of certain socioeconomic backgrounds, a chartered education makes more sense.

But for a school model to be truly successful, it has to work anywhere: it has to be as effective for students in the Trillium Lakelands District School Board as it is for students in Harlem. Even as it continues to flourish in the United States and Canada, it's clear even to advocates that the Nathan-Kolderie model isn't the solution everyone was hoping it would be. But if not charter schools, then what?

The classic debate, of course, is public versus private.

For most of the last thirty years, private schools were thought to be categorically superior. Beginning in 2002, the National Assessment of Educational Progress reported that "private school students generally perform higher than their public school counterparts on standardized achievements tests." Moreover, private school students were found to be more likely to complete advanced-level academic coursework, and more likely to finish an advanced degree by the age of twenty-five.

This fit with most people's impression: that private schools are inherently better, either because they have more money, better teachers, or some combination of factors public schools do not. But more recently, studies have begun showing that this is not the case.

In 2006, Educational Testing Service and the United States Department of Education compared the math and reading scores of fourth- and eighth-grade students from both public and private institutions. The result was that "children in public schools generally performed as well or better in reading and mathematics than comparable children in private schools." To arrive at this conclusion, researchers had to remove such adverse factors as race, income, and social background: "When student-level covariates are included in the model, the difference in adjusted averages between private and public schools is not significantly different from zero." In other words, public schools were only equal to private ones under certain conditions.

The following year, the nonpartisan, Washington-based Center on Education Policy studied a thousand low-income students who attend public urban high schools, and found they "did as well academically and on long-term indicators as their peers from private high schools ..." But like the 2006 study, researchers first removed such factors as parental expectation, income, and eighth-grade test scores. "When these were taken into account, the private-school advantage went away." After effectively nullifying their own report, researchers nevertheless managed to find the audacity to claim that, better than either public or academically private schools, were "Catholic schools run by holy orders such as the Jesuits."

The problem, of course, is that when it comes to public and private schooling, a student's background is the whole point. When researchers remove criteria like income and parental education levels, they're removing the primary determining factors in a student's success. Private schools such as Exeter and Andover, UCC and Appleby College, were built for privileged students, and taking that out of the equation ignores their history, mandate, and purpose. A statistically neutered student from one system might outperform a statistically neutered student from the other, but by then a larger point has been missed: that when it comes to an education—when it comes to something as precious and precarious and extraordinary—everything counts.

If private schools can't be compared to public ones, are there two systems that can? Waldorf and Montessori share some similarities: both attract parents who want an education for the "whole child," head, heart, and soul. Unfortunately, in terms of comparing the two approaches objectively, no studies exist. While at first this would appear to be an oversight, since both education systems are manifest in the public as well as private categories, not to mention charter and magnet, posing the question of which is better, Montessori or Waldorf, is just another way of asking if private is better than public. The answer is that they are different systems, with different students for whom there is a different agenda.

Then there are the homeschoolers. While many studies have been conducted that contrast home- and public schoolers, it hasn't been until fairly recently that a consensus seems to have developed within the academic community, beginning, in 1999, with a study of over twenty thousand homeschooled students. The results showed the homeschoolers' median scores on standardized tests were in the seventieth to eightieth percentile, or 20 to 30 percent above the American national average. Notably, the study also found that five thousand of those same homeschoolers were one or more grades above their age level in both public *and* private schools.

In 2008, it was reported that homeschool students "score 15 to 30 percent higher on standardized tests than their public school counterparts …" By the following year, the number had jumped to between 34 and 39 percent—or at least this was the claim of Brian D. Ray. As founder and president of the National Home Education Research Institute, Ray very seriously claimed his study had shown that homeschoolers "consistently outperform their public school peers. Even with variables that are linked to higher or lower levels of student achievement in public schools—such as whether a parent is college educated—homeschoolers still score well above the norm."

There was just one catch. Ray had been commissioned by Michael Farris.

In the kitchen of his home, O'Toole returned a bottle of ale to the counter. "What it all comes down to is this: get out of the way."

O'Toole is an exceptional teacher because he knows that getting out of the way is what good teachers do. Decent or bad teachers have no incentive to deviate from the path of ministry-made material. "Instead of taking a chance with something exciting that can genuinely grab kids and give them a reason to get excited about going to your class, they're just going to play it safe, and the kids will turn off. And it'll just be one more lousy education that won't be an education at all."

Ray Budde's idea of education by charter is like Hanushek's hypothesis that removing the worst teachers—the teachers who play it safe, the teachers who deliver a lousy education—would improve the overall level of education. Both make intuitive sense: fewer bad teachers means fewer students are receiving a bad education, and a less bureaucratic system means more teachers are able to deliver a good one. Despite how these ideas are implemented—in charter schools or in a merit-instead-of-tenure system—they are, in essence, seemingly good. But are they good enough? Are they enough to transform a nineteenth-century school model into a twenty-first-century system of education?

The answer is probably no. With all the reforms and reformers, the studies and reports, the findings and debates, one or two ideas probably won't make the difference we need—the difference that will give all students an education, not just the ones who survive the system, not just the ones lucky enough to have a teacher like O'Toole. If change is going to come to the system, it has to come from within; it has to transform every aspect of schooling, from the inside out. "It all comes back to the Prussian military model," O'Toole says. "That is at the foundation of our education system."

The Prussian public school model is the original system of education. It's where most people get their education and most people don't. It has more students than all the other systems combined. It has obtained universality: public schools in the Trillium Lakelands District School Board are the same as public schools in Harlem, or Hartford, or Harvard. In structure, the public school system in the Faroe Islands is the same as the public school system in Fiji. It follows the same design. It has the same characteristics. It produces the same overall effect. And it hasn't changed in almost two hundred years.

THE END OF HISTORY?

After Prussia helped defeat Napoleon at the Battle of Waterloo, the world wanted the answer to a single question: how did they do it?

Until recently, Prussia had been a ghost of its former self: its money was gone, its land was halved, and its people were broken. Such had been the defeat of Prussia at the hands of Napoleon that Hegel had called it "the end of history." But thanks to the Treaty of Tilsit, it had no future either: it could keep only forty-two thousand soldiers, a mere fraction of what it had before.

Then Gerhard von Scharnhorst had convinced the government to educate its army. To circumvent the number cap, Scharnhorst had cleverly devised a new system, the *Krümpersystem*, which trained soldiers as students. While the army would never grow beyond forty-two thousand troops, it would have an endless supply of new recruits with which to replenish itself.

But the *Krümpersystem* was only half the equation.

Spurred on by the philosopher Johann Fichte, Prussia had become the first country to institutionalize the learning process. Using both a compulsory system of military training, and a compulsory system of education, the whole country had been converted into an army—a single mass of people who didn't think for themselves or question their orders. School in particular had the effect of converting students into soldiers or citizens or whatever else its regulators desired. With such a system, Prussia had risen from the ashes, its people united, and defeated Napoleon—an almost unimaginable comeback.

Now other people wanted that power for themselves.

———————

In the summer of 1831, Victor Cousin traveled to Berlin.

The Battle of Waterloo had been fought fifteen years before, and Napoleon had been dead for ten. Word had leaked that the secret of Prussia's success was its system of education, and as a member of the Royal Council of Public Instruction, it was Cousin's job to figure out if France should use the same model.

In his 333-page "Report on the State of Public Instruction in Prussia," Cousin strongly recommended that France adopt the Prussian system. As was reasoned at the time, "We constantly imitate England ... why, then, should we blush to borrow something from kind, honest, pious, learned Germany ...?"

Cousin wasn't recommending that France borrow some small part of the Prussian education system, but the system itself. The system was what made Prussia different from France, England, and the rest. As early as 1736—some ninety-five years before Cousin's visit—Prussia had some semblance of organized schooling, but at the time it was an offshoot of the Church. Cousin was reporting on the fact that, by making education a branch of the government, and not the Church, Prussia had institutionalized all learning. This was what he was now urging France to do: adopt the Prussian *system* of education.

It was no small task.

Central to the Prussian system were four key points: First, a branch of the government, called the Ministry of Public Instruction, was now in charge of the country's education. For the first time in over a thousand years of Christian rule, the Church no longer dictated what people did and did not learn—that was now the government's domain. Second, there were to be different grade levels, with qualified teachers for each. Third, each municipal district would have its own schools, and finally, students would be required to attend them by law. Until then, no other country in the modern world had made school compulsory. No other country had an education *system*.

Each of these parts, of course, had plenty of subparts. For instance, to build schools in each municipal district required money. This money would be collected from taxpayers—or more specifically, land owners who paid tax—with minimal support from the federal government. To have separate grades required separate scholastic stages, with primary education lasting eight years, secondary education lasting four, and technical or higher education beyond that. Moreover, there was now ministry-approved coursework, ministry-approved teachers, and ministry-approved grading. Depending on a student's marks in school, he would be steered in the direction of employment that best represented his ability (or as it was thought at the time, his intelligence).

Cousin's report, which contained these observations and more, was deeply influential. It led to the French primary education law of 1833—"the foundation upon which a national system of elementary education was developed in France ..." And that was just the beginning. In 1834, Cousin's "Report on the State of Public Instruction in Prussia" was translated into English. The translator was a woman named Sarah Austin who, in a lengthy preface to Cousin's report, helped build momentum for the adoption of the Prussian model in the United States. When the head of the public education system in Michigan, John D. Pierce, assumed office, he created the same centralized vision advocated by Cousin, and remarked that it was Cousin who had inspired him to do so.

Following Cousin's return to France, an American named Calvin E. Stowe also went to Prussia, and came back to give "the clearest and the most succinct account of the Prussian school system to be found in American literature …" In 1837, Stowe submitted his "Report on Elementary Public Instruction in Europe to the Governor and Legislature of Ohio." Like Victor Cousin, Stowe admired the "perfect order, neatness, and frugality" of the Prussian education system. "It is impossible to contemplate the system without admiring the completeness and beauty of the plan," he noted. Like Cousin, Stowe was a persuasive writer: the Ohio legislature is said to have ordered 8,500 copies of Stowe's report—or one for each of the state's school board districts.

In 1837, Horace Mann was appointed secretary of the Massachusetts Board of Education. For five months in 1843, he toured, among other countries, England, Ireland, Belgium, Holland, France, and Prussia. As was noted at the time, "Among the nations of Europe, Prussia has long enjoyed the most distinguished reputation for excellence of its schools." These schools were "models for the imitation of the rest of Christendom." Published in 1844, Mann's "Report of an Educational Tour in Germany, and Parts of Great Britain and Ireland" has since become known as "The Seventh Annual Report." These as well as Mann's other studies led to the adoption of the Prussian school system throughout the United States.

Beginning in 1844, Egerton Ryerson spent fourteen months in the United States and Europe. His job, like that of Cousin, Stowe, and Mann, was to find "the most efficient system of Instruction" and bring it back to his own country. He found such a system in Prussia. After making the customary school inspections, meeting with the minister of public instruction, and watching ten thousand soldiers march through Berlin, Ryerson returned home to publish his findings as "A System of Public Elementary Instruction for Upper Canada, 1846." The impact of Ryerson's report was such that it led to both common-school legislation for European Canadians, and residential-school legislation for the Native ones.

In the 1850s, Britain sent Mark Pattison to Prussia, in order to bring back "an authoritative account of German Education ..." Like the reformers before him, Pattison was impressed by "the substantial administrative structure" of the Prussian school model, and recommended it to his commissioners. Published in 1861, the so-called Newcastle Report led to the Elementary Education Act of 1870. The administrative system of Prussia was now implemented in Britain: 2,500 school boards were established, with further legislative additions—compulsory attendance, funding through taxation—accumulating over the following decades.

With the Prussian model's adoption in France, the United States, Canada, and Britain, the rest of the world soon followed: Japan, Italy, New Zealand, Russia, Austria, even Thailand and the Philippines. Today, any country with the four originating principles—a devoted governmental branch; qualified, state-employed teachers for each grade; schools in every municipality; and students who legally have to attend them—uses the Prussian school system. Which isn't to suggest there was an absence of opposition.

The nineteenth-century travel writer Samuel Laing argued that the Prussian model was "a deception practised for the paltry political end of rearing the individual to be part and parcel of an artificial and despotic system of government, of training him to be either its instrument or its slave, according to his social station." Laing had spent some time in Prussia, and watched as one reformer after another visited the country. "They have only looked at the obvious, almost mechanical means of diffusing instruction. In their admiration of the wheels and machinery, these literary men have forgotten *to look under the table, and see what kind of web all this was producing.*"

The problem, the web, was that while it looked like school was giving people an education, it actually wasn't. This too was George Brown's perception when Egerton Ryerson adopted the Prussian model in Canada. From November 1846 to February 1847, Brown and others assailed Ryerson in Toronto's newspapers. Public schooling was said "to prepare the minds of the rising generation for submitting to despotism." Because education was now in the hands of the government, and the government decided what was taught, it could convert "the mind of men into a mass of plastic material to be operated on by a central power, and turned to whatever purpose."

British papers were similarly opposed, "not merely calling in question, but strongly denouncing, the whole plan of education in Prussia, as being not only designed to produce, but as actually producing, a spirit of blind acquiescence to arbitrary power ..." The Prussian model was "a system of education adapted to enslave, and not to enfranchise, the human mind." In a work entitled *The Age of Great Cities*, Robert Vaughn, a minister and professor of history at the University of London, warned that public schools could become "engines of oppression," run by the government to "serve its own evil purpose ..."

Vaughn even noted the original purpose of school: to convert students into soldiers. "Thus, in Prussia, every man is a soldier, and the whole country is as a camp." School was likened to a kind of factory, whose products were useful only to a point, at which time they became disposable. "Men were counted as so much machinery, as such they were to obey, as such they were to be used, and as such were they reckoned when they were worn out or destroyed."

Despite these criticisms, the desire to be in possession of such a machine was overwhelming. A system that was powerful enough to train soldiers could achieve other aims as well: it could produce a compliant citizenry, an educated labor pool, a pious clergy. These were the initial objectives sought by reformers—and the governments who commissioned them were willing to fight for it. Critics of the Prussian model were defeated, and by the following century, the whole thing was forgotten. By the time school entered the modern era, it had achieved ubiquity, while its own history—understandably, perhaps—was never taught inside its classrooms.

This has been the story of school.

If there is a moral to the story, perhaps it could be summarized the following way: When Prussians needed an army, they invented schools. When governments needed voters, students became citizens, and when capital was needed, citizens became workers. When the governments went to war, workers became soldiers, and when governments called for peace, soldiers went back to work.

When schools stopped teaching Greek and Latin, high literacy began to fall. When schools started teaching shop and home ec, low literacy began to rise. When a middle class was needed, there were schools for the general public, and when an upper class was needed, there were schools for a privileged few.

When universities needed money they went to corporations, who gave it to them in exchange for science. When science was applied to learning, knowledge became information, and wisdom was history.

And we wonder why there's so little education.

Over the course of this book, we've heard about people whose desire it was to shape students, not give them an education. This has led to a system in which *training* and *educating* are treated as synonymous terms. In considering the extent of this problem, it's difficult not to arrive at a seemingly paradoxical conclusion: the emergence of school has appeared to result not in the diffusion of enlightenment but in its tamping out. Instead of awakening our minds and hearts—and piquing our curiosity—school seems to have had the opposite effect. Examples of this may be found in either the present or the past: in the type of education we have today or the type of education we seem to have had not that long ago.

Before the Newcastle Report made school compulsory in Britain, the Royal Commission sent Matthew Arnold to visit a lyceum in Toulouse, where "In the sixth, or lowest class, the boys have to learn French, Latin, and Greek Grammar, and their reading is Cornelius, Nepos, and Phaedrus, and, along with the fables of Phaedrus, those of La Fontaine."

> For the next, or fifth class, the reading is Ovid in Latin, Lucian's *Dialogues and Isocrates* in Greek, and *Télémaque* in French. For the fourth ... Virgil in Latin and Xenophon in Greek; in French, Voltaire's *Charles XII*. For the third, Sallust and Cicero are added in Latin; Homer and Plutarch's *Moralia* in Greek; in French, Voltaire's *Siècle de Louis XIV*, Massilon's *Petit Carême*, Boileau, and extracts from Buffon. For the second class ... Horace, Livy, and Tacitus in Latin; in Greek, Sophocles and Euripides, Plato and Demosthenes; in French, Bossuet's *Histoire Universelle*, and Montesquieu's *Grandeur et Décadence des Romains*.

And that wasn't even the highest class. There, chemistry, physics, and mathematics were also taught, as well as history, geography, natural science, botany, zoology, physiology, and the language arts, in addition to the usual recitations from the New Testament (in both Latin and Greek).

Yet—and here's the salient point—this wasn't all that different from anywhere else.

In the United States in 1851, a year before education was institutionalized, one college was teaching philosophy, rhetoric, math, the natural sciences, physics, chemistry, economics, history, geography, bookkeeping, literature in three languages, grammar, logic, arithmetic, geometry, algebra, mythology, and more. In Canada in 1865, before there was a widespread system of education, a women's academy in Ottawa was teaching the harp, guitar, piano, melodeon, and organ, as well as painting and drawing, in addition to "the theory and practice of domestic economy," business, literature, and languages. In contrast to today, these subjects appeared to constitute an actual education—they broadened the mind, they enriched the spirit.

In the nineteenth century, popular books included *Wuthering Heights*, *Sense and Sensibility*, and *The Picture of Dorian Gray*. By the twenty-first, it was *The Hunger Games*, *Twilight*, and *Harry Potter*. The twentieth president of the United States, James Garfield, could write in two foreign languages simultaneously, one with each hand; its forty-third president, George W. Bush, seemed to have enough trouble with the one he was given. The fifteenth prime minister of Canada, Pierre Elliott Trudeau, was a renowned intellectual, poised extemporaneous speaker, and wide reader; its twenty-second prime minister, Stephen Harper, didn't once respond to author Yann Martel's four-year-long campaign to get him to read a single book.

Today, one in ten Canadian students have "a capacity to deal only with simple, clear material involving uncomplicated tasks." Twenty percent of the country's university graduates have skills "adequate to cope with the demands of everyday life …" and nothing more. In fact, nearly 15 percent of the population can't read the writing on a medicine bottle. In 2006, a survey by Statistics Canada found that 42 percent of Canadians are semi-illiterate. In 2009, the figure was 48 percent, or twelve million people, and by 2031, the number is expected to rise to over fifteen million.

And Canada is one of the best-educated countries on earth.

In the United States, nearly half of its eighteen- to twenty-four-year-olds don't read books for pleasure. In 1982, more than 80 percent of college graduates read literature (novels, short stories, plays, or poetry); twenty years later it had dropped to 67 percent. Within roughly the same period of time, the percentage of seventeen-year-olds who didn't read when they didn't have to doubled, while in the span of just ten years, the percentage of eighteen- to forty-four-year-olds who read a book fell seven points. Between 2006 and 2007, just 47 percent of American adults read a single work of literature. As a report by the National Endowment for the Arts concluded, "Literacy reading (has) declined in both genders, across all education levels, and in virtually all age groups."

Culture, wisdom, and ancient knowledge are also in decline.

Over 40 percent of the world's languages are currently endangered. The world loses one of its languages every 14 days. Of the 7,000 spoken today, more than half will be extinct by century's end. Eighty percent of the globe's population speaks just 80 languages, while 0.2 percent keeps the remaining ones alive. Australia was once the home of 700 languages; today it has 150, and only 20 are in constant use. Canada has over 50 Aboriginal languages, but just 3 are considered strong enough to survive. While globalization is said to be the main factor in language death, other considerations include "war, ethnic cleansing and compulsory schooling in a national tongue."

But still there's more.

Today, the rate of plant and animal extinction is a hundred to a thousand times the historic average. Not in sixty-five million years has life been so rapidly expunged from Earth. By 2050, it's estimated that 15 to 37 percent of all currently existing species will be extinct. A child born today could witness the obliteration of half the total plant and animal species within his or her lifetime. At the beginning of the twentieth century, there were a hundred thousand tigers in China; at the beginning of the twenty-first, there were approximately twenty. In Kenya, lions may become extinct in just a few years. In New York City, there is slightly more than half the total number of native plant species there was when the city was settled.

In the face of these facts, it's impossible not to wonder if they represent the choices of an educated planet. Equipped with an education, wouldn't we choose to read more often, and more widely? Wouldn't we choose to preserve our past and ensure our future? Wouldn't we make education a priority, with the recognition that it's this finest of qualities—this elixir of being—that affects not only our enjoyment of life but our very survival on the planet? No species in its right mind would seemingly choose its own extinction. The fact that humans appear to be on this very path speaks to the profound inadequacy of regular, everyday education. The institution we've relied on for this service is clearly not living up to its job.

Perhaps that's because, for almost two hundred years, the Prussian system has engineered students to be things, not people. At the hands of churches, armies, governments, and corporations, school has sought to turn its students into priests, soldiers, citizens, and workers. With each reformer, and each reform, there has always been an agenda, always a purpose, a point, a motive. No matter the organization, third party, or special interest group, the idea has been to look at what is needed and then make sure school manufactures the intended result. The idea has been to focus on what students can do, their end benefit to society, their value as human capital.

The result is clearly a problem without precedent or parallel: an erosion of language and culture, environment and history, identity and purpose. The result is a planet that doesn't know where it came from, what it's doing here, or where it'll be tomorrow. (Or, for that matter, if it'll be here at all.)

After all these years, Hegel's prediction seems to have taken on a new meaning: without an education, this might just be the end of our history, as well as our present and future. But that, of course, is up to us.

EPILOGUE

ONE RECENT AFTERNOON, I visited the home of Thomas H. B. Symons.

Now in his eighties, Symons has spent his life in the service of education. After graduating Oxford and Harvard, he became the founding president of Trent University, where he remains a Vanier professor emeritus. Over the course of an exceedingly distinguished academic career, Symons has received an Office of the Order of Canada, an Award for Merit from the Association of Canadian Studies, the Governor General's International Award for Canadian Studies, and the Order of Ontario. In just the few weeks between my query and when we sat down in the library of his home in Peterborough, he had received the Queen Elizabeth II Diamond Jubilee Medal and been made a Knight of the Order of St. Sylvester. (Asked if he should be addressed as "sir," Symons quite seriously responded, "Only in Italy.")

Yet at the end of the interview, it wasn't his education Symons wanted to discuss, but mine.

"Where did you study?"

And where did I study? Where did anyone? We probably learn as much in the schoolyard as we do in the classroom. Or on our own, lost in the pages of a good book. When it comes right down to it, learning can happen anywhere—or rather, everywhere. It isn't a matter of "Where did you study?" but "Where *didn't* you?"

When it happens that we actually receive an education from school, it's often more of a happy coincidence than a deliberate design. Most of us are lucky if we manage to extract even a speck of knowledge from a dozen years of institutionalized learning. The fact that our education system doesn't reliably do the one thing it's supposed to doesn't speak very highly of its effectiveness.

But what is an education, anyway? If this book has shown one thing, it's that we know what an education is *not*: from Prussia to Princeton, the peculiar pedagogues who advocated the annihilation of autonomy, supported the sterilization of society, are definitely *not* improving our educational welfare. The same goes for diploma mills, student-debt serfdom, and the world of high-stakes standardized testing. The one unassailably true thing we can say about education is that it's easy to identify its absence: we experience it all the time.

Saying what an education *is*, though, is considerably more difficult. Philosophers have grappled with the question for eons. The Greek atomist Democritus believed education was identical to nature, "for education transforms the man, and in transforming, creates his nature." Learning was part of living. Like taking a breath, it was the simple and extraordinary result of being alive. There was no reason to learn other than that it brought pleasure, and that it led to more learning. Out of this love of learning—this love of wisdom—life was enhanced, enriched, emboldened.

"The unexamined life is not worth living"—that's the way Socrates put it. Not that Socrates should get the final word on a topic that has changed considerably in the two and a half millennia since his passing. But for him the point of an education was that it helped determine the right way to live. His student, Plato, developed the idea further with the "Allegory of the Cave": the story of a man who somehow manages to discern the grotesque error and superstition that is accepted as knowledge—symbolized by shadows flickering against the cave wall. Stumbling into the dazzling light of the sun is disorienting and painful, but still infinitely preferable to the darkness and ignorance of the cave. So what does the enlightened escapee do? He ventures back underground to unshackle the other prisoners of ignorance.

Of course, part of Plato's story is a warning: back in the cave, the prisoners resent being told they've been wrong all along, and kill the guy who's come to free them. Enlightenment can be dangerous work. But as with all dangerous and important work, its rewards are all the greater. According to the Greeks, those who achieve wisdom are able to tell right from wrong. Part of this necessarily involves challenging the established order. Perhaps an education, then, is about a tension between being sure of what's wrong on one hand, and skeptical of what's generally held to be right on the other.

Let's call this spirit of impassioned inquiry "curiosity." Curiosity is the great motivator of an education. It's the how of learning: how we go from not knowing something to knowing it inside and out. You don't need ancient Greek philosophy to get the picture. To witness curiosity in action all you have to do is watch children at play. They pick up a ball or skipping rope (or their parents' iPhone), spend a nano-second scrutinizing it, and then proceed to master its every feature.

And here's the salient point: education is fun. Watch curious kids figuring things out—you can tell they're having a good time. The same goes for puppies and penguins and all kinds of creatures investigating the world around them. We love to learn because learning feels good. It both satisfies and stimulates curiosity. Reading a good book, having a meaningful conversation, listening to great music—just doing these things make us happy. They have no extrinsic purpose. To give them one takes away from their joy.

This is the problem with school in a nutshell. Education has no external purpose because it *is* purpose. It's a good unto itself. It's probably unfair to blame Prussia for ruining all formalized education, but if we want to identify the moment when education became viewed as good only so long as it was *useful*—to armies, to governments, to corporations—Prussia was it. With the advent of the Prussian system, education was acceptable only if it had a point. It had to go somewhere, it had to lead to something. Education for its own sake was forbidden, and as a result, curiosity—and the pleasure of learning—were repressed.

When education is infused with purpose, we agree it has a beginning and an end: that it's finite. It's as if we believe we can ever get to a point where we say, "Finally! Now I have an education." But of course we can't. As long as we're alive, we're learning, and as long as we're learning, we're experiencing joy. Children know this well. And so do parents, who often feel caught between wanting to give their child an education and wanting their child to succeed. But does there have to be a difference? In the twenty-first century, we use a nineteenth-century school model with twentieth-century values. There's clearly something wrong with this picture.

Finland is an example of a country that seems to have it down. Finns view school as assisting with an education, not delivering one in a lecture. Education is viewed as a means only to greater means. It's a natural, joyous activity that promotes life individually as well as collectively. One benefit of an educated person is an educated society. One benefit of an educated society is a creative workforce. And one benefit of a creative workforce is a healthy economic system, which in turn sustains everyday life on the planet. These are means, not ends. They are the *effect* of an education—what it can do when it's done right—and not a root cause.

Consider, for a moment, how profound is an education: every human-made object in the world is the result of one. Every car, computer, particle accelerator, thatched hut, hairstyle, soufflé, piano concerto. These are the products not only of the skilled hands and nimble minds of their creators, but the result of whole traditions and systems of education. Change education, and you change the world. That's not an article of faith—if this book has made one thing clear, it's that the reformers who set out to change the world by changing school were right. They accomplished exactly what they intended. It's just that the world they came up with leaves little to be desired.

Now consider the opposite: a world that values education for its own sake. That trusts in the magic of curiosity, that relishes the thrill of discovery. Consider a world where schools have the interests of their students in mind. Imagine children actually wanting to go there, and parents being excited to send them, knowing their children are developing an education that will lead them to happiness and fulfillment and success. Imagine a system where the emphasis is on promoting individuality, creativity, and compassion. Imagine a system in which the whole point is to get an education, because an education is the starting place, the beginning, the origin of everything.

But of course, this was too much to tell Tom Symons.

"Where did you study?"

And I answered, finally, that I'd been homeschooled. Apart from a few years in high school, that was it in terms of a formal education.

"Good for you," he said. "Honestly, I think you may be lucky."

The interview was over, but as I stood to leave, Symons kept me back a minute longer.

"I think it's simply wonderful and amazing that you're doing this," he said, meaning the book you've just finished reading. After a moment of reflection he added, "It speaks well about your homeschooling. It must have given you some bugs that are useful."

"What it really gave me is an insatiable curiosity," I told him.

"Well that's just grand," he said.

And we left it at that.

BIBLIOGRAPHY

BECAUSE I'VE INTENDED this work to be both informative and entertaining, I've built it around a variety of sources that, generally speaking, fall into five categories: books, scholarly articles, reports, news stories, and personal interviews. Each chapter uses hundreds of these sources, and including them all here would make for a very long bibliography indeed. What I've decided to do instead is offer a selection of some of the most relevant sources overall, and annotate each part of this bibliography with an explanation of how I came to have the perspective I did. To the extent possible, I hope this frames my knowledge of the subject, so that others may re-create a similar picture should they wish.

INTRODUCTION

For this section, I've relied most heavily on Christopher J. Lucas's exceptional history of higher education, which begins with the establishment of the scribal class and advances through thousands of years of formalization and development. I also read Urban and Wagoner's accessible and informative history, which focuses on social issues including the plight of minorities, and was particularly helpful in its discussion of Puritans. The rest is mostly cumulative knowledge acquired throughout my readings for the remainder of the book.

Conlin, Joseph R. *The American Past: A Survey of American History*. Boston: Wadsworth, 2009. Print.

Karras, Ruth Mazo. *From Boys to Men: Formations of Masculinity in Late Medieval Europe*. Philadelphia: U of Pennsylvania P, 2003. Print.

Lauria, Lisa M. "Sexual Misconduct in Plymouth Colony." *The Plymouth Colony Archive Project*. 1998. Web. 28 Apr. 2011.

Lucas, Christopher J. *American Higher Education: A History*. New York: St. Martin's, 1996. Print.

Otis, James. *Mary of Plymouth: The Story of the Pilgrim Settlement*. New York: American, 1910. Print.

Urban, Wayne J., and Jennings L. Wagoner. *American Education: A History*. New York: Routledge, 2009. Print.

1: CURIOUS BEGINNINGS

The End of History

For the biographical sketch of Gerhard von Scharnhorst, I found a paper by Michael Schoy particularly instructive; Schoy conveniently translated some of his own references from German to English. For the construction of period-specific language, sentiment, and facts, I used *The New York Times'* superlative archives (as I have throughout this work). With similar reliance, for the adoption of the Prussian system to Canada, I've referenced Sherman F. Balogh's master's thesis for the University of Toronto.

"Affairs in Germany." *New York Times* 6 Aug. 1867. Web. 15 Aug. 2010.

Balogh, Sherman F. *Ontario Educators' Observations of the German System of Education: 1834–1918*. Toronto: U of Toronto P, 1997. Print.

Fichte, Johann Gottlieb, and Daniel Breazeale. *Fichte: Early Philosophical Writings*. Ithaca: Cornell UP, 1993. Print.

"Education for All." *New York Times* 21 Nov. 1870. Web. 15 Aug. 2010.

Fichte, Johann Gottlieb. *Addresses to the German Nation*. Trans. R. F. Jones & G. H. Turnbull. Chicago: U of Chicago P, 1922. Print.

"Proposed Changes in the Public School System." *New York Times* 8 July 1869. Print.

"The Prussian Army after Jena." *New York Times* 19 Aug. 1883. Web. 31 Jan. 2011.

"Rigid Schools of Prussia." *New York Times* 11 Oct. 1896. Print.

Ryback, Timothy W. *Hitler's Private Library: The Books That Shaped His Life*. London: Bodley Head, 2009. Print.

Ryerson, Egerton, et al., eds. *Journal of Education for Upper Canada*. Vol. 19. Toronto: Lovell, 1806. Print.

Schoy, Michael. "Gerhard von Scharnhorst: Mentor of Clausewitz and Father of the Prussian-German General Staff." *Canadian Forces College Review*. 2003. n. pag. Web. 13 Feb. 2011.

Taber, John A. *Transformative Philosophy: A Study of Sankara, Fichte, and Heidegger*. Honolulu: U of Hawaii P, 1983. Print.

"The Victory of Prussian Administration." *New York Times* 23 Aug. 1870. Web. 2 Feb. 2011.

The Greatest Invention Ever Made by Mann

Jonathan Messerli's definitive biography of Horace Mann was an obvious starting point for my own portrait, and Megan Marshall's *The Peabody Sisters* provided further context and insight. I also went back to Urban and Wagoner, as well as the relevant passages in Balogh's thesis, and where possible relied on Horace Mann himself. Other sources include Paul E. Peterson's history of public education.

"The Common School Code." *New York Times* 17 Jan. 1852. Web. 24 Mar. 2011.

Compayri, Gabriel. *Horace Mann and the Public School in the United States*. Honolulu: UP of the Pacific. 2002. Print.

Drexler, Paul. *The German Puzzle*. Bloomington: Xlibris, 2010. Print.

"Horace Mann a 'Modern'" *New York Times* 29 July 1934. Web. 24 Mar. 2011.

Mann, Horace, ed. *The Common School Journal*. Vol. 2. Boston: Marsh, 1840. Print.

Mann, Mary Tyler Peabody. *Life of Horace Mann*. Boston: Walker. 1865. Print.

Marshall, Megan. *The Peabody Sisters: Three Women Who Ignited American Romanticism*. New York: Houghton, 2005. Print.

Messerli, Jonathan. *Horace Mann: A Biography*. New York: Knopf, 1972. Print.

Peterson, Paul E. *Saving Schools: From Horace Mann to Virtual Learning*. Cambridge: Harvard UP, 2010. Print.

Urban, Wayne J., and Jennings L. Wagoner. *American Education: A History*. New York: Routledge, 2009. Print.

Kerschensteiner's School

Derek S. Linton and Philipp Gonon were valuable resources and were kind enough to answer my follow-up questions about Georg Kerschensteiner and the industrial school model. *The Encyclopedia of Educational Reform and Dissent* was useful in the discussion of the General Education Board and has been a resource elsewhere as well. The mock auction between Carnegie and Rockefeller is the result of a selection from dozens of headlines from the period, too numerous to list here, but easily searchable on the internet.

"Education: Pritchett on Pensions." *Time* 21 Apr. 1 1930. Web. 1 Apr. 2011.

Geitz, Henry, et al. *German Influences on Education in the United States to 1917*. Cambridge: Cambridge UP, 2006. Print.

"German Educator Revolutionizes School Methods." *New York Times* 4 Dec. 1910. Web. 8 Dec. 2009.

Gonon, Philipp. *The Quest for Modern Vocational Education: Georg Kerschensteiner between Dewey, Weber and Simmel*. Bern: Peter Lang, 2009. Print.

Harper, Elizabeth P. "General Education Board." *Encyclopedia of Educational Reform and Dissent*. Ed. Thomas C. Hunt, et al. Thousand Oaks: Sage, 2010. Print.

Linton, Derek S. *Who Has the Youth, Has the Future: The Campaign to Save Young Workers in Imperial Germany*. Cambridge: Cambridge UP, 1991. Print.

2: THE TEST, AND WHAT IT'S ON
Binet's Scale

The historical anecdotes at the beginning of the chapter were derived mainly from news articles. Parts of the biographical sketches of Terman and Yerkes came from their own self-portraits, while Stephen Jay Gould's enduring critique of biological determinism and the inheritability of intelligence provided more information and context. Joel Vilensky's book about lewisite was one of the sources for the James Conant story. The shocking history of the SAT is well-documented, and authors like Nicholas Lemann, Jerome Karabel, and Jacques Steinberg have devoted whole works to its telling.

"Conant for 'Plan in Terms of Men;' Sees Wide Change in Education." *New York Times* 24 Jan. 1936. Web. 21 Apr. 2011.

Gould, Stephen Jay. *The Mismeasure of Man*. New York: Norton, 1996. Print.

Lemann, Nicholas. *The Big Test: The Secret History of the American Meritocracy*. New York: Farrar, 1999. Print.

Morion, Samuel Eliot. *The Founding of Harvard College*. Cambridge: Harvard UP, 1935. Print.

Terman, Lewis M. "Autobiography of Lewis M. Terman." *History of Psychology in Autobiography* 2 (1930): 297–331. Print.

Vilensky, Joel A. *Dew of Death: The Story of Lewisite, America's World War I Weapon of Mass Destruction*. Bloomington: Indiana UP, 2005. Print.

Whipple, Guy M. "The National Intelligence Tests." *Journal of Educational Research*. Vol. 4, No. 1. June 1921: 16–31. Print.

Yerkes, Robert Mearns. "Autobiography of Robert Mearns Yerkes." *History of Psychology in Autobiography* 2 (1930): 381–407. Print.

Serious Business

The horrific stories of students committing suicide over exam results came from many sources, from *The New York Times* to *The Times of India*. I've listed some of the more recent ones here, with the small hope that seeing them in succession will galvanize a modicum of awareness of the high-stakes epidemic and the multibillion dollar industry that supports it. Otherwise, I relied on the exceptional journalism of Nicholas Lemann, Malcolm Gladwell, and Steven Brill, as well as reports from ETS itself.

Brill, Steven. "The Secrecy behind the College Boards." *New York* 7 Oct. 1974: 67–83. Print.

"Exam Fear Drives Dharavi Teenager to Suicide. *Hindustan Times* 6 Jan. 2012. Web. 22 Jan. 2012.

"'Exam Stress' Drives Teen to Suicide." *Times of India* 26 Feb. 2008. Web. 28 Mar. 2012.

Gabriel, Trip. "After 3 Suspected Suicides, Cornell Reaches Out." *New York Times* 16 Mar. 2010. Web. 22 Jan. 2012.

Gladwell, Malcolm. "Examined Life: What Stanley H. Kaplan Taught Us about the S.A.T." *The New Yorker* 17 Dec. 2001. Web. 4 Jan. 2010

Lemann, Nicholas. "The Structure of Success in America." *Atlantic* Aug. 1995. Web. 17 Dec. 2009.

"MBA Student Commits Suicide." *Times of India* 17 Feb. 2011. Web. 28 Mar. 2012.

Nicholas, Lemann. "The Great Sorting." *Atlantic* Sept. 1995. Web. 18 Dec. 2009.

Owen, David. *None of the Above: The Truth Behind the SATs*. Lanham: Rowman, 1999. Print.

"Overdose of Internet Drugs Killed Talented Student, 18." *Sentinel* 18 Jan. 2012. Web. 22 Jan. 2012.

Qiang, Guo. "Three Die amid Gaokao Test." *Global Times* 9 June 2010. Web. 22 Jan. 2012.

"Teen Kills Self Due to Exam Stress." *Times of India* 16 Mar. 2009. Web. 28 Mar. 2012.

Curriculum Vitae

Where possible, I've sourced Franklin Bobbitt's work directly. Since very little is known of Bobbitt's life, I've had to rely on the family genealogist John William Bobbitt, as well as Franklin himself in his rare concessions of personal information. Otherwise, I found an article by Philip Jackson, a professor emeritus at the University of Chicago, relevant and helpful, and used Edwin Tunis's pictorial history of wheels in the introduction, in addition to the usual newsworthy anecdotes of the day.

Bobbitt, Franklin. "Foreign Service Effects." *Phi Delta Kappan* 27.9 (1946): 249–51, 263. Print.

Bobbitt, Franklin. "The Actual Objectives of the Present-Day High School." *American Journal of Education* 91.4 (1983): 450–67. Print.

Bobbitt, Franklin. *The Curriculum*. Boston: Houghton, 1918. Print.

Bobbitt, John William. *The Bobbitt Family in America*. 2001. Web. 20 July 2010.

Jackson, Philip W. "Shifting Visions of the Curriculum: Notes on the Aging of Franklin Bobbitt." *Elementary School Journal* 75 (1975): 118–33. Print.

Malewski, Erik, ed. *Curriculum Studies Handbook: The Next Moment*. New York: Routledge, 2010. Print.

Tunis, Edwin. *Wheels: A Pictorial History*. Baltimore: Johns Hopkins UP, 2002. Print.

Winfield, Ann Gibson. *Eugenics and Education: Implications of Ideology, Memory, and History for Education in the United States*. Raleigh: North Carolina State UP, 2004. Print.

The Rise of Low Literacy

For this section, I was grateful for the assistance of Ulrike Hanemann, and especially Peter Roberts at the University of Canterbury. The move to end the teaching of Latin and Greek was a popular subject of debate in the early twentieth century, and I've only highlighted some of the more pertinent articles here. Otherwise, I've quoted mainly from scholarly articles, including Abraham Flexner's work on the modern curriculum.

Austin, David M. "The Flexner Myth and the History of Social Work." *Social Service Review* 57.3 (1983): 357–77. Print.

"Charges Flexner Misused Statistics." *New York Times* 8 July 1917. Web. 29 Sept. 2010.

"Churchill Calls Schools Mediaeval." *New York Times*. 4 Apr. 1916. Web. 29 Sept. 2010.

C. K. "A Plea for the Classics: And Remarks on Formal Discipline." *Classical Weekly* 11.17 (1918): 129–31. Print.

Flexner, Abraham. *A Modern School*. New York: General Education Board, 1916. Print.

Jenner, William A. "The Modern Psychology and Formal Discipline." *Classical Weekly* 8. 4 (1914): 26–29. Print.

Lewis, F.C. "A Study in Formal Discipline." *School Review* 13.4. Apr. 1905: 281–92. Print.

Parker, Franklin. "Abraham Flexner, 1866–1959." *History of Education Quarterly* 2.4. Dec. 1962: 199–209. Print.

"Radical and Dangerous." Editorial. *New York Times* 21 Jan. 1917. Web. 29 Sept. 2010.

Roberts, Peter. "Defining Literacy: Paradise, Nightmare or Red Herring?" *British Journal of Educational Studies* 43.4 (1995): 412–32. Print.

"Rockefeller Board to Revise Education." *New York Times* 20 Jan. 1917. Web. 29 Sept. 2010.

3: CITIZENS AND SOLDIERS

Indian Troubles

The portrait of Egerton Ryerson came primarily from his own writings and journal entries, and his commissioned reports were referenced to show the influence of his writing on the Canadian public and residential school models. *The New York Times'* articles are an obvious feature of the introduction and closing, and even for Stephen Harper's 2008 apology, I found the *Times* offered better coverage than Canadian sources. I returned to Balogh's thesis for the Prussian connection and elsewhere relied on Sarah de Leeuw, John Leslie, and Douglas Owram. The Bagot and Davin reports are referenced in their original context.

"Canada Offers an Apology for Native Students' Abuse." *New York Times* 12 June. 2008. Web. 18 Jan. 2012.

"Editorial: Residential Schools: The Full Story." *Regina Leader-Post* 18 Jan. 2012. Web. 18 Jan. 2012.

"An Indian Encounter." *New York Times* 22 Sept. 1851. Web. 8 Aug. 2010.

"Indian Lawsuits on School Abuse May Bankrupt Canada Churches." *New York Times* 2 Nov. 2000. Web. 18 Jan. 2012.

Leslie, John. "The Bagot Commission: Developing a Corporate Memory for the Indian Department." *Historical Papers* 17.1 (1982): 31–52. Print.

Nixon, Virginia. "Egerton Ryerson and the Old Master Copy as an Instrument of Public Education." *Journal of Canadian Art History* 27 (2006): 94–113. Print.

"Our Bad Indian Policy." Editorial. *New York Times* 27 Oct. 1886. Web. 8 Aug. 2010.

"Our Indian Troubles—How to Meet Them." Editorial. *New York Times* 19 Jul. 1867. Web. 8 Aug. 2010.

Owram, Douglas. "Strachan & Ryerson: Guardians of the Future." *Canadian Literature* 83 (1979): 21–29. Print.

"Qualification for Citizenship." Editorial. *New York Times* 13 Mar. 1880. Web. 8 Aug. 2010.

Ryerson, Egerton. *Dr. Ryerson's Letters in Reply to Hon. George Brown.* Toronto: Lovell & Gibson, 1859. Print.

Ryerson, Egerton. *The Story of My Life.* Ed. J. George Hodgins. Toronto: William Briggs, 1883. Print.

Old-School Discipline

I benefited from my conversation with James FitzGerald, among many other, less formal talks with older generations. I relied on the reports of organizations like Human Rights Watch and the Global Initiative to End All Corporal Punishment of Children. Both the historic and modern anecdotes or instances of specific punishment were derived mainly through present and archival news articles, but also through the aforementioned organizations and occasionally from printed volumes.

"Corporal Punishment Damages Kids' Cognitive Functions—Study." *Toronto Sun* 27 July 2011. Web. 17 Jan. 2012.

"A Violent Education: Corporal Punishment of Children in US Public Schools." New York: Human Rights Watch, 2008. Print.

FitzGerald, James. *"Old Boys: The Powerful Legacy of Upper Canada College*—Excerpts." James Fitzgerald website. 17 Jan. 2012.

Hinchey, Patricia H. "Corporal Punishment: Legalities, Realities, and Implications." *Clearing House* 77.3 (2004): 96–100. Print.

Pearson, Patricia. "Review—What Disturbs Our Blood, by James Fitzgerald." *Globe and Mail* 3 Jun. 2010. Web. 17 Jan. 2012.

Reilly, Emma. "School Staff Facing Assault Charges." *Toronto Star*. 16 Feb. 2008. Web. 17 Jan. 2012.

"Smacking Children Reduces Their Emotional Intelligence and Makes Their Behaviour Even Worse." *Telegraph* 28 July 2011. Web. 18 Jan. 2012.

The War Machine

The militarization of public education had a tremendous impact on World War I. As the chief architect of this transformation, Newton Baker deserves more literary consideration than he's received. Aside from referencing the sole biography by C. H. Cramer, I contextualized the life of Baker through his activities as secretary of war, which were recorded by both the popular press and standard histories of World War I.

Baker, Newton. *Why We Went to War*. New York: Harper, 1936. Print.

Craig, Douglas. "Newton D. Baker and the Democratic Malaise, 1920–1937." *Australian Journal of American Studies* 25.1 (2006): 49–64. Print.

Cramer, C. H. *Newton D. Baker: A Biography*. Cleveland: World, 1961. Print.

Doenecke, Justus, D. *Nothing Less Than War: A New History of America's Entry into World War I*. Lexington: UP of Kentucky, 2011. Print.

"Plans to Mobilize Schools to Aid War." *New York Times* 17 Feb. 1918. Web. 1 Dec. 2009.

United States War Department. Committee on Education and Special

Training. "Committee on Education and Special Training: A Review of Its Work During 1918." 1919. Charleston: Nabu, 2010. Print.

"War School for 100,000 Soldiers." *New York Times* 28 Apr. 1918. Web. 10 Apr. 2010.

Westwell, Ian, and Dennis Cove, eds. *History of World War 1.* Vol. 1. Tarrytown: Marshall Cavendish, 2002. Print.

"Will Run Colleges Like Army Posts." *New York Times* 8 Sept. 1918. Web. 13 Apr. 2010.

4: THE CORPORATE EQUATION

Mount A+

Where possible, I've gone to Mount Allison for information about its history, finances, and board of directors, most of which is publicly available. Nancy Heckman and Indira Samarasekera gave generously of their time, as did my tour guide, Fraser Orr-Brown. Biographical information came from Catherine Thompson's portrait of Margaret Norrie; John G. Reid's study of Charles Frederick Allison; and the Gordon and Nicholson work on family feuds. Ranking universities is an increasingly controversial practice, and shortly after my visit to Mount Allison, I was pleased to discover Malcolm Gladwell's critique of the American system in *The New Yorker*.

"Charles Frederick Allison." *Dictionary of Canadian Biography Online.* 2000. Web. 12 May 2011.

Gladwell, Malcolm. "The Order of Things." *New Yorker* 14 Feb. 2011. Web. 14 Feb. 2012.

Gordon, Grant, and Nigel Nicholson. *Family Wars: The Real Stories behind the Most Famous Family Business Feuds.* London: Kogan, 2008. Print.

Maclean's Ranking of Canadian Universities. Ed. Nancy Heckman, et al. Oct. 1999. Web. 16 May 2011.

Mount Allison University. "Review of Operations (Unaudited)." 30 Apr. 2010. Print.

Samarasekera, Indira. "Rising Up Against the Rankings." *Inside Higher*

Ed. 2 Apr. 2007. Web. 5 Feb. 2012.

Thompson, Catherine. *The Prize for Learning Love: The Life of Margaret Fawcett Norrie, Nova Scotia's First Female Senator.* Saint John: Trinity, 2006. Print.

The Corporate Equation

For this section, I relied on the considerable expertise of Lawrence Busch and Sheldon Krimsky, in addition to the below-listed scholarly treatments of corporate–university partnerships. I also benefited from the press such controversies generated, including the book-length endeavors they led to. In the case of *Olivieri vs. Apotex*, I found Peg Tittle's brief overview the clearest.

Culliton, Barbara J. "Harvard and Monsanto: The $23-Million Alliance." *Science, New Series* 195.4280 (1977): 759–63. Print.

Lau, Edie. "Report: Five-Year Deal with Novartis Hurt UC Berkeley." *Sacramento Bee* 1 Aug. 2004. Web. 25 Jan. 2011.

McDermott, W. F., and J. C. Furnas. "About a Man Who Gave a Million-dollar 'No!'" *Rotarian* Jan. 1940: 18–54. Print.

Prusoff, William. "The Scientist's Story." *New York Times* 19 Mar. 2011. Web. 26 Jan. 2012. Print.

Tittle, Peg. *Ethical Issues in Business: Inquiries, Cases, and Readings.* Peterborough: Broadview, 2000. Print.

Washburn, Jennifer. *University, Inc.: The Corporate Corruption of American Higher Education.* New York: Basic, 2006. Print.

A Billion-Dollar Idea

Most of my account of John Sperling's life come from Sperling himself. Otherwise, I went to the journalists Hanna Rosin and James Traub for context, and more recent accounts for facts, including education writer Kayla Webley's 2012 article for *Time*. For the small but growing contingent of Canadian for-profit universities, I was assisted by reporting from the *Winnipeg Free Press* and *Maclean's*.

Bartlett, Thomas. "Phoenix Risen: How a History Professor Became the Pioneer of the For-Profit Revolution." *Chronicle of Higher Education* 6 July 2009. Web. 20 Nov. 2010.

Hechinger, John. "Battle Over Academic Standards Weighs on For-Profit Colleges." *Wall Street Journal* 30 Sept. 2005. Web. 23 Nov. 2010.

Millar, Erin. "Apollo Group Launches New University in New Brunswick." 14 May 2008. Web. 30 Jan. 2012.

"'Private Faculty' Sets Up Shop at U of M." *Winnipeg Free Press* 1 Feb. 2008. Web. 29 Jan. 2012.

Rosin, Hanna. "Red, Blue and Lots of Green: John Sperling Divides America Into 'Metro' and 'Retro.' His Money's on 'Metro.'" *Washington Post*. 26 Oct. 2004. Web. 19 Nov. 2010.

Sperling, John G. *Rebel with a Cause: The Entrepreneur Who Created the University of Phoenix and the For-profit Revolution in Higher Education.* New York: Wiley, 2000. Print.

Traub, James. "Drive-Thru U: Higher Education for People Who Mean Business." *New Yorker* 20 & 27 Oct. 1997:114–23. Print.

Webley, Kayla. "For-Profit-Schools: 'Agile Predators' or Just Business Savvy?" *Time Moneyland* 9 Jan. 2012. Web. 31 Jan. 2012.

Gratefully Indebted

Most of the tuition figures from the introductory segment are quoted from schools directly or, when impossible, through reliable secondhand sources (as is the case with Le Rosey, which isn't in the habit of disclosing the price of admittance). Larry Leslie's dated but still relevant work in the *Journal of Higher Education* provided the historical context I was looking for, and Leslie was also patient with my follow-up questions, as was Alan Collinge. Instances of student debt are as tragic as they are numerous. The stories repeated came from news articles, scholarly works, or book-length treatments of the student-loan industry.

"Bracing for $40,000 at New York City Private Schools." *New York Times* 27 Jan. 2012. Web. 29 Jan. 2012.

Brown, Louise. "Ontario Students to Protest High Tuition Wednesday." *Toronto Star* 31 Jan. 2012. Web. 31 Jan. 2012.

Collinge, Alan. *The Student Loan Scam: The Most Oppressive Debt in U.S. History—and How We Can Fight Back.* Boston: Beacon Press, 2009. Print.

Dewan, Diptiman. "UK Schools Woo Indian Students." *Times of India* 20 Jan. 2012. Web. 1 Feb. 2012.

Leslie, Larry L., and Jonathan D. Fife. "The College Student Grant Study: The Enrollment and Attendance Impacts of Student Grant and Scholarship Programs." *Journal of Education* 45.9 (1974): 651–71. Print.

Leslie, Larry L., and Gary P. Johnson. "The Market Model and Higher Education." *Journal of Higher Education* 45.1 (1974): 1–20. Print.

Spaeth, Robert L. "Disturbing Aspects of Private Power." *Improving College and University Teaching* 32.2 (1984): 109. Print.

5: POWERFUL PEDAGOGIES
The Weird World of Rudolf Steiner

As always, I tried to let the primary biographical subject speak for him- or herself, and in the case of Rudolf Steiner, there's certainly no paucity of introspection. I've referenced only the bare minimum here, in the hopes enthusiastic readers will explore more for themselves. Additionally, a few incidental sources are included below, such as the strange and wonderful *Encyclopedia of Reincarnation and Karma*.

Gidley, Jennifer, Debra Bateman, and Caroline Smith. *Futures in Education: Principles, Practice and Potential.* Melbourne: Swinburne, 2004.

Hemleben, Johannes, and Leo Twyman. *Rudolf Steiner: An Illustrated Biography.* London: Sophia, 2000. Print.

Jongeneel, Jan A. B. *Jesus Christ in World History: His Presence and Representation in Cyclical and Linear Settings.* Frankfurt: Peter Lang, 2009. Print.

McClelland, Norman C. *Encyclopedia of Reincarnation and Karma.* Jefferson: McFarland, 2010. Print.

"New Scheme of Social Organization." *New York Times* 14 Jan. 1923. Web. 19 Apr. 2011.

Penczak, Christopher. *Ascension Magick: Ritual, Myth & Healing for the New Aeon*. Woodbury: Llewellyn, 2007. Print.

PLANS, Inc. v. Sacramento City Unified School District, Twin Ridges Elementary School District. No. CIV. S-98-0266. Eastern District of California, US District Ct. 13 Sept. 2005. Print.

Steiner, Rudolf. *Christianity as Mystical Fact: And the Mysteries of Antiquity*. Teddington: Echo, 2008. Print.

Steiner, Rudolf. *The Dead Are with Us*. London: Rudolf Steiner, 2006. Print.

Steiner, Rudolf. *From Elephants to Einstein: Answers to Questions*. London: Rudolf Steiner, 1998. Print.

Steiner, Rudolf. *The Incarnation of Ahriman: The Embodiment of Evil on Earth*. London: Rudolf Steiner, 2006. Print.

Steiner, Rudolf. *Nutrition: Food, Health, and Spiritual Development*. London: Rudolf Steiner, 2008. Print.

Steiner, Rudolf. *Staying Connected: How to Continue Your Relationships with Those Who Have Died*. Ed. Christopher Bamford. Great Barrington: Anthroposophic, 1999. Print.

The Montessori Method

Alison Smith, at Dearcroft Montessori in Oakville, was incredibly kind and accommodating, and provided a great introduction to the Montessori Method. The classic *Maria Montessori: A Biography*, by Rita Kramer, was the natural place to begin a more academic inquiry (though, as it was originally published in 1976, we're due for a new definitive work). I found Gerald L. Gutek's chapter in the standard *Educational Psychology* particularly informative and elsewhere relied on scholarly texts from the period, particularly the work of Philip W. L. Cox and Paul Willcott. Montessori's relationship with Mussolini is evidently an area scholars have overlooked, and the subject deserves the attention of the next definitive biographer.

Babini, Valeria, Sarah Morgan, and Daniel Pick. "Science, Feminism and Education: The Early Work of Maria Montessori." *History Workshop Journal* 49 (2000): 44–67. Print.

Cox, Philip W. L. "Fascism, Liberalism, and Individuality in Italy." *Junior-Senior High School Clearing House* 10.2 (1935): 85–89. Print.

"Dr. Montessori Talks of Her Mode of 'Auto Education.'" *New York Times* 7 Dec. 1913. Web. 23 Oct. 2010.

Gutek, Gerald L. "Maria Montessori: Contributions to Educational Psychology." *Educational Psychology: A Century of Contributions*. Eds. Barry J. Zimmerman and Dale H. Schunk. Mahwah: Lawrence Erlbaum, 2003. 171–86.

Hall, Clifton L. "The First Lady of Education." *History of Education Journal* 4.4 (1953): 124–28. Print.

Kramer, Rita. *Maria Montessori*. Chicago: U of Chicago P, 1976. Print.

"Montessori and the Fascists." *Glasgow Herald* 14 Apr. 1930. Web. 3 Feb. 2012.

Willcott, Paul. "The Initial American Reception of the Montessori Method." *The School Review* 76.2 (1968): 147–65. Print.

A House on Summer Hill

My sketch of A. S. Neill came mostly from his brief and enjoyable auto-biography. As a reference, I returned to the *Encyclopedia of Educational Reform and Dissent* and found further context in an article by Jean-François Suffange. Regarding Neill's work on Summerhill, Ian Stronach's scholarly treatment was a good source of information, and Stronach himself was kind enough to let me bother him with questions over the holidays. I used the original Ofsted reports, and the media they generated, to show opposition to the school during its long and colorful history.

"Summerhill Revisited." *New York Times* 7 Nov. 1999. Web. 8 Oct. 2010.

Cassebaum, Anne. "Revisiting Summerhill." *The Phi Delta Kappan* 84.8 (2003): 575–78. Print.

Neill, Alexander Sutherland. *Neil! Neil! Orange Peel! An Autobiography*. Oxford: Hart, 1972. Print.

Rampton, James. "Summerhill: The School Where Lessons Are Optional." *Telegraph* 19 Jan. 2008. Web. 17 Mar. 2012.

Suffange, Jean-François. "Alexander Sutherland Neill." *Prospects: The Quarterly Review of Comparative Education* 24 (1994): 217–29. Print.

United Kingdom. Office for Standards in Education. *Summerhill School* (inspection report). London: Ofsted Publications Centre, 1999. Print.

Wan, Guofang. "A. S. Neill (1883–1972)." *Encyclopedia of Educational Reform and Dissent.* Eds. Thomas C. Hunt et al. Thousand Oaks: Sage, 2010. Print.

A Private Elite

For this segment, I had valuable conversations with Michaele Robertson, Barry Wansbrough, Thomas H. B. Symons, and James FitzGerald. John Strachan's biographical portrait came from his memoirs as well as sketches by John Moir and G. M. Craig. I found further coverage in the work of Douglas Owram and Alan Taylor. Alan Wilson's entry in the *Dictionary of Canadian Biography Online* was my primary source for the John Colborne story. The Coleman Report has received much attention, but I preferred the quiet succinctness of Judith Kleinfeld's review in the *Anthropology & Education Quarterly*. The story of the founding of the Roxbury Latin School came from the *Journal of Education*. Charles Bell's history of Exeter provided the details of its founding. The wealth of comparisons between private and public schools was the result of extracting and matching facts from a variety of sources, including many recent news articles. The bit about Harvard having more money than the sum of Africa's poorest countries is the result of comparing combined GDPs with Harvard's 2011 endowment.

"John Colborne." *Dictionary of Canadian Biography Online.* 2000. Web. 8 Feb. 2012.

Barnard, Henry, ed. *The American Journal of Education.* Vol. 27. Hartford: Office of *American Journal of Education,* 1877. Print.

Bell, Charles. *Phillips Exeter Academy in New Hampshire: A Historical Sketch.* Exeter: Morrill, 1883. Print.

Bethune, Alexander Neil. *Memoirs of the Right Reverend John Strachan, First Bishop of Toronto*. Toronto: Rowsell, 1870. Print.

Craig, G. M. *Dictionary of Canadian Biography Online*. 2000. Web. 5 Feb. 2012.

Dillon, Sam. "As Budgets Are Trimmed, Time in Class Is Shortened." *New York Times* 5 Jul. 2011. Web. 19 Feb. 2012.

Drummond, Don. "Commission on the Reform of Ontario's Public Services: A Path to Sustainability and Excellence." Toronto: Queen's Printer, 2012. Print.

Kleinfeld, Judith. "Book Reviews." *Anthropology & Education Quarterly* 16.3 (1985): 244–46. Print.

Moir, John. "John Strachan." *Canada: Portraits of Faith*. Ed. Michael D. Clarke. Nashville: Reel to Real, 1998. Print.

Taylor, Alan. *The Civil War of 1812: American Citizens, British Subjects, Irish Rebels, & Indian Allies*. New York: Knopf, 2010. Print.

Winerip, Michael. "In Public School Efforts, a Common Background: Private Education." *New York Times* 17 Apr. 2011. Web. 10 Feb. 2012.

God's Army

The story of John Holt came partly through his personal correspondence, edited by Susannah Sheffer. Pat Farenga and Milton Gaither provided additional support, both in writing and to me personally. Marci McDonald's *The Armageddon Factor* was evidently a source for the religious homeschooling movement in Canada. In the United States, it was Hanna Rosin's 2005 piece in *The New Yorker* and subsequent volume from Houghton Mifflin Harcourt, though I've also drawn from a wider variety of articles and sources.

Buncombe, Andrew. "The Bible College That Leads to the White House." *Independent/UK* 21 Apr. 2004. Web. 17 Feb. 2011.

Holt, John. *A Life Worth Living: The Selected Letters of John Holt*. Ed. Susannah Sheffer. Columbus: Ohio State UP, 1990. Print.

Jackson, Daniel. "Muslim Families Turn to Home-Schooling." *Washington Times* 21 Feb. 2012. Web. 28 Feb. 2012.

McDonald, Marci. *The Armageddon Factor: The Rise of Christian Nationalism in Canada*. Toronto: Random, 2010. Print.

Rosin, Hanna. "God and Country: A College that Trains Young Christians to Be Politicians." *The New Yorker* 27 June 2005. Web. 17 Feb. 2011.

Rosin, Hanna. *God's Harvard: A Christian College on a Mission to Save America*. Boston: Houghton, 2007. Print.

6: A MODERN AGENDA

Standardized Students

The story of standards in education is well known: corporations exert pressure on the government to produce a report, which the government then uses to initiate reforms. In Canada, I relied on the substantial work and research of Margaret Dagenais, Heather-jane Robertson, and Maude Barlow. In the United States, Neal McCluskey and Yong Zhao provided valuable perspectives in both this segment and the following. There is a huge amount of literature on educational standards, and my references below represent a cursory selection.

Barlow, Maude, and Heather-jane Robertson. *Class Warfare: The Assault on Canada's Schools*. Bolton: Key Porter, 1994. Print.

Dagenais, Margaret. *An Effective and Critical History of Canada's National Standardized Testing Program*. Regina: U of Regina P, 2011. Print.

Duncan, Arne. "Education Reform's Moon Shot." *Washington Post* 24 July 2009. Web. 24 Sept. 2009.

Salutin, Rick. "Standard Tests: More Questions than Answers." *Toronto Star* 1 Apr. 2011. Web. 20 Jan. 2012.

Taylor, Alison. *The Politics of Educational Reform in Alberta*. Toronto: U of Toronto P, 2001. Print.

The National Commission on Excellence in Education. *A Nation at Risk: The Imperative for Educational Reform*. Washington: U.S. Government, 1983. Print.

Winerip, Michael. "Despite Focus on Data, Standards for Diploma May Still Lack Rigor." *New York Times* 4 Feb. 2012. Web. 7 Mar. 2012.

An Army of Nerds

In addition to the continuation of my discussions with Dagenais and Zhao, I gained from conversations with Thomas H. B. Symons, Hal Salzman, and B. Lindsay Lowell. In a world that has largely accepted the validity of STEM-based reforms, Salzman and Lowell's research provides the context for a much-needed second opinion. In other areas, I selected information from the Augustine reports, the Flaherty paper, and some of the news they generated. For the evolution of the standards-based reform movement into STEM-based initiatives, I relied on Dagenais's doctoral thesis and her knowledge of *Sputnik*-era politics.

Dehaas, Josh. "Students Are Fleeing STEM Degrees." *Maclean's* 7 Nov. 2011. Web. 11 Mar. 2012.

Department of Finance Canada. *Advantage Canada: Building a Strong Economy for Canadians.* Ottawa: Department of Finance Canada: 2006. Print.

Hauch, Valerie. "Philanthropist Donates $100M for University Scholarships." *Toronto Star.* 14 Oct. 2011. Web. 11 Mar. 2012.

Lowell, B. Lindsay, and Hal Salzman. *Into the Eye of the Storm: Assessing the Evidence on Science and Engineering Education, Quality, and Workforce Demand.* Washington: Urban Institute, 2007. Print.

Lowell, B. Lindsay, et al. *Steady as She Goes? Three Generations of Students through the Science and Engineering Pipeline.* Washington: Georgetown UP, 2009. Print.

National Academy of Sciences. *Rising Above the Gathering Storm, Revisited: Rapidly Approaching Category 5.* Washington: National Academies, 2010. Print.

National Academy of Sciences. *Rising Above the Gathering Storm: Energizing and Employing America for a Brighter Future.* Washington: National Academies, 2005. Print.

Salzman, Hal, and B. Lindsay Lowell. "A Size That Fits All for the Science-and-Technology Pipeline." *Chronicle of Higher Education* 31 July 2011. Web. 13 Mar. 2012.

Zhao, Yong. *Catching Up or Leading the Way: American Education in the Age of Globalization*. Alexandria: Association for Supervision & Curriculum Development, 2009. Print.

The Finnish Model

I'm grateful to the Finnish educators I interviewed, especially George Malaty Marcus, Jussi Välimaa, and Jaana Palojärvi. Information about the Finnish model, particularly in the introduction, was culled from a number of sources, but among the most relevant were Anu Partanen's piece in *The Atlantic* and Diane Ravitch's contribution to *The New York Review of Books*. My brief and simplistic history of Finland was the product of an amalgamation of antiquated and contemporary sources, which I've provided only in rough below. Of particular use in the former category were articles in *The Ohinemuri Gazette* and *The New York Times*, and in the latter, Välimaa's chapter in *Academic Staff in Europe: Changing Contexts and Conditions*.

Anderson, Jenny. "From Finland, an Intriguing School-Reform Model." *New York Times* 12 Dec. 2011. Web. 15 Mar. 2012.

Juhani Tuovinen. *Teaching and Learning: International Best Practice*. Eds. Dennis M. McInerney and Arief Darmanegara Liem. Charlotte: Information Age, 2008. Print.

Nilsson, Victor Alfred. *Sweden*. Cork: Lee, 2010. Print.

"Oppressed Finland." *Ohinemuri Gazette* 14 Sept. 1903. Web. 8 Nov. 2010.

Partanen, Anu. "What Americans Keep Ignoring about Finland's School Success." *Atlantic* 29 Dec. 2011. Web. 16 Mar. 2012.

Ravitch, Diane. "Schools We Can Envy." *New York Review of Books* 8 Mar. 2012. Web. 16 Mar. 2012.

Rushowy, Kristin. "Finland's Secrets to Educational Success." *Toronto Star* 14 Sept. 2010. Web. 15 Mar. 2012.

"Russia Alarmed by Finland's Move." *New York Times* 14 July 1917. Web. 11 Nov. 2010.

Välimaa, Jussi. "The Changing Nature of Academic Employment in Finnish Higher Education." *Academic Staff in Europe: Changing Contexts and Conditions.* Ed. Jürgen Enders. Westport: Greenwood, 2001. Print.

7: THE SYSTEM

An Educated Guess

The examples of knowledge in decline come either directly from surveys and reports or from the news they generated. Articles in *Reason, Maclean's,* and *Time* provided a variety of perspectives, and of course Hanushek's idea of teacher deselection was valuable as well. The history of the NEA and the anecdotes of female employees being subjected to outrageous prejudice came from the archives.

de Rugy, Veronique. "Losing the Brains Race." *Reason* 22 Feb. 2011. Web. 5 Mar. 2011.

Dillon, Sam. "Survey Finds Teenagers Ignorant on Basic History and Literature Questions." *New York Times* 27 Feb. 2008. Web. 5 Mar. 2011.

Greene, Jay P. *Education Myths: What Special-Interest Groups Want You to Believe About Our Schools—And Why it Isn't So.* Lanham: Rowman, 2005. Print.

Hanushek, Eric. "Teacher Deselection." *Creating a New Teaching Profession.* Eds. Dan Goldhaber and Jane Hannaway. Washington: Urban Institute, 2009. Print.

Hollingsworth, Barbara. "Majority of American Students Flunk Civics Test." *Washington Examiner* 5 Mar. 2011. Web. 5 Mar. 2011.

Mendleson, Rachel. "Why It's so Hard to Fire Bad Teachers." *Maclean's* 8 July 2009. Web. 6 Mar. 2011.

Stephey, M. J. "A Brief History of Tenure." *Time* 17 Nov. 2008. Web. 9 Mar. 2011.

Homework

Sean O'Toole offered substantial help with my knowledge of the teaching profession in Ontario. Since the charter school idea was only just gaining popularity during the final years of Ray Budde's life, biographical information came mainly from articles published at the time of his death. Otherwise, Budde's "Education by Charter" was the original point of my research on charter schooling, and from there I went through the reports that measured their success and the resulting avalanche of media, including the documentary *Waiting for Superman*. The comparisons between other school models and methods was the result of knowledge accumulated throughout my research for the rest of the book.

Budde, Ray. "Education by Charter." *Phi Delta Kappan* 70.7 (1989): 518–20. Print.

Cloud, John. "Are Private Schools Really Better?" *Time* 10 Oct. 2007. Web. 15 Mar. 2011.

Greene, Jay P., Greg Forster, and Marcus A. Winters. *Apples to Apples: An Evaluation of Charter Schools Serving General Student Populations*. New York: Center for Civic Innovation, 2003. Print.

"The Push-Back on Charter Schools." *New York Times* 14 Mar. 2010. Web. 3 Mar. 2012.

Saulny, Susan. "Ray Budde, 82, First to Propose Charter Schools, Dies." *New York Times* 21 June 2005. Web. 13 Mar. 2011.

Weaver, Reg. "Study Finds Public, Private Schools Equal." *The Spokesman-Review* 25 July 2006. Web. 15 Mar. 2011.

The End of History?

Here, I returned to my sources for the book's opening: Balogh's thesis once again provided the historical context I've attempted to bring to the entire work. Likewise, I returned to Ryerson and Mann's original reports and studies, and brought in other strands from Robert Vaughan's *The Age of Great Cities* and John R. Davis's *The Victorians and Germany*, to hint at the tremendously controversial decision to implement the Prussian model abroad. The idea that institutionalized education has eroded our physical and mental landscapes and that this is at least partially a product of the Prussian school system is of course contextualized by many of the sources I've referenced, but in the closing paragraphs of the book, I compiled figures mainly from scientific studies, and their resultant media, to show the rapidity of language death and the evident fact that we live in a time of great educational privation. We are clearly in need of a whole new way of doing things.

Arnold, Matthew. *A French Eton*. London and Cambridge: MacMillan, 1864. Print.

Balogh, Sherman F. *Ontario Educators' Observations of the German System of Education: 1834–1918*. Toronto: U of Toronto P, 1997. Print.

Davis, John R. *The Victorians and Germany*. Bern: Peter Lang. 2007. Print.

Draaisma, Muriel. "Endangered Languages." *CBC Online* 22 Feb. 2008. Web. 5 Mar. 2012.

Jones, H. S. *Intellect and Character in Victorian England: Mark Pattison and the Invention of the Don*. Cambridge: Cambridge UP, 2007. Print.

"The Languages of Extinction: The World's Endangered Tongues." *The Independent* 19 Sept. 2007. Web. 5 Mar. 2012.

MacFarquhar, Neil. "UN to Reduce the Extinction Rate." *New York Times*. 29 Oct. 2010. Web. 5 Mar. 2012.

Vaughan, Robert. *The Age of Great Cities*. London: Jackson, 1843. Print.

"Young Ladies' Academy of the Grey Sisters. *Daily Union* 26 Aug. 1865. Web. 5 Mar. 2012.

Zimmer, Carl. "Multitudes of Species Face Climate Threat." *New York Times* 4 Apr. 2011. Web. 5 Mar. 2012.

ACKNOWLEDGMENTS

WORKS OF THIS KIND are communal efforts, and I'm incredibly grateful to everyone involved. First and foremost, I'd like to acknowledge the whole staff at Penguin Canada, who believed in this book from the beginning and transformed my manuscript into the finished volume before you. Thank you especially to my editor Nick Garrison, who lent his tremendous vision to this work and to whom I'm deeply grateful. Thank you as well to Shona Cook, Sandra Tooze, Tara Tovell, Mary Opper, Justin Stoller, and everyone else; I couldn't have asked for a better home than Penguin.

Another special acknowledgment is reserved for my agent, Meghan Macdonald, whose extraordinary kindness and patience have been hallmarks of our working relationship. I'm thankful as well to the people at TLA, who've lent their considerable knowledge and skill to the present title. Thank you very much indeed.

I'd like to single out the many scholars, writers, and educators who let me inundate them with questions, giving generously of their time and expertise with nothing in return. In roughly the order in which they appeared, thank you to Derek S. Linton, Philipp Gonon, Ulrike Hanemann, Peter Roberts, James FitzGerald, Sarah de Leeuw, Nancy Heckman, Indira Samarasekera, Lawrence Busch, Sheldon Krimsky, Larry L. Leslie, Alan Collinge, Dan Dugan, Alison Smith,

Ian Stronach, Michaele Robertson, Barry Wansbrough, Thomas H. B. Symons, Pat Farenga, Milton Gaither, Margaret Dagenais, Neal McCluskey, Yong Zhao, Hal Salzman, B. Lindsay Lowell, George Malaty Marcus, Jussi Välimaa, and Jaana Palojärvi. Thank you as well to the others who provided information that didn't end up making it into the final work; your contributions were no less appreciated and no less valuable.

Thank you to Guy Sprung for translating the epigraph at the beginning of this book. Thank you to my friend and former English teacher, Sean O'Toole, who read early drafts of this book and to whom I'm particularly grateful. Thank you to my mother and father, who homeschooled me long before it was popular and provided me with the means to create my own education. Thank you to my friends Jessica Wright, Kevan Anne Murray, Chris and Rory Jordan-Stevens, Leah Long, Jonathan Moseney, and Joel Rendall.

Thank you to all students of wisdom and teachers of curiosity, and thank you for reading.

INDEX